TWENTIETH CENTURY VIEWS

The aim of this series is to present the best in contemporary critical opinion on major authors, providing a twentieth century perspective on their changing status in an era of profound revaluation.

Maynard Mack, *Series Editor*
Yale University

SHELLEY

SHELLEY

A COLLECTION OF CRITICAL ESSAYS

Edited by

George M. Ridenour

Prentice-Hall, Inc. *Englewood Cliffs, N. J.*

Contents

Contents

Introduction
Shelley's Optimism

by George M. Ridenour

Let us believe in a kind of optimism in which we are our own gods.
Shelley to Maria Gisborne, October 1819

I am one of those whom nothing will fully satisfy, but who am ready to
be partially satisfied by all that is practicable.
Shelley to Leigh Hunt, November 1819[1]

There is at present no consensus about Shelley, and there may not be
one soon. Some undergraduates, in any case, still come to Shelley with a
disposition to disapprove that is not always easy to analyze. How much of
it is a natural response, and how much is picked up from instructors whose
attitudes were formed by anti-Shelleyan critics? To some extent it may be
part of the attempt of intelligent young people to realize the special qualities
of their own time—that is, to "be modern." And since the modern sensibility
as we have thought of it was largely developed in the 1920s and '30s, the
period which developed the hostile critical attitudes, it is not remarkable
that undergraduates should recapitulate what may now seem to be old-
fashioned points of view.

Among older readers of Shelley there is not only the inheritance of hostile
criticism, but also the reaction against optimistic liberalism experienced by
heirs of two wars and the dislike of revolutionaries felt by those who are
eager to preserve an ideology or a social order that they believe in or are
used to. Objections of this sort must be treated respectfully. The literary
critic can point out misreadings; he may call attention to the complexity of
the relationship between an ideology considered in itself and as it enters into
a poem; he may even advise, on general principle, the entertaining of alien
points of view. But it must finally be admitted that only limited mediation
is possible between opposed visions of the nature of man and his world.

[1] Shelley's letters are cited from the edition of F. L. Jones (Oxford, 1964).

Other objections, however, are frivolous. They are often based on an objection to the kind of poem Shelley wrote, generically, and to the kind of person one conceives him to have been. Some critics resent romantic poetry in general, and dismiss it as self-delusion, "ventriloquism," an attempt to "escape reality"—and, to be sure, it is an attempt to escape the reality of such critics. They point to the difficulty the romantics had in maintaining their positions and cite it as proof that the positions are mistaken. It is, of course, evidence that the positions are difficult.

In a similar way, the tendency of the romantics to concentrate on central human problems and situations, to the neglect of individual story and characterization, can lead to their being accused of being abstract, uninterested in real human beings. Their art does not seem to meet the demands of either the drama or the novel, and these forms dictate our unexamined expectations in literature to a surprising extent. The elevation of "dramatic," in fact, from a descriptive to an evaluative term has become as pernicious as the similar elevation of "concrete." If concern with individual personality is your standard, then obviously the novel is your form, and the Byron of *Don Juan* is superior to the Shelley of *Prometheus Unbound* (or to Aeschylus, for that matter). But in that case, Trollope is better than any of them.

It is strange that, with all our consciousness of critical fallacy, comment such as this is still offered. But the personal argument may be equally influential. It assumes that we can reduce a poem to what we take to be the impulse behind it and then judge it as a poem on the basis of our judgment of that impulse. This is another version of the assumption that we can understand and judge a poem on the basis of our understanding and judgment of what we take to be the ideas behind it. We have only to state the two positions to see that they constitute a denial of the imagination's fundamental claim of opening "unknown modes of being." There is, in fact, no reason why imagining of a high order should not involve ideas and attitudes which might not win much respect outside the poem (the poet's loss could be our gain), while there is much reason to fear that the reader may be insensitive to the imaginative value of ideas and attitudes he dislikes.

Critics who dislike Shelley, for example, are often hostile to youth (they say "adolescence"), and rationalize their difficulty with the poet by calling him immature. But what we call maturity often seems to be made up of equal parts of cowardice and exhaustion. We finally give up our own insistence that the world be a human world and then make fun of people who are still working at it. We tell them they are immature. When Shelley met Southey in Keswick the elder poet told the younger that the difference in their views was the difference between their ages. Shelley wrote drily to Godwin: "I do not feel the least disposition to be Mr. S's proselyte." And surely this indocility is one of his gifts to us—his refusal to give in, accept, be mature. In his refusal, for example, to accept monopoly in personal relationships, as expressed in the rhetoric of appropriation ("You're mine," "I'm yours"), he provides a model for Emily Brontë's Catherine Linton, who will not understand that she cannot live with both of the men she loves and needs in different ways. Already in *Wuthering Heights* the motif, as they say, is "domesticated," and in *David Copperfield* it appears in fully respectable form in the hero's two marriages. (Browning plays with the notion more directly, but ironically, for protection.) But the classical expression is Shelley's, primarily in *Epipsychidion*, which is his witness to the possibility of a fully human love, free from possession and jealousy. His first wife wrote of Shelley's plan of living with both her and Mary Godwin: "He had the folly to believe this possible." Shelley certainly felt that a relation of the sort should be possible, and he was determined to make it possible, to make us the kinds of people for whom it would be possible. It is not evident that his imaginings would be more valuable if their point were a mature recognition of limitation, though such recognition clearly has its merit. One of Shelley's great values for us is a fine childlike intransigence, an unwillingness to settle quickly for less than what men really want.

This is Shelley's "utopianism," and it does not seem to me strictly a defense of Shelley to point out that when we examine his utopian utterances carefully we find that they are in various ways qualified. Part of the irony of Shelley's depreciation by the New Critics is that his view of things tends to be at least as ironic—in the sense of "qualified," "aware of alternative points of view" —as their own. And while there is no reason to suppose that such irony has a predictable relation to the value of imagining, it is certainly part of what we admire in Shelley. But for Shelley, unlike some poets, irony is not in itself a condition of poetry. It does not call attention to itself as content, and this has misled some of his critics. Rather, as Wordsworth refuses to allow his poems to "mean" the paradoxes they contain (and the imagining lies in the refusal), the value of Shelley's ironies lies largely in the effort he makes to deny them. He works to make the biggest statement he can, to claim the most for man that he is able, but at his most characteristic the statement is circumscribed: the paradise is a limited one, or he fails to achieve it, or it collapses after having been achieved. His hopes are infinite, but he is sober in expectation.

Shelley's poems, however, deal with his hopes, and the embodiment of Shelley's hopes could only be a god. So his poems often treat, from various points of view, the implications of man's ability to imagine a divine nature. At no point does Shelley imagine a creator god or an omnipotent god. The first would be a Father and the second a King, and these he saw as images of evil. The divine was the actualizing of freedom, while fathers and kings were obstacles to freedom. The only good monarchy is that of each man over himself, that is, when there is no monarchy at all.[2] Furthermore, God's goodness implies his limitation, since an all-powerful god must also be responsible for evil. Shelley's visionary poetry, therefore, bothers readers of very different points of view. The orthodox are apt to find it offensively independent, while unbelievers find it excessively religious. Agnostics may like "Mont Blanc," for example, but resist "Intellectual Beauty." In fact, these poems contain values both believer and infidel claim to admire, and we can all learn from so powerful a theological imagination.

I have touched on two sources of resistance in Shelley to the idea of an all-powerful god, one imaginative and one philosophical, and both more or less external to the poems. But there are others, developed in the poems themselves. Readers are struck first of all by the flickering, undependable nature of Shelleyan deities. The classic example is "Intellectual Beauty," who

> . . . visits with inconstant glance
> Each human heart and countenance;
> Like hues and harmonies of evening,—
> Like clouds in starlight widely spread,—
> Like memory of music fled,—
> Like aught that for its grace may be
> Dear, and yet dearer for its mystery.[3]
>
> (ll. 6–12)

"Intellectual Beauty" is an attempt to account for, or to give an adequate account of, moments of joy and satisfaction which, by comparison with the ordinary level of life, seem to be of a different order, "supernatural" or "superhuman." Their relative infrequency and impermanence call attention to them as divine visitations, but at the same time cause us to wonder about the god who is so sparing of his favors. There is no suggestion, for example, that there is any proportion between the coming of the power and the worthiness of the devotee, except that it clearly would not have come at all if he were not generally deserving. One resists the suspicion that a cruel game is being played, but the feeling of being teased is hard to overcome. That is one reason why the god is not apprehended as personal, or why the element of personality is played down. A person who conducted himself in that way would be called at best thoughtless.

[2] For Shelley dominion of any kind is inherently evil, and men's tendency toward the exercise of dominion is basic to what he means by moral evil. (A character in the novel *Porius* by John Cowper Powys makes the very Shelleyan suggestion that "the Devil is every god who exacts obedience.")

[3] Shelley's poems are cited from the edition of Thomas Hutchinson (Oxford, 1905).

This is the situation Shelley treats with such sophistication in *The Witch of Atlas*. Shelley is trying to make the best case for a god that he can, without resorting to what seem to him dishonest dodges for exculpating an all-powerful deity from responsibility for imperfections in his creation. The Witch is the best kind of god he feels justified in imagining on the basis of his own knowledge and experience. That means a god whose nature is carefully qualified, presented in a myth qualified by its playfulness.

At his most anti-religious Shelley never thinks of the idea of divinity as irrelevant to man. He regularly assumes that there are kinds of experience that call attention to themselves for their qualitative difference from the rest of life, and which seem to demand a theological vocabulary. They intimate the possibility of a richer and more satisfying life of tranquility and fulfilment. As we work toward the realization of these possibilities, we come to think of them as "out there," already fulfilled, beckoning us on and as "within us," inspiring us toward fulfilment. In both cases the power is experienced as in some sense detached from us, and it gradually takes on the characteristics of a god, separate and tantalizing. This development is the story of *Alastor*, where the Poet is drawn beyond nature, and finally beyond life, by a pair of "starry eyes" that beckon him "with their serene and azure smiles." The serenity of this loveliness is what he seeks, to be sure, but it may also be the reason he does not find it. (Compare the still serenity of the "inaccessible" Power at the summit of Mont Blanc.)

In both *Alastor* and (presumably) "Intellectual Beauty," the deity sought is feminine not merely because there are sexual elements in both imaginings. Shelley's myth of feminine deity expresses charm, but also limitation. This is most fully developed in the *Witch of Atlas*, where it is used to account for the transience of divine visitations. For the Witch has a woman's beauty and vivacity, charm and graciousness, but also a woman's fickleness, and something of the self-centered arbitrariness of a rich and spoiled young lady. (She is a bossy little thing, who tells her boatman, "Sit there!") The Witch is trapped by her own immortality, which imposes a radical distinction between her and other orders of being. It is with real grief that she rejects the love of beings that can die, but she rejects it because the grief would be too great for her. Similarly, she clearly means well toward men and wants to help them, but the very playfulness that is so much of her charm leads her to be arbitrary and inconstant in her ministrations. In neither case do we blame her much. It is a necessary limitation in divinity; she cannot really understand. (Thomas Hardy inherited this motif from Shelley, just as Browning, in "Numpholeptos," carries on the notion of tantalizing purity, and Swinburne —see "A Nympholept," developed from lines 420–492 of *Alastor*—that of beneficent amorality.) There is a suggestion that in after times she learned to love (stanza 68), but Shelley is not sure of it, which means he cannot yet imagine it. Now at least she is a "sexless bee" who passes "with an eye serene and heart unladen" (recalling the tantalizing vision of *Alastor*):

> But other troubled forms of sleep she saw,
>   Not to be mirrored in a holy song—
> Distortions foul of supernatural awe,
>   And pale imaginings of visioned wrong;
> And all the code of Custom's lawless law
>   Written upon the brows of old and young:
> "This," said the wizard maiden, "is the strife
> Which stirs the liquid surface of man's life."
>
> And little did the sight disturb her soul,—
>   We, the weak mariners of that wide lake
> Where'er its shores extend or billows roll,
>   Our course unpiloted and starless make
> O'er its wild surface to an unknown goal:—
>   But she in the calm depths her way could take,
> Where in bright bowers immortal forms abide
> Beneath the weltering of the restless tide.
>
> (stanzas 62–63)

The graceful, controlled bitterness of stanza sixty-three is unique in the language. One would have to turn to ancient Greece, perhaps, for this kind of sophistication in theology. The closest parallel might be Euripides, at once skeptical and pious, whose reverence for the gods is blended with resentment toward them—the *Ion*, or the *Bacchae*. The Apollo of Greek myth, furthermore, is a particularly striking blend of cruelty and beneficence (see the essay by Milton Wilson in this volume), and the Witch is something of her father's daughter. (Compare the coarser myth developed by Robert Graves.)

The Witch of Atlas is Shelley's most brilliant interweaving of hope and expectation, but the most comprehensive expression is found in the last two acts of *Prometheus Unbound*. Here the situation presents itself partly as a discrepancy between manner and content. If Wordsworth will make the most extraordinary statement with the utmost blandness, as if nothing unusual were being said, Shelley is apt to give enthusiastic utterance to a statement which, when examined, seems unexpectedly sober. It is hard to believe that this is simply a matter of imposing a "poetic" tone on unlikely subject matter; Shelley might, after all, have claimed more. Had he sought an exercise in grandiose rhetoric, it should not have been hard to hit upon a suitably extravagant content. The discrepancy partly reflects a contrast in Shelley's vision between exuberant hope and sober expectation, but it is also an expression of his delight in even limited gains. They are something to rejoice about.

In these final acts Shelley has set himself to imagine what kind of world we would live in if we really became all we have it in us to be. As usual, he is trying to claim as much as he can while being responsible to his awareness of limiting factors. This poses special problems for the poet, who must show everything different and still much the same. In passages of rapturous celebration he will be careful to point out that the physical alteration has been slight. The Spirit of the Earth asks:

> . . . wouldst thou think that toads, and snakes, and efts,
> Could e'er be beautiful? yet so they were,
> And that with little change of shape or hue:
> All things had put their evil nature off. . . .
>
> (III, iv, 74–77)

And the Spirit of the Hour:

> I wandering went
> Among the haunts and dwellings of mankind,
> And first was disappointed not to see
> Such mighty change as I had felt within
> Expressed in outward things; but soon I looked
> And behold, thrones were kingless, and men walked
> One with the other even as spirits do. . . .
>
> And women, too, frank, beautiful, and kind
> As the free heaven which rains fresh light and dew
> On the wide earth, past; gentle radiant forms,
> From custom's evil taint exempt and pure;
> Speaking the wisdom once they could not think,
> Looking emotions once they feared to feel,
> And changed to all which once they dared not be,
> Yet being now, made earth like heaven. . . .
>
> (III, iv, 126–132, 153–160)

In the fourth act he makes more sweeping claims, but it is clear that the change is largely in our seeing. The interaction of internal and external forces this implies can be conceived most readily in terms of time. The new world of *Prometheus Unbound* is in a sense eternal—qualitatively, and conditionally so in duration—but it is not immobile or immune from pain and death. Time remains, but is experienced differently. In a world free from remorse or anxiety there is only a richly realized present, whose blending of objective and subjective elements may be expressed as dance. (Compare Shelley on paradisal time in his "Assassins" fragment.) The pattern is both human (dance as art) and natural (the movement of the stars). Dance also expresses that union of masculine reason (the abstract pattern) and feminine love (the affective content) that is basic to the transformation of men which makes the dance possible.

The formality of the dance echoes also the formality of the drama as a whole. It is a masque or (as John Holloway suggests) a pageant, and not everyone will care for so ceremonious a poem. Shelley has strong affinities with the baroque, and *Prometheus* is his most mannered and extravagant creation.[4] But if the characters are flamboyant, stagey, larger than life, that is perhaps a comment on fatigued normality. Trotsky speculated that in time "Man will grow incomparably stronger, wiser, subtler; his body will become more harmonious; his movements more rhythmical; his voice more musical. The forms of his existence will acquire a dynamic theatrical quality."[5] *Prometheus Unbound* is a ritual in which we are invited to join in order to develop the qualities whose consequences it embodies, and to limit the obstacles it incorporates. As Shelley wrote to Elizabeth Hitchiner (July 25, 1811): "You say that equality is unattainable, so will I observe is perfection; yet they both symbolize in their nature, they both demand that an unremitting tendency towards themselves should be made, and the nearer Society approaches towards this point the happier will it be."

A number of these considerations are evident in Shelley's treatment of Prometheus himself. Prometheus is the ideal protagonist for Shelley's purposes because of his equivocal position between the gods and men. He can be god and man in the way Shelley needed for his statement without the difficulties that bothered Shelley in the corresponding Christian doctrine. He can embody man's potentiality for deity in such a way that his humanity is never compromised. The serenity and eternity of divine life is his by right as a god and by virtue of his moral and intellectual achievement as a man. For this reason there does not attach to him any of the bitterness one feels

---

[4] "There are . . . times when he writes like a poet of the Catholic reaction." A. Clutton-Brock, Introduction to C. D. Locock's ed. of the *Poems* (London, 1911), I, xxvii. Admirers of Bernini might have difficulty being embarrassed by the mannered intensity of lines such as: "I fall upon the thorns of life! I bleed!" or even, "I shrieked, and clasped my hands in ecstasy!"

[5] *Literature and Revolution*, cited by Isaac Deutscher, *The Prophet Unarmed* (second vol. of the biography of Trotsky) (London, 1959), p. 197. Deutscher, p. 195, quotes from the closing lines of the third act of *Prometheus Unbound*. It may be worth pointing out that the analogy with Blake, valuable in many ways, breaks down here, since Blake does not characteristically attempt sustained elaboration of what life in a new heaven and earth would be like. He presents it largely negatively, through our understanding of opposed states. Compare with both Shelley and Trotsky (and Blake) the doctrine of St. Maximus the Confessor, presented by Vladimir Lossky, *The Mystical Theology of the Eastern Church* (trans.) (London, 1957), pp. 108–110, 137–138. Shelley occupies a position between the saint and the revolutionary.

toward even so engaging a deity as the later Witch of Atlas. He enters the paradisal cave as Oedipus enters the grove at Colonus, a tragic hero whose suffering is done. His absence is not resented because man as a whole has approximated his level, and his personal aid is no longer needed. He remains valuable, however, as an ideal of detachment in involvement, of the active at one with the contemplative, the social with the individual—areas of experience that he has earned for man and which he holds open to him. He remains in a sense the norm to which the rest of the drama approximates. We learn to see things as Prometheus does by being as he is.

Shelley's optimism is based on chances for exacting benefit from an order of things not obviously concerned with man. As he himself observes at the beginning of his "Proposals for an Association of Philanthropists": "Man cannot make occasions, but he may seize those that offer." This is classical, as Shelley knew. He expanded a cynical epigram of the Palatine Anthology: "Under Heaven's High cope/ Fortune is God—all you endure and do/ Depends on circumstance as much as you." But it is possible to reverse the emphasis and point out that it depends on you as much as circumstance, and this is Shelley's usual way. He assumes that while man's mind and what it experiences concur only imperfectly, the extent of disproportion can be at least reduced. Art, science, and social organization can reshape the experienced world nearer to the heart's desire. But as we have noticed, Shelley's emphasis falls on what, for want of better terms, we must call the spiritual or psychological. He hopes it is possible to exercise the mind in such a way that, without deception, the elements favorable to man may be strengthened, the hostile reduced, and man find the good he seeks. The strategy is a delicate one, involving a complex interplay of active and passive, inner and outer, mind and experience, as in the intricate "gearings" of *Alastor*, "Intellectual Beauty," or "Mont Blanc." (See the essays by R. H. Fogle, Frederick A. Pottle, and Earl R. Wasserman in this volume.) The movement outward of the mind often involves an imaginative projection of what ought to be, which is itself to some extent "received"—e.g., the vision in *Alastor*. The passive aspect involves an inner disposition that Shelley usually calls love: roughly the affective correlative to the more consciously shaping power. Together they make up man's capacity for integrated experience, i.e., imagination. Shelley points out that even limited success is evidence that the nonhuman world is at least amenable to human purposes, and he hopes that it may suggest an ultimate identity in nature.

One of the characteristics of Shelley's imagination is fidelity to the hypotheses it constructs. Shelley says, in effect: "Put it this way and see what you've got," and he is usually careful to stay within the terms of the proposition. He will put it that way with all his passion and ingenuity, testing the statement by his sense of probability, and offering it for the test of our contemplation. With all his ardor for unified experience, Shelley is un-expectedly patient in working out systems that make no pretense to being comprehensive statements. He seems to have been in fact a good deal of a pluralist, in the sense of a person who believes that the closest we can come to truth about our whole experience is through accounts from different points of view that may be hard to fit together. The most problematic ex-pression of this is found in *Alastor*, where, for example, it is impossible to be sure what is meant by the fact that the eyes of the maiden who beckons the hero-Poet on to his death are experienced by him as tantalizing. It could be that his own vision is weakening, that she is luring him on for his own good, or that she is revealing herself in her true nature, as cruel. In the same way, it is impossible to decide whether the rapport between the Poet's experience and the natural world is an illusion of the Poet's perception, is a sign of an ultimate unity of being, or is a necessary device of the narrator's. Shelley suggests all of these possibilities, and his unwillingness to choose between them is part of the meaning of the poem. (This is the best example of con-tinental "romantic irony" I have noticed in the English romantic poets.) The closest thing to a comprehensive statement in Shelley is in *Prometheus Unbound*, where "what happens" (or Demogorgon) is largely, though not wholly, how you see it and what you make of it (Asia's Demogorgon is very different from Jupiter's), and the god you "get" is the god you are able to imagine.

The most dogmatically optimistic of Shelley's poems is *Adonais*, but its optimism is of a desperate sort, operative within the limits set by the situ-ation. The situation here of course is the death of a poet. Though for the romantics the poet was both a person set apart by his gifts and also, since we all live by imagination, a representative of man in general, the former is the more emphasized in *Adonais*. This puts the universal problem of the meaning of human death in a radical form. The poem is concerned with the death of an elect spirit who dies before his gifts can be fully exercised. It is the problem of the death of a saint in a world where there is not surely a God.

Hypotheses such as "the Eternal" (stanza 38) or "the One" (stanza 52) are the product of (implicit) ontological arguments, from conditioned to unconditioned being, and of analogical argument developed through a contrast between the *being* of Adonais and that of the enemies of the imagi-native life, represented by the dragon-critic, even as the gods of earlier poems are inferences from qualities of experience undergone by the poet himself. Eternity and integrity are perceived as qualities of Adonais, so that to see the world under the aspect of Adonais is to see it in relation to an

"Eternal" and a "One." The "Power" (stanza 42) and "one Spirit's plastic stress" (stanza 43) correspond similarly to the shaping power of his work. The specific theology of the poem is an answer to the question posed by the death of Adonais. It would have only problematic existence outside the poem, or with regard to other poems by Shelley.

The relation between "the One" and the "plastic stress" is not wholly clear, and Shelley may have been remembering the passage toward the end of the first book of the *Essay on Man* where the doctrine of permeating deity exemplifies the oneness of the chain of being. The discrepancy, if it is one, is to the point. Even here, in his most ambitious assertion, he is far from conceiving an all-powerful deity, or even a creative one.[6] Such a god would be hard to exculpate from the evil Shelley's poem emphasizes so strongly. And although this god is more loving than the Witch of Atlas, he is also more inhuman. The god is limited in power and nature, according to the Humean rule, to precisely those qualities demanded by the terms of the analogy. The poet's apparent injunction to haste toward death (stanzas 51ff.) must be understood in this manner. Shelley is following out in imagination the implications of his hypothesis. To be sure, when we contemplate reality by means of the poem, our final judgment of the perspective it offers will take account of all it seems to involve, practically, but this is not in any simple way a judgment of the poem. *Adonais* could not have the value it has for us if its terms were less radical and its choices less absolute, whether or not we are minded to accept the terms or to act on the choices.

Adonais is a baroque apotheosis, echoing the earlier period in its blending of the sensuous and the ascetic, the ceremonial and the moral. Its hope for man is in the cleansing and directing of his imaginative powers, to create, in effect, the god whose sanction it invokes. It is a more exigent vision than *Prometheus*, and more individual. But if it lacks the social emphasis of the earlier poems, the difference is no greater than is the case with many works that treat corresponding areas of orthodox revelation, which has its own problems of accommodating the individual and the corporate. There is every suggestion that the accomplishments of Adonais are open to all, if on a less heroic level. We are offered a mode of being that we can all to some extent live ourselves into, an optimism for man as his own god, as the saving god of *Adonais* is an inference from the nature of Adonais himself.

If there is any justice in this argument at all, it should be possible to make a fairly ambitious claim for Shelley's "value at the present time." It would be hard to think of another figure who mediates to such effect between so

[6] The God who dawns on Chaos in stanza 19 is more a function of the rhetoric than of the theology of the poem.

many of our major concerns—theist and humanist, theologian and politician, collectivist and individualist, conservative and radical. He appeals both to our idealism and to our sense of crushing circumstance, providing a vision well adapted, one would think, to a modern sensibility. His commitment is to man, rather than to system, but he knows man cannot live without system, and he is fertile in evolving systems in terms of which experience can be shaped, as much as may be, to man's will. Instead of sacrificing either natural or supernatural perspectives, he is apt to present a focus that will exploit the values of both, avoiding the exclusions. His success is not uniform, but that is to be expected. For good or ill, Shelley's imagination is in many ways a modern one, and it is our fault if we do not grasp the extent to which his view is directed toward us in the twentieth century.

The Abstractness of Shelley

by Richard Harter Fogle

Critical opinion has been unanimous in terming the poetry of Shelley "abstract." As "abstract" has among modern critics almost universally become synonymous with "bad," an analysis of his "abstractness" which is also a defense of his poetic qualities seems not inappropriate at the present time. I shall attempt, therefore, in this essay to examine the question of what this abstractness of his consists; and, I hope, to demonstrate that it implies no lack of value.

Shelley's poetic world is not a literal transcription of his perceptions of the natural world, but a conscious arrangement and composition of these perceptions. Keats, who believes fully in the deep truth of appearances, seldom feels called upon to alter them or go beyond them. Shelley, however, has less confidence in appearances, although he is fascinated by them.[1] To put this difference in another way, Shelley does not believe so thoroughly as Keats in the correspondence of the human mind to what it perceives. While Keats permits things to rest in their complexity, Shelley consciously imposes upon them the order of his intellect, reshaping them according to his restless and masterful will.

He is sometimes concerned less with the world as it is than with the world as he would have it.[2] In *Prometheus Unbound*, for example, he is the architect

---

"The Abstractness of Shelley." From *Philological Quarterly*, XXIV (1945), 362–79. Reprinted in Fogle, *The Imagery of Keats and Shelley* (Chapel Hill, 1949), pp. 215–40. Reprinted here by permission of the author, of *Philological Quarterly*, and of the University of North Carolina Press.

[1] "The natural scenery of Shelley has a quality very different from Wordsworth's. It is less realistic, less familiar. It is an imaginative composite of features taken from nature and put together in a pattern suitable to the poetic thought and mood. . . . The sensory appeal is as rich and constant in Shelley as in Wordsworth; but it is on a different level of experience, less familiar. . . ." (J. W. Beach, *The Concept of Nature in Nineteenth Century English Poetry* [New York, 1936], p. 210.)

[2] The relationship of Shelley's reforming instincts to his poetry is perhaps most wisely to be left to himself to define: "Let this opportunity be conceded to me of acknowledging that I have what a Scotch philosopher characteristically terms 'a passion for reforming the world.' . . . But it is a mistake to suppose that I dedicate my poetical compositions solely to the direct enforcement of reform. . . . Didactic poetry is my abhorrence. . . . My purpose has hitherto been simply to familiarize the highly refined imagination of the

of a universe idealized by Love, in which accident disappears, incongruous and conflicting elements vanish, and all is harmony. Man is not, indeed, exempt from "chance, and death, and mutability," but he rules them like slaves (III, iv, 200–201). They are subjugated to the pattern of the whole. His conception of the relationship between man and nature, between subject and object, is not fixed, however, but varies and shifts. If one cares to describe this relationship in philosophic terms, one may declare Shelley to be at varying periods idealistic and materialistic, Platonic and neo-Platonic, Naturalistic and Necessitarian. To apply any of these terms too rigidly to his poetry, however, is unfortunate. Obviously there is a slow and steady motion away from the bald mechanism and necessitarianism of the juvenile *Queen Mab*, with its recurring image of "the chain of being," [3] its emphasis on cold geometrical symmetry; but Shelley does not lend himself to labeling. He escapes from under the hand of the philosophic critic.

The elusiveness of his poetic thought is reflected in the disagreement which obtains among many of his commentators. Professor Gingerich considers Shelley a deep-dyed and unredeemed Necessitarian, who covers his traces with a thin layer of superficial Platonism.[4] To A. T. Strong and Miss Winstanley he is a Platonist of the inner circle.[5] Joseph Warren Beach discerns in his poetry an unresolved conflict between Platonism and Naturalism.[6] A. E. Powell expounds the doctrine of the Platonic forms to account for his imagery,[7] a view of the question which Professor Solve appears to share.[8] Carl Grabo emphasizes the neo-platonic elements of Shelley's poetry, while admitting an appreciable amount of Platonism as well.[9] A. A. Jack in an essay written in 1904 declared that Shelley's Nature is the cold mechanistic world of science, suggesting also a touch of Platonism in Shelley by remarking that "the secret of things is what has charm for him, not the things themselves." [10]

---

more select classes of poetical readers with beautiful idealisms of moral excellence; aware that, until the mind can love, and admire, and trust, and hope, and endure, reasoned principles of moral conduct are seeds cast upon the highway of life which the unconscious passenger tramples into dust, although they would bear the harvest of his happiness" (Preface to *Prometheus Unbound*).

[3] Cf. Pope, *Essay on Man*; A. O. Lovejoy, *The Great Chain of Being* (Cambridge, Mass., 1936).

[4] S. F. Gingerich, *Essays in the Romantic Poets* (New York, 1929), p. 217, *passim*.

[5] A. T. Strong, *Three Studies in Shelley* (London, 1921); Lilian Winstanley, "Platonism in Shelley," *Essays and Studies by Members of the English Association*, IV (1913), 72–100.

[6] *Op. cit.*, pp. 242ff.

[7] A. E. Powell, *The Romantic Theory of Poetry* (London, 1926), pp. 206–16.

[8] ". . . to the mature Shelley, art was not copying mundane forms, but imitation of the infinite and archetypal forms, so far as imagination was able to apprehend them" (M. T. Solve, *Shelley: His Theory of Poetry* [Chicago, 1927], p. 115).

[9] Carl Grabo, *The Magic Plant* (Chapel Hill, N. C., 1936), pp. 412–38.

[10] A. A. Jack, *Shelley: an Essay* (London, 1904), pp. 33–34, 38ff., 127.

This brief chronicle of divergence in criticism might easily be extended. The moral is, I believe, that as a poet Shelley is not to be confined to any single set of beliefs. His deep interest in philosophy is undeniable; but his poetry is a refractory creature which takes the bit between its teeth and seeks its ends after its own fashion. This is as much as to say that Shelley is a philosophic poet, not a poetic philosopher. His imagery is intellectual and consciously symbolic to an unusual degree, but it should not be regarded as a set of fixed counters used to objectify and visualize a philosophic system. Neither is his verse a rhymed manual of natural science. Professor Grabo is guilty of this form of didactic fallacy in his self-revealing comment upon "The Cloud":

> Shelley elaborates the theme with much ingenuity, with beautiful color effects and varied imagery, but the essential facts under the fanciful dress are sound. It is good meteorology. Therefore it is an excellent brief instance of Shelley's poetic processes, his ability to raise a beautiful and imaginative superstructure upon a basis of fact.[11]

He appears to believe that by justifying Shelley as a scientific observer he is establishing his value as a poet. This method of defense, however, is essentially irrelevant.

Shelley, indeed, seeks Truth in poetry. But it is a poetic Truth which he pursues, by means of the creative imagination, synthetic and intuitional, which is embodied in "vitally metaphoric" poetic language, in itself creative insofar as it "marks the before unapprehended relations of things." Shelley's distinction between reason and imagination[12] should be sufficient warning for those who insist upon making his poetry a hanger-on of philosophy and science, unless they believe that he misrepresented his own creative processes.

The Truth toward which Shelley's poetry from first to last aspires is a shifting, tantalizing, elusive thing which he is always striving to catch and clothe in words. It seems to him so close that he grasps for it as for a mirage, yet it is at the same time evident to him that through words he can never attain it, the means being inadequate to the end. For although at one point in the *Defence of Poetry* he declares that "language is arbitrarily produced by the imagination, and has relation to thoughts alone," that it is "as a mirror which reflects" the light of which it is the medium, the quality and substance of his own poetry is better represented by his statement in the same essay of the relationship between inspiration and expression:

---

[11] *Op. cit.*, pp. 282–83. Grabo is echoing what had previously been said by Stopford Brooke: "Strip off the imaginative clothing from 'The Cloud' and Science will support every word of it" (Introduction, *Selections from Shelley* [London, 1926], pp. xli–xlii). To this A. A. Jack very properly retorted, "Yes, but what then?" (*Op. cit.*, p. 42.)

[12] *A Defence of Poetry.*

. . . the mind in creation is as a fading coal, which some invisible influence, like an inconstant wind, awakens to transitory brightness; this power arises from within, like the colour of a flower which fades and changes as it is developed, and the conscious portions of our natures are unprophetic either of its approach or its departure. Could this influence be durable in its original purity and force, it is impossible to predict the greatness of the results; but when composition begins, inspiration is already on the decline, and the most glorious poetry that has ever been communicated to the world is probably a feeble shadow of the original conceptions of the poet.

The characteristic imagery of Shelley seeks through "vitally metaphorical" and creative language to grasp and express an unseen and unattainable truth. To this restless energy of aspiration is to be attributed both his virtue and defect: fierce power and a wearing lack of repose. Feeling the inadequacy of language to produce the precise effect at which he is aiming (and little wonder, for he seeks absolute Truth), he nevertheless indomitably goes on trying. He cannot tell, as he would wish, exactly what manner of creature the skylark is:

> What thou art we know not;
> What is most like thee?

But by creative imagery he can roughly approximate his archetypal conception of it, as far as the resources of language will aid. The bird is like a Poet hidden in the light of thought, a high-born maiden in a palace tower, a glowworm golden, and so on. The skylark itself, a symbol of Perfection and Truth, is significantly unseen and remote.

This passage combines the abstract and the concrete in a fashion very typical of Shelley. For while the figures are concrete, each one is emblematic of the remoteness and the invisibility of the lark. The poet is *hidden* in the light of thought; the maiden is secluded in a tower, symbol of withdrawal from actuality; the glowworm scatters *unbeholden* its aërial hue; the rose is concealed within its own green leaves. This concrete-abstract dualism is notably present elsewhere. One may not pierce to the secret being of the west wind, for it is an "unseen presence." In the visible world it is objectified by the leaves, the seeds, the clouds, the waters upon which it acts. In the "Hymn to Intellectual Beauty" the subject of the poem is at two removes from our perceptions:

> The awful shadow of some unseen Power
> Floats though unseen among us. . . .

As in "The Skylark," the images through which Shelley attempts to come at the quality of Beauty themselves embody the unseen; Beauty is

> As summer winds that creep from flower to flower;
> Like moonbeams that *behind* some piny mountain shower.

This Beauty becomes visible only through its effects upon perceptible objects:

> It visits with inconstant glance
> Each human heart and countenance . . .
> Like hues and harmonies of evening,
> Like clouds in starlight widely spread.

In the "Ode to Heaven" Shelley is frankly hopeless of doing justice to his immense subject. He throws out a variety of imaginal suggestions almost at random. These suggestions are voiced by three Spirits of decidedly diverse opinions. To the First Spirit Heaven is the boundless space above us, a "palace-roof of cloudless nights," a "paradise of golden lights," a

> Presence-chamber, temple, home,
> Every-canopying dome
> Of acts and ages yet to come. . . .

It is the physical void, but more than physical in that it is eternal, transcending actuality. The Second Spirit holds that Heaven is

> But a dim and noonday gleam
> From the shadow of a dream

of reality to come; it is "the mind's first chamber," giving only a faint notion of the "world of new delights" stretching out to the infinite capacity of the human mind. This confidence in human potentialities is abruptly rejected by the Third Spirit:

> Peace! the abyss is wreathed with scorn
> At your presumption, atom-born! [13]

Heaven is embodied and symbolized in "a globe of dew," a flower, insofar as it can be grasped by the human intellect. Essentially, however, it cannot be known at all.

Shelley's poetry strives continually to express by images an absolute truth or beauty beyond the scope of imagery. Face to face with this ultimate reality, he is unable to summon the words which will fix its identity; he falls back in defeat. Demogorgon, the symbol of the Absolute, is a "mighty

---

[13] According to Mrs. Shelley, in these lines Shelley "expresses his despair of being able to conceive, far less express, all of variety, majesty, and beauty, which is veiled from our senses in the unknown realm, the mystery of which his poetic vision sought in vain to penetrate" (Quoted in *The Complete Poetical Works of Percy Bysshe Shelley*, ed. G. E. Woodberry [Boston and New York, 1901], p. 366).

darkness," without limb, form, or outline, and his answers to the questions of Asia and Panthea are shadowy, ambiguous, and inconclusive (*Prometheus Unbound* II, iv). The answer of Demogorgon to Asia's query, "Whom called'st thou God? " reflects most exactly Shelley's dilemma:

> If the abyss
> Could vomit forth its secrets—but a voice
> Is wanting, *the deep truth is imageless.*
>
> (ll. 113–115)

Shelley, then, is abstract in that his poetry continually climbs toward abstraction on steps of concrete imagery. He is abstract also in that mind is as real to him as matter.[14] He is abstract, too, because in his poetry mind and matter are not fused as they are, for example, in Keats, who is able to speak with perfect and instinctive spontaneity of the soul as a web upon which Man should "weave a tapestry empyrean full of symbols for his spiritual eye, of softness for his spiritual touch, of space for his wandering, of distinctness for his luxury." [15] Instead of finding the subject within the object, as does Keats, Shelley often goes directly to the subject itself as a separate and distinct entity. Quite frequently he terminates a rising succession of concrete images with an abstraction, to which he apparently assigns a poetical value identical with them.

I cite two closely adjoining passages from *Prometheus Unbound* to demonstrate this tendency, which could be pointed out in almost any poem of Shelley's. The Earth, exulting over the fallen tyrant Jupiter, anathematizes him as a

> Sceptred *curse*
> Who all our green and azure *universe*
> Threatenedst to muffle round with black *destruction* . . .
>
> (IV, 338–340)

She cries to him,

> How thou art sunk, withdrawn, covered, drunk up
> By thirsty *nothing*, as the brackish cup
> Drained by a desert troop, a little drop for all;

[14] Cf. "Speculations on Metaphysics": "It has commonly been supposed that those distinct thoughts which affect a number of persons, at regular intervals, during the passage of a multitude of other thoughts, which are called *real* or *external objects*, are totally different in kind from those which affect only a few persons, and which recur at irregular intervals, and are usually more obscure and distinct, such as hallucinations, dreams, and the ideas of madness. No essential distinction between any one of these ideas, or any class of them, is founded on a correct observation of the nature of things. . . ."

[15] *The Letters of John Keats*, ed. M. B. Forman, 2nd ed. (London and New York, 1935), p. 103.

> And from beneath, around, within, above,
> Filling thy void annihilation, love
> Bursts in like light on caves cloven by the thunderball!
> (IV, 350–355)[16]

Since Shelley believes that the mind is as real as the external world, and of the same order of reality, he often begins with subjective ideas and states and clothes them with natural and concrete imagery. This is the converse of what I believe to be the typical procedure of Keats, who begins with sensuous perception and goes on to build upon it. In the Preface to *Prometheus Unbound* Shelley declares that

> The imagery which I have employed will be found, in many instances, to have been drawn from the operations of the human mind, or from those external actions by which they are expressed. This is unusual in modern poetry, although Dante and Shakespeare are full of instances of the same kind; Dante indeed more than any other poet, and with greater success. But the Greek poets, as writers to whom no resource of awakening the sympathy of their contemporaries was unknown, were in the habitual use of this power; and it is the study of their works (since a higher merit would probably be denied me) to which I am willing that my readers should impute this singularity.

To pass over the problem of Shelley's antecedents in Dante, Shakespeare, and the Greek dramatists, I believe that the difference he mentions between his procedure and that of his contemporaries arises from a greater than usual consciousness of mind as a separate entity. To him mind is co-equal with the phenomenal world and of the same order, but the two are not identical, nor are they fused. There is always a gap between them. To bridge this gap Shelley is forced to make greater and more conscious adjustments than are necessary to other poets, notably Keats. *Prometheus Unbound* is a drama of the mind in a sense in which Keats's *Hyperion*, for example, is not. Its characters are a step closer to the abstractions of allegory; they have less reality independent of the mind of their creator.

Prometheus Unbound is "expressionistic."[17] Prometheus on his rock is mentally tortured by Furies[18] "From the all-miscreative brain of Jove," who is

---

[16] Cf. William Empson's unfavorable interpretation of this Shelleyan usage: ". . . not being able to think of a comparison fast enough he compares the thing to a vaguer or more abstract notion of itself . . . he was too helplessly excited by one thing at a time, and that one thing was too often a mere notion not conceived in action or environment" (*Seven Types of Ambiguity* [London, 1930], p. 203).

[17] In the modern theatrical sense, as Eugene O'Neill's *Emperor Jones* is expressionistic. Subjective moods, concepts, and mental states are projected into dramatic visibility. As Jones is done to death by Little Formless Fears, scenes from his past, and so on, Prometheus is tortured by his own mind.

[18] These Furies are one indication of Shelley's indebtedness to Greek drama in his imagery. The Furies who hounded Orestes are their obvious parents, and are employed in precisely the same fashion.

himself simply that quality of the mind of Prometheus which inhibits the
free play of his spirit until by conquering himself he shall win release. The
Furies have form and reality only in the minds of their victims:

> So from our victim's destined agony
> The shade which is our form invests us round;
> Else we are shapeless as our mother Night.
>   (I, 470–472)

The spiritual sufferings inflicted by them upon Prometheus, are transposed
into vivid organic imagery: they will rend him bone from bone and nerve
from nerve, working like fire within. The ambiguous relationship which here
obtains between the physical and mental is best displayed in a speech of the
Third Fury:

> Thou think'st we will live through thee, one by one,
> Like animal life, and though we can obscure not
> The soul which burns within, that we will dwell
> Beside it, like a vain loud multitude,
> Vexing the self-content of wisest men;
> That we will be dread thought beneath thy brain,
> And foul desire round thine astonished heart,
> And blood within thy labyrinthine veins
> Crawling like agony?
>   (I, 483–491)

The poet tells us plainly what he is doing in his initial simile, *"like* animal
life." The agonies are purely subjective. Yet so nice a balance is maintained
that one never quite decides to relegate them entirely to the realm of mere
abstraction. The powerful sensuous realization of the last four lines sees to
that.

Shelley is also abstract in his conscious and consistent use of symbolism.
Of all the elements of his poetic style this is perhaps the most essential. By his
recurring use of the veil, the lyre, the stream, the boat, the cloud, and like
images, his poetry is most easily and confidently to be identified. Henry Salt
was the first, to my knowledge, to mark this fact:

> The repetition of certain images and words is one of Shelley's most marked
> characteristics. Among metaphors frequently used are those drawn from the
> instruments of weaving, the warp, woof, and web; from a lyre or Aeolian harp
> hung up to the wind; an eagle and serpent locked together in fight. The refer-
> ences to serpents are very numerous. Perhaps the strangest instance of Shelley's
> recurrence to a favourite idea is in his references to Ahasuerus, the Wandering
> Jew.[19]

---

[19] Henry Salt, *A Shelley Primer* (London, 1887), pp. 42–43.

A. T. Strong repeated this observation in 1921, mentioning as of special significance the veil image, which he interprets as an emblem of the thinness of the barrier separating the finite and the infinite; the eagle and the serpent; the meteor; poison and the scorpion as images of evil; the boat, the stream, and the guardian spirit; and the moon, as a symbol of loveliness.[20] A. C. Bradley pointed out in his essay, "Shelley's View of Poetry," that "the light of hidden power" was one of Shelley's favorite metaphors.[21] In *The Magic Plant* Carl Grabo devoted considerable attention to Shelley's symbolism, with particular reference to their sources in the neo-Platonists. The value of his comment is, in my opinion, damaged by his insistence upon regarding Shelley's images as inflexible and inert scientific and philosophic counters:[22] a type of emphasis which implicitly denies the independent validity of poetry as a mode of meaning.

G. Wilson Knight offers a more productive and less rigidly bounded interpretation of Shelley's symbolism, paying particular heed to Shelley's domes, his image of the chariot, his treatment of sleep, and his sea-river-cave journeys.[23] Bennett Weaver interprets the Shelleyan cave anew, and calls attention to Shelley's symbolic use of kings, priests, and judges.[24] Newman Ivey White, like Professor Grabo, is interested primarily in the intellectual content and sources of Shelley's imagery, while admitting that poetry is more than logic.[25]

W. B. Yeats, aided by the insight of his poetic genius, has given the most fully satisfying account of Shelley's symbols, although his view is perhaps colored overmuch by mysticism. To him a symbol is an image "that has transcended particular time and place," and "passes beyond death, as it were, and becomes a living soul." By this transcendence of time and place the poet, who is a mystic striving always to be absorbed into the surrounding universe, through reverie places himself in contact with the vast reservoir

[20] "Shelley's Symbolism," *op. cit.*, pp. 68–106.

[21] A. C. Bradley, *Oxford Lectures on Poetry* (London, 1917), p. 152.

[22] Note the emphasis in such statements as the following: "Shelley's fondness for certain images and symbols and his repeated use of them in a form increasingly adequate to his thought is one of his marked characteristics as a poet" (p. 104). ". . . Shelley was, unconsciously perhaps, preparing for his use a medium of peculiar efficacy in the expression of philosophic ideas in the form needful for poetry" (p. 169). ". . . in later poems, he employs these symbols and others kin to them, and with a growing sense of their suitability as poetic counters, expressing both physical facts and metaphysical theories" (p. 176).

[23] G. Wilson Knight, "The Naked Seraph—an Essay on Shelley," *The Starlit Dome* (London and New York, 1941).

[24] Bennett Weaver, *Toward the Understanding of Shelley* (Ann Arbor, Mich., 1932), pp. 69, 189.

[25] Newman Ivey White, "Words in their logical meaning being by nature often inadequate to the uses of great poetry, images and symbols may sometimes be employed to speak more directly to the imagination and intuition" (*Shelley* [New York, 1940], 1, 425).

of world-memory, from which his symbols are drawn.[26] These symbols are valuable because of their depth and universality. By means of them the poet passes beyond the limitations of his own personality,[27] and is linked to all the human heritage of past and present. By virtue of this deep-rooted kinship with all that is, the poet's imagery grows infinitely rich, flexible, and meaningful, drawing upon the connotations with which his symbols have been invested by a thousand poets before him. It is not merely fantastic or capricious, but is based upon enduring verities.[28] Such symbolism as this, then, is essentially private and unique,[29] but nevertheless universal in its significance.

The worth of Yeats's interpretation of Shelley's symbols is primarily that he conceives them to be poetic, not in the narrow sense philosophical: fluid, not fixed: emotional and sensuous as well as intellectual. Shelley's symbols are expressive of his search for Truth, but a poetic Truth imaginatively pursued. It is this pursuit which evokes the deepest feelings of Shelley's spirit. His most characteristic imagery embodies an attempt to establish the relationship between the finite and the infinite. This relationship is variable according to his mood; it is not exclusively Platonic, nor neo-Platonic, nor Naturalistic, but is all by turns, or partakes of all simultaneously. Shelley's philosophic studies furnish an important part of the subject matter of his verse, but a part not more important than does his love of and response to natural beauty; and the result, when Shelley is writing well, is always poetry.

It is not too daring, I think, to assert that this finite-infinite relationship is the focal point of Shelley's imagery. Shelley is intellectually a Monist,

[26] W. B. Yeats, "The Philosophy of Shelley's Poetry," *Ideas of Good and Evil* (London, 1914), pp. 80–81.
    Cf. Shelley, "On Life": "Those who are subject to the state called reverie, feel as if their nature were dissolved into the surrounding universe, or as if the surrounding universe were absorbed into their being. They are conscious of no distinction."
[27] Cf. *Prometheus Unbound*, IV, 394ff.:
> Man, oh, not men! a chain of linked thought,
> Of love and might to be divided not,
> Compelling the elements with adamantine stress; . . .
> Man, one harmonious soul of many a soul,
> Whose nature is its own divine control,
> Where all things flow to all, as rivers to the sea. . . .
[28] "It is only by ancient symbols, by symbols that have numberless meanings beside the one or two the writer lays an emphasis upon, or the half-score he knows of, that any highly subjective art can escape from the barrenness and shallowness of a too conscious arrangement, into the abundance and depth of nature. . . .
    ". . . his [Shelley's] poetry becomes the richer, the more emotional . . . when I remember that these are ancient symbols, and still come to visionaries in their dreams" (Yeats, *op. cit.*, pp. 90, 92).
[29] ". . . voices would have told him how there is for every man some one scene, some one adventure, some one picture that is the image of his secret life, for wisdom speaks first in images. . . ." (*Ibid.*, p. 98.)

emotionally and instinctively a Dualist. He is always attempting to reconcile these two poles of his nature, and never quite succeeding. He is continually putting together Time and Eternity, Relative and Absolute, Fluctuating and Fixed, Seen and Unseen, to determine how they will relate and interact. The stress thus set up is the essential condition of his poetry, the climate in which it exists.

This relationship appears perhaps most frequently in the image of the veil, and in this form is plainly evident as early as *Queen Mab*. The "glowing limbs" (I, 32) of the sleeping Ianthe are an envelope covering a secret light, perceptible only through this fleshly mask. The Fairy Queen, herself supernatural, has it in her power "to rend The veil of mortal frailty" and set free the spirit, "Clothed in its changeless purity" (I, 180–182). The ocean acts as a mirror to reflect the "pale and waning stars," the fiery wake of the Fairy's chariot, and the light of morn; this foreshadows other, more conscious images of reflection (I, 225–230). In this case fleeting appearances are caught and held fast in a changeless medium, but there are other images in which eternity is mirrored in shifting waters emblematic of time. Time and Eternity are contrasted in the figure of the Spirit of Ianthe peering down from above at the earth:

> The Spirit seemed to stand
> High on an isolated pinnacle;
> The flood of ages combating below. . . .
> (II, 253–255)

Images of curtaining, canopies, and robes, not infrequent in Shelley, are probably merely descriptive in *Queen Mab*, innocent of an ulterior meaning. Yet as variations of the veil image they have their interest. "Heaven's ebon vault" is like a canopy "which love had spread To curtain her sleeping world" (IV, 4–8); the hills are "Robed in a garment of untrodden snow" (IV, 9). It should be noted that in these instances the covering itself is beneficent and significant, not something to be torn away.

The Time-Eternity contrast is explicit in

> . . . the storm of change, that ceaselessly
> Rolls round the eternal universe and shakes
> Its undecaying battlement. . . .
> (VI, 160–162)

It is somewhat confusedly presented in

> Soul of the Universe! eternal spring
> Of life and death, of happiness and woe,
> Of all that chequers the phantasmal scene

> That floats before our eyes in wavering light,
> Which gleams but on the darkness of our prison
> Whose chains and massy walls
> We feel but cannot see.
>
> (VI, 190–196)

This image seems to be derivative from Plato's image of the cave, without reference to which it is barely intelligible.

The image of the veil as a delusive covering hiding reality occurs in Ahasuerus's bitter description of the Christ:

> . . . humbly he came,
> Veiling his horrible Godhead in the shape
> Of man, scorned by the world. . . .
>
> (VII, 163–165)

It may be remarked in passing that the figure of Ahasuerus himself, the wandering Jew, which had a singular fascination for Shelley, is an ironic symbol of the Time-Eternity relationship. This relationship, faintly adumbrated in an image of a giant oak braving a wintry storm (VII, 259–263), is direct in

> . . . the cradles of eternity
> Where millions lie lulled to their portioned sleep
> By the deep murmuring stream of passing things,
>
> (VIII, 6–8)

is pictured in a shroud ("Tear thou that gloomy shroud" [VIII, 9]), in a veil ("Through the wide rent in Time's eternal veil" [VIII, 12]), and in a lighthouse:

> And, 'midst the ebb and flow of human things,
> Show somewhat stable, somewhat certain still,
> A light-house o'er the wild of dreary waves.
>
> (VIII, 55–57)

To trace the course and ramifications of this basic image in its various forms throughout the body of Shelley's poetry would be work for a book rather than an essay. I shall therefore confine myself to citing a few instances of it in significant poems. In *Alastor*, the visioned maid who appears to the poet in dreams is *veiled* (l. 151). Her body, like the body of Ianthe in *Queen Mab*, is a covering concealing yet permeated by an inner fire:

> Soon the solemn mood
> Of her pure mind kindled through all her frame
> A permeating fire. . . .
>
> (ll. 161–163)

In like fashion her "eloquent blood" tells "an ineffable tale" in "the branching veins" of her fair hands (ll. 166–169). The poet, viewing the maid, sees

> . . . by the warm light of their own life
> Her glowing limbs beneath the sinuous veil
> Of woven wind. . . .
>
> (ll. 174–176)

I have previously cited the statement of A. T. Strong that the veil is emblematic of the thinness of the barrier between the finite and the infinite. That is doubtless in some cases true, but the matter is not quite so simple, as the present passage shows. It is equally true that this image betrays Shelley's hopelessness of piercing the barrier, or even forming a clear notion of what lies beyond it, for there is here not one veil but many. One grasps at seeming reality only to find it merely the covering of a still deeper truth. The maid is the object of attainment, "beneath the sinuous veil," yet her "glowing limbs" are themselves merely the veil for a purer essence, in itself composed of complex elements, as is indicated by the "self-inwoven" image,[30] "the warm light of their own life."

Something of this complexity is present also in the lament for the poet with which *Alastor* ends:

> But thou art fled,
> Like some frail exhalation, which the dawn
> Robes in its golden beams. . . .
>
> (ll. 687–689)

Which is the essence, the exhalation or that which robes it? The relationship between covering and the thing covered is ambiguous.

Prometheus Unbound is rich in images of the finite-infinite relationship. The sea is "Heaven's ever-changing shadow" (I, 27–28). The Earth tells Prometheus of a world which is the shadow of our world,

> . . . where do inhabit
> The shadows of all forms that think and live,
> Till death unite them and they part no more.
>
> (I, 197–199)

One is not quite sure which is the shadow, which the reality; and the last line hints that both "shadows" and "forms" are but shadows of a truth still more remote. Prometheus calls before him not Jupiter but the Phantasm of Jupiter from the world of shades, while in the world of appearances Pain and Ruin are the shadows of Love (I, 779–780).

---

[30] I am indebted for this term to William Empson's *Seven Types of Ambiguity*.

The dizzying elusiveness of an essence or absolute concealed from perception beneath many veils is powerfully suggested in such images as

> Those eyes which burn in smiles that fade in tears,
> Like stars half-quenched in mists of silver dew.
> Beloved and most beautiful, who wearest
> The shadow of that soul by which I live. . . .
>
> (II, i, 28–31)

The whirling, overlapping syntax of the first line perfectly represents the bewildering involutions of the thought.

In some instances the veil itself is the essential element, notably in Panthea's dream of Prometheus:

> . . . the overpowering light
> Of that immortal shape was shadowed o'er
> By love; which from his soft and flowing limbs,
> And passion-parted lips, and keen, faint eyes,
> Steamed forth like vaporous fire. . . .
>
> (II, i, 71–75)

The finite-infinite image lies at the heart of the dazzling "Life of Life" lyric, from which one may strip off layer after layer without arriving at any solid certainty:

> Life of Life, thy lips enkindle
> With their love the breath between them;
> And thy smiles before they dwindle
> Make the cold air fire; then screen them
> In those looks, where whoso gazes
> Faints, entangled in their mazes.
>
> Child of Light! thy limbs are burning
> Through the vest which seems to hide them;
> As the radiant lines of morning
> Through the clouds, ere they divide them;
> And this atmosphere divinest
> Shrouds thee whereso'er thou shinest. . . .
>
> Lamp of Earth! where'er thou movest
> Its dim shapes are clad with brightness,
> And the souls of whom thou lovest
> Walk upon the winds with lightness,
> Till they fail, as I am failing,
> Dizzy, lost, yet unbewailing!

This song celebrates the quest, and not the gaining of the quarry. "Life of Life" is itself a finite-infinite image, portraying an essence within outer coverings. Yet in what does this essence lie? "Thy lips enkindle With their love the breath between them." It seems, however, equally likely that the breath may enkindle both. And why, if the smiles of the spirit "make the cold air fire," should they be screened

> In those looks, where whoso gazes
> Faints, entangled in their mazes?

For these "smiles" and "looks" are presumably identical, and both presumably derive from a deeper source.

Then, the limbs of the Child of Light are burning "Through the vest which seems to hide them": obviously the container and its contents. But these limbs themselves seem merely a veil for a further reality; and this burning does not reveal the naked truth, but conceals it: "this atmosphere divinest Shrouds thee whereso'er thou shinest." The "Lamp of Earth" indeed infuses the merely human with divinity, but the divine is known only as it manifests itself in the "dim shapes" of humanity. The source of this secret fire remains hidden. The souls whom this spirit loves "walk upon the winds with lightness," indeed, but whence their blessedness comes is unknown to them.

In the later stages of *Prometheus Unbound* the image of the veil becomes more simply an opposition of the accidental and imperfect to the perfect and permanent, as Shelley depicts the world of his desire:

> And, veil by veil, evil and error fall.
> (III, iii, 62)

Even in this confident speech, however, evil and error do not fall instantaneously; there is a suggestion of layer upon layer to be stripped off. There is, of course, the famous

> . . . painted veil, by those who were, called life,
> Which mimicked, as with colors idly spread,
> All men believed and hoped, is torn aside,
> (IV, 189–191)

in which reform and revelation are immediate.

In *Adonais* still another aspect of the finite-infinite relationship appears: dread of the consequences of success in the pursuit of the absolute. In his self-portrait he refers to himself as one who

> Had gazed on Nature's naked loveliness
> Actaeon-like, and now he fled astray. . . .
> (ll. 283–285)

A few lines later he characterizes himself as "A love in desolation masked"

—an unusual variation of the container-content theme, but reminiscent of the mingling of love with desolation and ruin in *Prometheus Unbound.*

The spirit of Keats is an essence hindered in life by its mortal covering:

> Dust to the dust! but the pure spirit shall flow
> Back to the burning fountain whence it came,
> A portion of the eternal. . . .
>
> (ll. 347–349)

The relationship between life and death is not constant, however, for

> . . . death is a low mist which cannot blot
> The brightness it may veil. . . .
>
> (ll. 400–401)

The temporal veil appears in a new guise in

> The One remains, the many change and pass;
> Heaven's light forever shines, Earth's shadows fly;
> Life, like a dome of many-colored glass,
> Stains the white radiance of Eternity,
> Until Death tramples it to fragments.
>
> (ll. 460–463)

It is to be noted that this veil has very decided attractions. Shelley, despite his brave words, is not wholly anxious to desert the beautiful world of appearances for the cold perfection of the One. There is a certain ambiguous emotion in "Until Death tramples it to fragments." This hesitation to take the final step, to tear the veil asunder once for all, pervades the last three stanzas of *Adonais*, striking an ominous note amid their joyous prophecy. "The soft sky smiles,—the low wind whispers near"—am I mistaken in imagining here a certain dread lest this invitation prove a betrayal? The next stanza is unquestionably a hymn to the One, a Light and a Beauty, a Benediction and a Love,

> Which through the web of being blindly wove
> By man and beast and earth and air and sea,
> Burns bright or dim, as each are mirrors of
> The fire for which all thirst. . . .

Yet the imagery betrays some mental conflict. The "web of being" is apparently at least in part opaque, and if it is "blindly wove" it is woven by creatures in some degree blind, who cannot in consequence be perfect mirrors of the fire. This fire, of course, "burns bright or dim" according to the stage of being in which it is reflected; nevertheless, the images of the web and the mirror do not entirely harmonize.

In the final stanza awe, exaltation, and repulsion are closely intertwined:

> The breath whose might I have invoked in song
> Descends on me; my spirit's bark is driven
> Far from the shore, far from the trembling throng
> Whose sails were never to the tempest given;
> The massy earth and sphered skies are riven!
> I am borne darkly, fearfully afar;
> Whilst, burning through the inmost veil of Heaven,
> The soul of Adonais, like a star,
> Beacons from the abode where the Eternal are.

The soul of Adonais is at once a strong wind which blows the bark of the spirit into dark, fearful waters and a fixed star which guides the mariner, comfortably like the beacon of a lighthouse. Yet before this light can be reached the poet must pierce not one, but many veils. "The massy earth and sphered skies are riven"; actuality disappears as at a thunder-clap before the divining perception of the seeker. The light, however, is still far to seek. Heaven itself is composed of layer within layer of mystery, veil beyond veil.

Of the various symbols which move constantly through Shelley's pages I have offered only a brief glimpse at that key-sumbol of his verse which is most typically represented by the image of the veil. This symbol, like his other symbols, is abstract insofar as it is, in the words of Yeats, an image "that has transcended particular time and place," and has a predetermined meaning not wholly dependent upon the sensuous and natural context in which it is framed. Like his other symbols, it is symptomatic of a fundamental dualism in Shelley's conception of the relationship between mind and nature—a dualism all the more evident because of his continuous efforts to resolve it into unity.

What I have chiefly attempted to show, however, is that Shelley's images are not lifeless pawns in a game of philosophic chess. They are living, flexible, various in the subtle shades of meaning which attach to them. Reflecting a consistent view of life, each image is nevertheless a response to a particular poetic stimulus and situation, dictated by a thousand considerations of mood, tone, and artistic necessity. Shelley's imagery is always dramatic, expressive of struggle and aspiration toward heights which he did not, as some would have, conceive as easy of attainment, but which he felt to be inexpressibly enchanting through the very difficulty of scaling them.[31] The stress beneath which it labors is the condition of its unique identity and value, for it is indicative of an appreciation of complexity and a love of natural beauty for which Shelley is not always given credit. The "dome of many-coloured glass" was perhaps as dear to him as the "white radiance of eternity," although he did not find the two compatible.

[31] Cf. the "Ode to Heaven" and Mrs. Shelley's comment, quoted above, note 13.

Shelley and the Creative Principle

by Leone Vivante

Shelley conceives life's radical aspects, which perpetually disclose its creative essence, as *real*. He conceives them as implying, directly or indirectly, all the problems of spirit and nature. And nobody is in closer contact with those aspects or this essence. No wonder, then, if he considers himself—and the Poet in general—as a researcher; and poetry, as highly contributive to knowledge. He expresses his conviction frequently (e.g., *Alastor*, 22, 37); and, in more general terms, his view is implied when he calls science and poetry "sisters" ("And Science, and her sister Poesy . . . ," *The Revolt of Islam*, 2255).

To maintain that his conviction depends on his incompetence concerning the meaning and methods of knowledge, or on a kind of self-delusion, would be absurd.

"Ode to the West Wind" (1819)

It is not only through obvious material associations that the poem almost begins with the image of scattered autumnal leaves,

> Yellow, and black, and pale, and hectic red,
> Pestilence-stricken multitudes. . . .
> ("Ode to the West Wind," 4)

The colors of the spring seem to be essentially connected with the moment of birth, of the first coming into being, as we may inwardly imagine it—revealing tenderness and grace, and, in each gem and bud, absolute faith, and newness, and innocence. But the beauty of autumn seems to be scarcely related to the processes by which it is determined or conditioned. There is something almost uncanny in it; something non-human and even heterogeneous from life. Hence, as it seems, through a spontaneous, deep kinship of concepts, the image anticipates in some way the ode, and fits in with its grandeur.

"Shelley and the Creative Principle" (Editor's title). From *English Poetry and its Contribution to the Knowledge of a Creative Principle* (1950). Excerpted and reprinted by permission of Leone Vivante. References to other parts of the work have been omitted.

> Thou on whose stream, mid the steep sky's commotion
> Loose clouds like earth's decaying leaves are shed. . . .
>
> (*Ibid.*, 15)

Self-surrender, through which everything is lost, and renewed, and identified with that power (the "wind") is here the *essential* moment expressed. We begin to be aware that the "Wind" is spirit itself—or a medium to its expression.

> Thou who didst waken from his summer dreams
> The blue Mediterranean, where he lay,
> Lulled by the coil of his crystàlline streams. . . .
>
> (*Ibid.*, 29)

Is the Mediterranean here depicted, or is it rather a means to express thought's elemental qualities? For that by which we are here allured and enlightened is thought's very transparency, rediscovered in and through the "object," and the element of form, however light it may be (cf. the "coil" of the sea's "crystalline streams") which is essential to the reality of thought itself and shares in that transparency. It may be objected that Shelley was unaware that thought's reality had anything to do with the "coil" and the "crystalline streams" of the sea. I maintain that consciousness of this is not entirely lacking either in the poet, or in the reader. Insofar as Shelley is concerned, the following passage, not belonging to the same poem, would seem to support my contention. The relation between the crystalline sea and thought is here more apparent, and intentional:

> But Greece and her foundations are
> Built below the tide of war,
> Based on the crystàlline sea
> Of thought and its eternity. . . .
>
> (*Hellas*, 696)

The above question reflects a problem which is always an open one in all arts—except in music and (in certain respects) in architecture. This is the problem, or rather the *riddle* of the represented "object"—which in itself, on the one hand, appears to be but a pretext, or an occasion, or a fecund medium, and yet, on the other hand, must be aimed at and loved in and for itself, otherwise thought's very power and all grace is forfeited.

> If I were a dead leaf thou mightest bear;
> If I were a swift cloud to fly with thee;
> A wave to pant beneath thy power, and share

> The impulse of thy strength, only less free
> Than thou, O uncontrollable! If even
> I were as in my boyhood, and could be
>
> The comrade of thy wanderings over Heaven. . . .
> ("Ode to the West Wind," 43)

Obviously, the personification of the West Wind would be impossible—or extremely fictitious and disturbing—were not the "object" (the "West Wind") merged in the spiritual reality it embodies. I would limit myself to pointing out here only one aspect of this reality, as expressed in the passage above quoted—that of dauntlessness (to use one of Shelley's words).

Self-oblivion, self-surrender, pity and tenderness, and all forms of one's identification with the active principle in its intrinsic or *eternal* nature, may seem in Shelley's poetry to efface, in some respects, individuality. He, in his own words, is "of hearts the weakest":

> When a voice said: "O thou of hearts the weakest. . . ."
> (*Epipsychidion*, 232)

What is there in Shelley that compensates or counteracts this (if spirit's harmony and reality must be restored)? It is not *pride*. It is not the *will* in the narrower sense of the word. It is not *control over thought*. I think that in this connection (in Shelley's poetry) the outstanding and characteristic factors are dauntlessness and disdain. As for *disdain*, let us quote (as demonstrating a particular shade of it) the following passage:

> There is the wisdom of a stern content
> When Poverty can blight the just and good,
> When Infamy dares mock the innocent,
> And cherished friends turn with the multitude
> To trample: this was ours, and we unshaken stood!
> (*The Revolt of Islam*, 68)

"The dauntless and the good" (cf. "The Daemon of the World," 314) seems to resume, and may be taken as symbolizing, the twofold aspect of value. Compare the following fragments:

> From hate and awe thy heart is free;
> Ardent and pure as day thou burnest. . . .
> ("The Daemon of the World," 91)

> For none than he a purer heart could have,
> Or that loved good more for itself alone;
> Of nought in heaven or earth was he the slave.
> ("Prince Athanase," 16)

Cf. also *The Revolt of Islam*, 710, 951; *Prometheus Unbound*, IV, 572–73. The West Wind is "uncontrollable," "wild," "fierce." In another passage of the Ode, a few lines further on, the concept-value I am referring to is even more distinctly expressed:

> A heavy weight of hours has chained and bowed
> One too like thee: tameless, and swift, and proud.
> ("Ode to the West Wind," 55)

Shelley explicitly calls the West Wind "Spirit," a "wild Spirit," which is "moving everywhere" (l. 13). Cf. also ll. 61–62 (quoted in the following passage). But this does not, or might not, mean very much; and "spirit" and "wind" are terms which possess an old common history. What matters is that the actual and yet self-transcending *cause* of life is real, and felt, and known, in the image of the Wind. The "Ode to the West Wind" sounds now as an invocation, now as a prayer—and this, again, would appear awkward, or fictitious, if that *reality* were not actually present.

Here are the last lines of the Ode:

> . . . Be thou, Spirit fierce,
> My spirit! Be thou me, impetuous one!
>
> Drive my dead thoughts over the universe
> Like withered leaves to quicken a new birth!
> And, by the incantation of this verse,
>
> Scatter, as from an unextinguished hearth
> Ashes and sparks, my words among mankind!
> Be through my lips to unawakened earth
>
> The trumpet of a prophecy! O, Wind,
> If Winter comes, can Spring be far behind?
> (*Ibid.*, 61)

May I draw attention to two concepts especially, which are most contributive to the meaning and poetical power of this passage.

A value of universality (which indeed inspires all Shelley's poetry) is here expressed, that finds in the image of the Wind a particularly apt means of expression. This image may convey a sense of self-transcendency and universality in many ways, but I would confine myself to emphasizing the following. Dissatisfaction with anything particularly local, and national, and human, a sense of homelessness, the wish for an endless wandering, these feelings may be suggested by the image of the Wind. We may understand that Shelley found in the West Wind a fit medium of expression, which his very soul was seeking for. Let us refer to other poems. He likes to speak of "homeless streams (*Alastor*, 566); of that which "cannot make abode" (*The Revolt of Islam*, 4759); of man "unclassed, tribeless, and nationless" (*Prometheus Unbound*, III, iv, 195). "The Aziola," also, I could hardly refrain from quoting in this connection—where he humorously says:

> . . . How elate
> I felt to know that it was nothing human,
> No mockery of myself to fear or hate. . . .
> ("The Aziola," 7)

Yet his heart is with mankind, and in the righteousness of his deepest claims, and above all in the original reality with which he is now in close contact, in the *felt* eternity, and universality, of a principle of inviolate freedom, he knows, he seeks, a power of prophecy. The actual cause itself is, in fact, embodied in the "Wind," "uncontrollable," "awaking," transparent and (in a sense) unattainable, simple, inviolable and most powerful. The actual cause is, on the other hand, immediately and essentially forging the temporal direction and, let us say, forward looking, stretching into the future; moveover, it is "the key of truths," and primal, i.e., self-characterizing *ad infinitum*. Hence, I think, the immediate feeling of a "prophetic" character in it.

"To a Skylark" (*1820*)

> Hail to thee, blithe Spirit!
> Bird thou never wert,
> That from Heaven, or near it,
> Pourest thy full heart
> In profuse strains of unpremeditated art.
> ("To a Skylark," 1)

"Unpremeditated," as here the word is used, not only conveys the feeling and the meaning of the creative and deeply new moment, self-imposing, intrinsically characterized; it also expresses in a distinctly high degree a temporal direction, a joyous and glorious opening of the gates of the future; and, again, it emphasizes the holocaust of the self (cf. "Pourest thy full heart . . .") in the essentially new act, and it seems to show that the latter's rich and wide content (cf. "In profuse strains . . .") depends just on this newness.

> Higher still and higher
> From the earth thou springest
> Like a cloud of fire;
> The blue deep thou wingest,
> And singing still dost soar, and soaring ever singest.
> (*Ibid.*, 6)

Indeed, height, and light, and song, and the glory of thought in the visioned
infinity of its bright original power, are here one identical reality: yet each
word carries its own problem, which is felt as a distinct reality and, in some
sense, a distinct mystery. Why is *height* a radical, essential value of mental
reality? Why does the feeling of *height* exist at all? We may try to explain
height pragmatically, with reference to eons of experiences of power and
freedom; but these, so far as we can conceive, would presuppose such value,
or such urge, and the attempt would be but to explain away the problem.
"Height" is the last name—the last standard—for our moral judgment; and
for the poet's inspiration. In the manifold aspect of original causality, *height*
is a non-deducible element. It points to a primal urge for intellectual life. It
seems a *cause* in history and evolution, and not only the outcome of it. It
constitutes a burning problem; hence, in part, the actuality and power of the
poem.

> In the golden lightning
> Of the sunken sun,
> O'er which clouds are bright'ning,
> Thou dost float and run;
> Like an unbodied joy whose race is just begun.
>
> (*Ibid.*, 11)

In the last line of the stanza, the first and most intense initial moment—in
the essentially ever-initial *activity*—is pointed out as the most significant.

> The pale purple even
> Melts around thy flight;
> Like a star of Heaven
> In the broad daylight
> Thou art unseen, but yet I hear thy shrill delight. . . .
>
> (*Ibid.*, 16)

"Unseen": cf. further on, verses 46 ff.;

> All the earth and air
> With thy voice is loud,
> As, when night is bare,
> From one lonely cloud
> The moon rains out her beams, and Heaven is overflowed.
>
> (*Ibid.*, 26)

Fullness of form and infinitude are here expressed in all their power and
indistinguishably blended; form is here as wide as infinitude, and infinitude
itself is form.

> What thou art we know not;
> What is most like thee?

> From rainbow clouds there flow not
>> Drops so bright to see
> As from thy presence showers a rain of melody.

> Like a Poet hidden
>> In the light of thought,
> Singing hymns unbidden,
>> Till the world is wrought
> To sympathy with hopes and fears it heeded not. . . .
>> *(Ibid.*, 31)

The concept expressed in the second of the two stanzas last quoted consists in two parts. (1) Creative thought overshadows the separate self. The poet is absorbed by it; he is identified with it. His past, his organism, his very life are but a *medium*—a fertile *medium* for an ever-new, exacting actuality. (2) The *Word*—the actual cause—carries within itself a seed of truths, an harmonious richness, which cannot be entirely absent, wherever a beginning of consciousness is found, and which can be awakened, or—if means of expression and other conditions are not widly different—*it seems impossible* that it should not be awakened. Original causality is here powerfully felt and asserted in its self-transcending character (cf. "a Poet hidden") and in its essential novelty (cf. "hymns unbidden"), but above all, owing, as I maintain, to its deep intrinsic character, a universal and almost prophetic quality in it is realized. It is perhaps from the consciousness of poetic reality, as expressed in this stanza, that Shelley drew first his inspiration for the whole poem. (Cf. verses 101–5, quoted further on, with ll. 39–40 in this stanza.)

> Like a glow-worm golden
>> In a dell of dew,
> Scattering unbeholden
>> Its aëreal hue
> Among the flowers and grass, which screen it from the view!

> Like a rose embowered
>> In its own green leaves,
> By warm winds deflowered,
>> Till the scent it gives
> Makes faint with too much sweet those heavy-wingèd thieves . . .
>> *(Ibid.*, 46)

Shelley seems to search here—yet as one who only looks after beauty!—for a high and still higher degree of indeterminacy. This is a positive value, a value in itself. It is elicited, enhanced, by every word and image. Invisibility, secretness and intimacy, which we here find expressed, are in fact essential aspects of indeterminacy—and of creative novelty.

> Sound of vernal showers
>   On the twinkling grass,
> Rain-awakened flowers,
>   All that ever was
> Joyous, and clear, and fresh, thy music doth surpass. . . .
>
> *(Ibid.,* 56)

It may be also emphasized that, especially, the words "Joyous, and clear, and fresh . . . ," as used here, reflect and witness a deep ontological reality, and depth of thought, but that they are lost, precisely in their poetical value, for anyone who, through pseudo-scientific preconceptions, makes himself deaf to any sense of the creative element in which they have their force and significance.

> Chorus Hymeneal,
>   Or triumphal chant,
> Matched with thine would be all
>   But an empty vaunt,
> A thing wherein we feel there is some hidden want.
>
> What objects are the fountains
>   Of thy happy strain?
> What fields, or waves, or mountains?
>   What shapes of sky or plain?
> What love of thine own kind? what ignorance of pain?
>
> With thy clear keen joyance
>   Languor cannot be:
> Shadow of annoyance
>   Never came near thee:
> Thou lovest—but ne'er knew love's sad satiety.
>
> Waking or asleep,
>   Thou of death must deem
> Things more true and deep
>   Than we mortals dream,
> Or how could thy notes flow in such a crystal stream?
>
> *(Ibid.,* 66)

Is the creative element to such a degree identified with the song's perpetual novelty—with the summit of the living present—that no shade of the past ever touches it? Or is it so deeply and powerfully identified with the intrinsic and eternal character of its very principle and essence, that this *character* becomes the only existing reality, and individual death is made insignificant? Or, again, are there transcendental explanations of that joy, which are entirely unknown to us? Shelley says that

Our sweetest songs are those that tell of saddest thought.

(*Ibid.*, 90)

Indeed sorrow calls for pity and for love or, more in general, for the vindi-
cation, and present reality, of the spirit—through its denial. But the "Bird"
does not need this. It does not feel this; and yet its song attains greater height
than ours. Obliviousness and ignorance are but negative values; and yet the
bird's song soars higher than anything of ours. It must not be really oblivion,
or ignorance, which sustains it, but truth. Shelley's question is not idle,
because the "key of truths" lies there—in the song. The criterion of truth
lies in the height, in that supreme reality which Shelley sees and hears and
which inspires him in these lines. He does not believe that it can deceive us.
And this conviction of his can probably be taken as the test of his identification with the spirit and of the intensity of his inspiration.

However this may be, a more definite truth becomes now apparent. That
"keen joyance" is the unconquerable *formative* power (the actual cause), the
quintessence of it. And, could we only learn "half" of that "gladness," the
truth for which we stand on this earth would be so powerfully recreated and
interpreted in and through it, that all men's unwillingness to hear should be
conquered:

> Teach me half the gladness
>   That thy brain must know,
> Such harmonious madness
>   From my lips would flow
> The world should listen then—as I am listening now.

(*Ibid.*, 101)

Epipsychidion (*1821*)

Here I shall select only a few [passages from *Epipsychidion*] which refer
especially to woman—as the object, so to say, in which spirit now is discovered by Shelley or revealed to him. Yet I leave aside the most relevant
aspect of his discovery, namely, that profound Oneness with the beloved
being—implying annihilation and renewal—to which already attention has
been called.

> Seraph of Heaven! too gentle to be human,
> Veiling beneath that radiant form of Woman
> All that is insupportable in thee
> Of light, and love, and immortality!

(*Epipsychidion*, 21)

The image is again suggested and constituted by the essential interplay between form and, on the other hand, the very principle of form—in its original, universal, and eternal character (distinctly signified by "light," "love," and "immortality"). Form (cf. "that radiant form of Woman") is eclipsed, but to such a degree of intensity, that we may doubt whether or not this transitory form represents the full reality of the principle itself. The image may remind us of that one in which Shelley says that life "stains" (not as here "veils") the "white radiance of Eternity." But here the "white radiance of Eternity" is not supposed to lie outside the beloved being itself. These concepts make up the warp and woof of Shelley s imagery—and, indeed, neither a transcendent nor an immanent view need be implied! This, however, does not mean that they have here no ontological significance. Here as elsewhere, in fact, they are most significant and revealing, in so far as thought's—and life's—irreplaceable and inimitable tissue is concerned.

> Sweet Benediction in the eternal Curse!
> *(Ibid.,* 25)

> Thou Wonder, and thou Beauty, and thou Terror!
> *(Ibid.,* 29)

He attempts to find images most like his beloved, and it is worth while noticing that they are the more powerful (as I would think) the more directly they elicit essential aspects of the original reality we are considering:

> A Solitude, a Refuge, a Delight . . .
> *(Ibid.,* 64)

> A cradle of young thoughts of wingless pleasure . . .
> *(Ibid.,* 68)

> A Metaphor of Spring and Youth and Morning . . .
> *(Ibid.,* 120)

> Her Spirit was the harmony of truth.
> *(Ibid.,* 216)

> . . . the brightness
> Of her divinest presence trembles through
> Her limbs, as underneath a cloud of dew . . .
> Amid the splendour-wingèd stars, the Moon
> Burns, inextinguishably beautiful. . . .
> *(Ibid.,* 77, 81)

As happens to many a man, from his first youth Shelley longs for an ideal and fully incarnate Form, in whom to find consent, his highest standard of values confirmed and the best of his soul made real and tangible; in whom to know, above all, that awful Simplicity, which cannot be known except in its self-revealing actuality, love, comparable only—in its infinitude—to Death.

> There was a Being whom my spirit oft
> Met on its visioned wanderings, far aloft,
> In the clear golden prime of my youth's dawn. . . .
> *(Ibid.,* 190)

The *active* principle, in love's passion as in art, is omnipresent; this original power calls from everywhere, lies in every object:

> . . . In solitudes
> Her voice came to me through the whispering woods, . . .
> And from the singing of the summer-birds,
> And from all sounds, all silence.
> *(Ibid.,* 200, 208)

Eventually,

> She met me, Stranger, upon life's rough way, . . .
> And called my Spirit, and the dreaming clay
> Was lifted by the thing that dreamed below . . .
> . . . and in her beauty's glow
> I stood, and felt the dawn of my long night
> Was penetrating me with living light. . . .
> *(Ibid.,* 72, 338)

"To Jane, The Recollection" (*1822*)

Inviolable quietness, presence infinite, silence, are suggested in the following lines and actually expressed, not only, but most especially, through the *absence* of wind and tempest, which are represented in their *possibility*—an allusion being made to their secret "nest" and "home." The "hour"—a most indeterminate noun—"from beyond the sky" conveys the sense of an even wider and purer presence:

> We wandered to the Pine Forest
> That skirts the Ocean's foam,
> The lightest wind was in its nest,
> The tempest in its home.
> The whispering waves were half asleep,
> The clouds were gone to play,
> And on the bosom of the deep
> The smile of Heaven lay;

> It seemed as if the hour were one
>   Sent from beyond the skies,
> Which scattered from above the sun
>   A light of Paradise.
>   ("To Jane, The Recollection," 9)

The "inviolable quietness" (cf. l. 37) is again expressed by the image which immediately follows in the poem. The "pines" are powerfully sculptured while being compared with "serpents interlaced." "Storms" and "serpents" suggest movement. The idea of it is not entirely absent and makes the immobility of the trees, our thought of it, *actively* and perpetually real:

> We paused amid the pines that stood
>   The giants of the waste,
> Tortured by storms to shapes as rude
>   As serpents interlaced. . . .
>
> Now all the tree-tops lay asleep,
>   Like green waves on the sea,
> As still as in the silent deep
>   The ocean woods may be.
>
> There seemed from the remotest seat
>   Of the white mountain waste,
> To the soft flower beneath our feet,
>   A magic circle traced,—
> A spirit interfused around,
>   A thrilling, silent life,
> To momentary peace it bound
>   Our mortal nature's strife. . . .
>   (*Ibid.*, 21, 29, 41)

"A thrilling, silent life": in the first draft Shelley had written: "A thinking, silent life." This may indicate how distinctly Shelley understood and felt as a reality of thought, or sharing in thought's nature, the present value of eternity which is expressed in the poem. (He replaced the word "thinking" perhaps only because the expression "thinking . . . life" would sound rather crude—as it is presented.)

> We paused beside the pools that lie
>   Under the forest bough,—
> Each seemed as 'twere a little sky
>   Gulfed in a world below;

> A firmament of purple light
>   Which in the dark earth lay,
> More boundless than the depth of night,
>   And purer than the day—
> In which the lovely forests grew,
>   As in the upper air,
> More perfect both in shape and hue
>   Than any spreading there.
>
> Sweet views which in our world above
>   Can never well be seen,
> Were imaged by the water's love
>   Of that fair forest green.
> And all was interfused beneath
>   With an Elysian glow,
> An atmosphere without a breath,
>   A softer day below.
> Like one beloved the scene had lent
>   To the dark water's breast,
> Its every leaf and lineament
>   With more than truth expressed; . . .
>   (*Ibid.*, 53, 69)

The image of "pools" mirroring the landscape occurs repeatedly in Shelley's poetry; while here it finds its fullest, perfect expression. The following passages are of special interest both with reference to this image and to the whole poem:

> . . . a well,
> Dark, gleaming, and of most translucent wave,
> Images all the woven boughs above . . .
>   (*Alastor*, 457)

> . . . the moveless wave
> Whose calm reflects all moving things that are . . .
>   (*The Revolt of Islam*, 3104)

> And many a fountain, rivulet, and pond,
> As clear as elemental diamond,
> Or serene morning air . . .
>   (*Epipsychidion*, 436)

> Quivering within the wave's intenser day. . . .
>   ("Ode to the West Wind," 34)

Indeed these pools reflecting the landscape seem to be an image of thought's very reality, in its radical aspects. There is *unity* in them, to a remarkable degree, more perceptibily than in the landscape directly seen. There is *depth* in them—unfathomable (cf. "More boundless than the depth of night"). There is *purity* (cf. "purer than the day"). This purity reflects both creative novelty—the uncorrupted, simple, non-composite character of thought in its live originality—and, on the other hand, the soul's primary quest, self-transcending, never concluded. In Shelley's images the intensity of the *serene* seems to get its quality from all his power of joy and, on the other hand, the keen and deep, fundamental dissatisfaction of a distinctly *ethical* nature, burdened with unsolved problems and with sorrow, seeking for atonement. Compare the lines:

> Pinnacled dim in the intense inane.
> (*Prometheus Unbound*, III, iv, 204)

> Or fragments of the day's intense serene. . . .
> (*Epipsychidion*, 506)

Cf. also "Rosalind and Helen," 957. In no other poet, I think, except in Leopardi, does the "serene" attain this intenseness of meaning and is to such a degree a reality.

Let us come back to the image of the pools that lie "under the forest bough." There is in them, again, perspicuity and distinctness of form—reflecting an intrinsic or *eternal* modality of thought, and not only belonging to the objects *qua* objects. There is in the pool's transparency, in the fact that the water is there, but is not seen as such—rather is converted in the image of the landscape, made invisible in it, yet delicately bears the image itself—a likeness of love (cf. "Were imaged by the water's love," and ll. 76–78). There is represented the distinct acquisition of a deeper truth (cf. "With more than truth expressed"). This is a fundamental character of artistic activity. For things become *truer, more real*, they acquire a new and different reality, when they are, in a non-subordinate way, transformed into intrinsic values and modes of thought. And here, in fact, there is a *clearness*, which is not that of the objects, but is more convincing and powerful, more real as a quality. Above all, not timelessness, but a time not measured by change, or not primarily constituted by change, seems to be suggested. Thought's perpetual identity through its manifold forms seems to be almost perceptible in the stainless mirror, no less, or even more, than in the silence and inviolable quietness of the forest.

Thus Shelley attained in four most memorable instances the closest and happiest contact with spirit or, more exactly, was absorbed in it, identified with it, *knowing* it. We may say that in the "Ode to the West Wind" spirit is discovered and expressed, above all, as *freedom;* in the poem "To a Skylark," as perpetual *novelty;* in the *Epipsychidion,* as *Oneness;* and in the quietness of the forest near Pisa, as "self-enshrined" *eternity.*

The Poet of Adolescence

by Humphry House

For thousands now alive a passionate love of Shelley was a major experience in their young development—a love not only for particular poems, but for an idea of Shelley and the Shelley style; yet there are few in whom this passion has lasted into later life. This is acknowledged even by Mr. Lea, who is opposed to all that it implies. The common view is, briefly, that the delight does not last because there is something immature in the poetry itself. This is not new; it was well and clearly stated by J. A. Symonds in 1878:

> There was no defect of power in him, but a defect of patience; and the final word to be pronounced in estimating the larger bulk of his poetry is the word immature.

That was written before Dowden's *Life* and before Arnold's essay, which was a review of it; before the "inspired child" critiques of the nineties and all that derived from them; it was written, in fact, in the middle of a century in which, according to Mr. Lea, eulogy was the rule, and long before 1933, when he says "a Bull was published declaring Shelley to be bad, after all." He adds, that disparagement now carries the day, and that "no satisfactory full-length study of either Shelley's work or his life has so far appeared in this country making use of all the available material." But there have been books and better essays on Shelley in England which do not all get caught on the dilemma of false eulogy or disparagement which Mr. Lea has prepared for them.

The immediately relevant question is: Why should it be thought any disparagement at all to say that Shelley is adolescent and the bulk of his work immature? For it is surely just this that gives it its unquestioned power, its unique character in our literature. His poetry enthralls boys (girls rather less, I fancy) as no other poetry enthralls them—the rush of images based on light, sea, clouds, and mountains; the impatience with authority; the "passion for reforming the world"; the "idealisms of moral excellence"; the unflagging fantasy; Greece for the classical side, astronomy and botany for the modern, and even for the Army Class the series of dream girls (in *Alastor*, *Epipsychidion*, etc.) who exalt Narcissistic imaginings into regions of beautiful mystery. The vagueness, profusion, and complexity of the images are among the greatest attractions; it is indeed poetry "not perfectly understood"; but it is poetry loved with greater intensity and passion than any poetry afterward. The strongest evidence of Shelley's essential immaturity is his unfailing popularity with the young. But adolescence is never wholly superseded in any man, not even in those who (to quote Mr. Lea) "have left behind with their youth less of their intolerance than their generosity." Not only can past experience be recalled by Shelley with peculiar vividness; but there is an immature element in most adult situations, and Shelley is the supreme poet of exactly that.

I find it hard to appraise this book because, of the two later phases of response to Shelley which Mr. Lea describes, I have experienced only one, and that imperfectly. Even in adolescence there seemed to be "an element of supreme value in *Adonais*," and I agree that Phase 2 is an attempt to explain whence this value derives; but I cannot agree that this attempt, by inducing us to follow Shelley into "an intellectual mysticism that leads straight to despair," must make Phase 2 intolerable as a lodging-place. For the contradictions and despair in face of death which *Adonais* expresses are only one mood of human feeling among many. We do not go to *Adonais*, or to Shelley at all, for a system, or for a final answer about anything, but for an experience. To be committed neck and crop to a considered philosophy of despair by reading the works of one poet is simply not a normal response at all.

In Phase 3, Shelley becomes for Mr. Lea not a man or a poet but a "pure phenomenon" (of the kind that D. H. Lawrence became for Mr. Middleton Murry, whose work colors all Mr. Lea's judgments) "all equally significant, because of the order to which he belongs." Here I resign; I claim to be temperamentally disqualified; and suggest the banal alternative that to understand Shelley we must see him whole and see him plain. To this end it is important to follow the way he seized on certain philosophical ideas and the use he made of them in his verse: Mr. Lea's book is for this purpose a useful and, so far as the matter permits, lucid guide. The genesis of these ideas is described more fully than before, with good quotations, especially from the less well-known prose. But the philosophical understanding is far less than in Miss Powell's admirable essay in *The Romantic Theory of Poetry*

(1926); and not all Mr. Lea's honest and painstaking revelation of contradictions, unresolved problems, imperfect arguments, and uncorrelated experiences can convince me that Shelley was as great a philosopher as he was a poet.

The Necessity of Love: *Alastor* and the Epipsyche

by Carlos Baker

> She disappear'd, and left me dark, I wak'd
> To find her, or for ever to deplore
> Her loss, and other pleasures all abjure.
> (Adam, in *Paradise Lost*)

> Egeria! sweet creation of some heart
> Which found no mortal resting-place so fair
> As thine ideal breast; whate'er thou art
> Or wert—a young Aurora of the air,
> The nympholepsy of some fond despair;
> Or, it might be, a beauty of the earth,
> Who found a more than common votary there
> Too much adoring; whatsoe'er thy birth,
> Thou wert a beautiful thought, and softly bodied forth.
> (Byron, in *Childe Harold's Pilgrimage*)

> Pray, are you yet cured of your Nympholepsy? 'Tis a sweet disease: but one as obstinate and dangerous as any.
> (Shelley to Peacock, August 1818)

I

The concept of a strictly materialistic necessity, with which Shelley had dealt as vigorously as he knew how in *Queen Mab*, was a sufficiently poetical subject, as Shelley's admired Lucretius had proved in *De Rerum Natura*. Yet the stress on natural law, however fundamental in the life of man, tended to de-emphasize another law of which Shelley had become deeply though imperfectly conscious in the period between 1813 and 1815. This was the law of love, and in composing *Alastor* Shelley was attempting to dramatize a conflict of allegiance between what might be called the law for thing (natural law) and the law for man (the law of love). The general failure to see that this is the purpose of Shelley's second major work has resulted in a misapprehension of its meaning; and though Shelley and Mary both insisted that the poem ought to be considered didactic rather than merely descriptive-narrative, readers have regularly found difficulty in deciding what lesson was intended.[1]

The problem has been to account for an apparent discrepancy between the poem and a sentence or two in the preface. The second paragraph of the prefatory remarks implies that a curse-motif is at work in the poem; yet neither the first paragraph nor the poem itself will support the implication.[2]

Medwin, Dowden, Peacock, and Peck have all passed over this problem as if it did not exist.[3] But it has bothered Mrs. Campbell, who notices that "in the preface the youth is condemned: in the poem he is glorified";[4] her opinion is echoed by White, who says that "no one who had not read the Preface would suppose that the author intended the poem as a criticism of him";[5] and Havens, after an extensive study of the poem, has concluded that *Alastor* is "not a unity, does not produce a single impression, and was not the offspring of a single dominating purpose." [6] Dissenters from this position have included Stovall, who regards as untenable Mrs. Campbell's view that "Shelley, in his preface, misinterprets his own poem"; and Hoffman, who believes that Havens is wrong, and that "we must not abandon the attempt to discover minute connections between it [the poem] and the Preface, for the Preface makes us aware that a meaning was intended." [7]

---

[1] Shelley's contemporary reviewers damned the poem for its obscurity. See N. I. White, *The Unextinguished Hearth* (Durham, N.C., 1938), pp. 105–16. Victorian critics still found it obscure, but admired its noble language; better a "dreamy mysticism" than Queen Mab's subversive propaganda. See F. C. Mason, *A Study in Shelley Criticism* (Mercersburg, Pa., 1937), pp. 109–10, 112, 120, 147.

[2] Peacock assisted in confounding the confusion.

[3] Thomas Medwin, *The Life of Percy Bysshe Shelley*, ed. H. Buxton-Forman (London, 1913), pp. 138–40; T. L. Peacock, *Memoirs of Shelley*, in *Works*, Halliford ed., VIII, 100; E. Dowden, *The Life of Percy Bysshe Shelley* (London, 1886), I, 531–33; W. E. Peck, *Shelley, His Life and Work* (Boston, Mass., 1927), I, 422–31.

[4] O. W. Campbell, *Shelley and the Unromantics* (London, 1924), p. 188.

[5] N. I. White, *Portrait of Shelley* (New York, 1945), p. 192.

[6] R. D. Havens, *PMLA*, XLV (1930), 1098–1115.

[7] Floyd Stovall, *Desire and Restraint in Shelley* (Durham, N.C., 1931), p. 150, note 21; H. L. Hoffman, *An Odyssey of the Soul* (New York, 1933), p. 3. Carl Grabo, *The Magic Plant* (Chapel Hill, N.C., 1936), p. 174, does his best to bring together the poem and the preface. Other studies of the poem include that of Mueschke and Griggs, *PMLA*, XLIX (1934), 229–45, which argues that Wordsworth is the prototype of Shelley's poet, an argument effectively answered by Marcel Kessel, *PMLA*, LI (1936), 302–10. There appear to be good grounds for the belief of F. L. Jones, *PMLA*, XLIX (1934), 969–71, that *Alastor* is to some extent foreshadowed in Shelley's early novel, *St. Irvyne*. Cf. also the article by A. E. Dubois, *Journal of English and Germanic Philology*, XXXV (1936), pp. 530–45, which answers Havens.

The real point at issue would seem to be this: when Shelley wrote the poem, did he mean it to be the story of a peerless youth's quest for the ideal maiden of his dreams, or did he mean to imply that the youth was in some way culpable, and that the quest was a punishment? All the evidence points to the probability that the poem was originally intended to be what the poem itself and the first paragraph of Shelley's preface indicate—the story of a youth who took natural philosophy as his province, and was happy enough until he suddenly awoke to the thought that he needed sympathetic association with an ideal. Having united into a single idealized but pleasantly voluptuous image all of the wonderful, wise, and beautiful ideas known to him, he became passionately attached to his creation. When she vanished, his disappointment at not being able to find her again was too great for his sensitive spirit. He descended "to an untimely grave." This quest-motif is really the central motif in the poem.

The first paragraph of the preface contains nothing that would suggest an avenging spirit of solitude. In the poem itself Professor Havens has noticed two passages which seem to show that in writing the poem Shelley had in mind the curse-motif. Yet neither of them is necessarily involved with the avenging *alastor* theme. The first has to do with the origin of the vision. The preface says that the poet "images to himself the Being whom he loves," neither stating nor implying that this being has been sent to punish him, or that any supernatural agency beyond the poet's own imagination is involved, or even that the poet has been really culpable in his neglect of love. The poem (203–205) states that the vision was sent by "the spirit of sweet human love" to a youth who had hitherto spurned her "choicest gifts." In terms of the curse-motif, these words would suggest that the vision was sent for punitive purposes. But if the poem were written in ignorance of the *alastor* theme, the lines would mean simply that the youth, long preoccupied with philosophical considerations, suddenly awoke to the notion that he had been neglecting love.

The second passage has been generally misunderstood. The problem hinges on the interpretation of the phrase "fair fiend" (297). Professor Havens believes that the words refer to the visionary maiden.[8] But they seem rather to refer to the enigmatic figure of death, whom the poet regards as a kind of *ignis fatuus*. In the preceding lines, the youth has watched a swan fly back to its mate. He thinks of its flight as a symbol of his own desire to rejoin the vanished maiden of his dream—a desire which leads him seriously to consider the notion of suicide. Why should he continue to waste his powers on an unresponsive earth when those powers would evoke sympathetic re-

[8] R. D. Havens, *op. cit.*, p. 1105.

sponse from his dream-maiden in some other world? But can he safely trust death? May not death be just as false to him as was sleep in snatching away and keeping "most relentlessly" her precious charge? He seems to see death with a mocking smile dangling before him a shadowy lure.

> Startled by his own thoughts, he looked around.
> There was no fair fiend near him, not a sight
> Or sound of awe but in his own deep mind. . . .

The figure of death, which for a moment he seemed to see, was only a phantasm conjured up from the depths of his imagination, a fiend who looked fair because he half promised reunion with the lady.

We have seen that the first paragraph of the preface has nothing to do with the curse-motif. We now discover that in the poem itself the only two passages that might suggest a curse-motif are perfectly amenable to other interpretations. The poem—aside from the title and the second paragraph of the preface—can without difficulty be regarded as the quest-poem whose argument is given in the first prefatory paragraph.

Much of the prevailing confusion about the meaning of the poem can be traced to Peacock's generally misunderstood explanation of the title, and to the second or final paragraph of the preface, which looks very much like an ex post facto attempt by Shelley to moralize his song and to justify Peacock's nomenclature. Peacock suggested the title, very likely after the poem was finished. Shelley, says his learned friend, was "at a loss for a title, and I proposed that which he adopted: Alastor, or the Spirit of Solitude. The Greek word *Alastor* is an evil genius. . . . The poem treated the spirit of solitude as a spirit of evil. I mention the true meaning of the word because many have supposed *Alastor* to be the name of the hero." [9]

Peacock's explanation, while it enlightened those who had mistakenly supposed that the poet had a name, also helped to obscure Shelley's intention, for it implied that a curse-motif was prominently at work in the poem, and one could thereby infer that the visionary maiden was sent to the poet on a kind of punitive expedition. In this interpretation, of course, the poet was punished for having ignored the demands of human sympathy.

But Shelley's poem does not represent "solitude" as "evil." The word *solitude* occurs only three times in the whole piece, and in only one of these (line 414) could it possibly be construed as having evil significance. We are told that the poet longed to deck his hair with flowers. "But on his heart its solitude returned/ And he forebore." Here again we encounter ambiguity, for the lines may mean simply that the feeling of solitude (i.e., empty loneliness in the absence of his beloved) returned to grip the poet's heart and to

[9] *Memoirs of Shelley* in *Works of Thomas Love Peacock*, Halliford ed., VIII, 100.

dissuade him from lingering over the flowers. The explanation immediately follows: his vivid remembrance of the maiden's charms still exercised too powerful an influence over his mind to let him interrupt his search for her, even though his ill-kempt hair was by this date badly in need of embellishment.

The Greek idea of an avenging spirit would not therefore appear to have been in Shelley's mind during the composition of the poem. "At a loss for a title," he accepted Peacock's rather esoteric suggestion. It then became his task to explain the poem in terms of the new title without the need of revising the text itself. The second paragraph of the preface contains the attempted explanation.

The pertinent sentences are the second and ninth. Sentence two reads: "The Poet's self-centered seclusion was avenged by the furies of an irresistible passion pursuing him to a speedy ruin." Sentence nine expands the idea: "Among those who attempt to exist without human sympathy, the pure and tender-hearted perish through the intensity and passion of their search after its communities, when the vacancy of their spirit suddenly makes itself felt." The first of these sentences clearly asserts Peacock's *alastor* idea. The poet was "self-centered" in his "seclusion" and the "furies of an irresistible passion" drove him to ruin. But in the second sentence the poet is called (at least by implication) "pure and tender-hearted," and he perishes, not through the ministrations of vengeful furies, but by "the intensity and passion" of his search after human sympathy. The two sentences do not cohere: the self-centered poet of the first could hardly be the "tender-hearted" creature alluded to in the second. One might guess—though it is only a guess—that Shelley inserted the sentence about the "furies of an irresistible passion" in order to justify Peacock's title. Nowhere else in the preface, and nowhere in the poem, is the curse-motif visible.

Hoffman thinks that the "idea of Solitude as an avenging genius" is the central theme of *Alastor.* But he significantly adds that Shelley did not have the classical conception of *alastor* in mind when he composed the poem. Instead, according to Hoffman, he was thinking of Wordsworthian solitude as set forth in the picture of the Solitary in *The Excursion.* "It was not," he says, "until Peacock supplied the Greek word that Shelley saw how admirably it fitted the idea he had already worked out." [10] It might be urged rather that the Greek word did *not* fit the idea Shelley had worked out; but it had a sufficient connection with his main theme so that he seized upon it. In seizing upon it, however, he unfortunately threw the emphasis away from his primary theme: the conflict in a sensitive individual between allegiance to a kind of materialism and allegiance to a kind of idealism.

[10] H. L. Hoffman, *An Odyssey of the Soul: Shelley's* Alastor (New York, 1933), p. 53.

The real driving force in the poem is love, which obtains a complete hold over the intellect, imagination, and senses of the protagonist. According to Shelley's preface,

> the intellectual faculties, the imagination, and the functions of the sense have their respective requisitions on the sympathy of corresponding powers in other human beings. The Poet is represented as uniting these requisitions and attaching them to a single image.

When that image appears in the form of a maiden, the poet responds on all levels.

Seated beside him, talking solemnly of "knowledge and truth and virtue," the maiden at first evokes intellectual response in the poet, for these are the "thoughts most dear to him." Soon the young lady, herself a poet, turns to the subject of poesy, and, in a voice partly stifled by sobs, raises "wild numbers" as she fingers her "strange harp." Poetry, the language of the imagination, is also familiar ground to a youth long since acquainted with all "great or good or lovely" things which the "sacred past in truth or fable consecrates." Presently, however, it is time for the "functions of the sense." Rising suddenly and impatiently to her feet, the maiden gives every indication of a desire to embrace the poet. Uninitiated though he is in the arts of courtship, the youth responds to her rather obvious mating signals. With that "frantic gesture and short breathless cry" not uncommon in early Shelley heroines, the maiden has just "folded his frame in her dissolving arms" when the now thoroughly erotic vision ends, dark sleep floods in, and the youth awakes into a dismal loneliness. His intellect, his imagination, and his senses have all established bonds with corresponding powers in the maiden, or to put the matter simply, he is in love. Thereafter his every effort is directed toward reunion with the dream-maiden, failing which he wastes away to death.

The poem is an attempt to show, more or less symbolically, the intensity of one highly sensitive being's search for the "communities" of sympathy. The curse-motif is in the title and the preface alone. The erotic vision leading to a passionate quest was originally, and remained finally, the real central motif of Shelley's poem.

II

Stopford Brooke long ago observed a fundamental dichotomy in Shelley's poetry which now becomes pertinent. Shelley, says Brooke, lived in two worlds.

One was the world of Mankind and its hopes, the other was the world of his own heart. His poetic life was an alternate changing from one of these worlds to the other. He passed from poetry written for the sake of mankind, to poetry written for his own sake and to express himself; from the Shelley who was inspired by moral aims and wrote in the hope of a regeneration of the world, to that other Shelley who, inspired only by his own ideas and regrets, wrote without any ethical end, and absolutely apart from humanity.[11]

Brooke states his idea too mechanically and applies it too rigidly. His picture of a Shelley who walks across the stage singing of mankind, disappears into the wings, reappears singing of himself, and disappears once more only to reappear singing of mankind, and so on, has too many overtones of the quick-change artist of vaudeville. But the insight is not without value, and its psychological implications have been developed at some length by Stovall in his *Desire and Restraint in Shelley*, a very searching study of the opposition of altruistic and egoistic strains in Shelley's nature.[12] Brooke, Stovall, and their followers are all in substantial agreement that *Alastor* is an egoistic poem in which Shelley was seeking to express himself, to give an account, as Hoffman calls it, of the odyssey of a soul very like his own.[13]

While it is unlikely that Shelley could have written *Alastor* without benefit of introspection, and while the portrait of the wandering poet inevitably suggests an idealized and somewhat sentimentalized Shelley, it is possible to push the egocentric argument too far. One need not suppose that the poem is basically autobiographical any more than one need imagine that Hamlet was intended as an idealized portrait of Shakespeare himself. Although an argument might be made to show that the *Alastor* poet is really T. J. Hogg in disguise, and although an argument has been presented to show that Shelley had Wordsworth in mind when he wrote the poem, neither of these arguments is any more impressive than the view that Hamlet is meant for Sir Philip Sidney, the perfect soldier-scholar-courtier of the Elizabethan age. Instead of trying to paint an idealized picture of anyone (himself included), Shelley meant, as the first paragraph of his preface indicates, to describe, in an objective parabolical fashion, a state of mind which he had observed both in himself and in Hogg during the period 1811–1815.[14]

Shelley was acquainted with that phenomenon of some impressionable minds in which the lover builds up in his consciousness an ideal of a woman. The real woman, whom he clothes with the light that never was on sea or

---

[11] Stopford A. Brooke, *Poems from Shelley* (London, 1880), Preface, pp. xi–xii.

[12] See esp. Chapter XII, and elsewhere *passim.*

[13] H. L. Hoffman, *op. cit.,* see esp. p. 3.

[14] Hoffman states (*op. cit.,* p. 10) that the poem is a "metaphorical representation of a mental state."

land, has little resemblance to the ideal. Shelley's own affair with Harriet
Grove in 1810–1811 provided one example: he had painfully observed the
discrepancy between the Harriet of his fond dreams, and the Harriet who
was so afraid of his iconoclasm that she quickly married a mere "clod." At
this same time he had tried, with a peculiar combination of sentimental and
experimental motives, to build up in Hogg's mind an ideal image of his
sister, Elizabeth Shelley. He wished to see Hogg and Elizabeth united outside
the marriage tie. By the summer of 1811 Elizabeth had withdrawn in much
the same manner as Harriet Grove, and for similar reasons, chiefly a fear of
the opinions of her elders. On June 2, the *deus ex machina* of Field Place explained to his presumably bewildered friend how the delusion about Elizabeth had arisen:

> You loved a being, an idea in your own mind. You concreted this abstract of
> perfection. . . . The being, whom that name signified, was by no means worthy
> of this. . . . You loved a being, the being, whom you loved, is not what she was,
> consequently, as love appertains to mind, and not body, she exists no longer.[15]

Two weeks later he all but admitted that he had built up an idea of
Elizabeth's perfection in Hogg's mind to see how his friend would react.
"I knew what an unstable, deceitfull thing Love is; but still did I wish to
involve you in the pleasing delusion." [16] In short, there were two events in
1811 which served to acquaint Shelley with the tendency in the youthful and
imaginative male mind to concrete abstracts of perfection, to love an idea.
At the same time Shelley realized that this tendency did not necessarily
require the activating agency of flesh and blood. For someone like himself
a literary heroine would serve. When he read Lady Morgan's novel, *The
Missionary*, he became ecstatic over the "divine Luxima." "What a pity," he
cried, "that we cannot incorporate these creations of fancy; the very thoughts
of them thrill the soul." [17]

Between 1811 and the composition of *Alastor* in 1815, these early experiences were duplicated several times over. Shelley had (and variously em-
braced) other opportunities to involve himself in what he had called the
"pleasing delusion." The foci were Harriet Westbrook, Elizabeth Hitchener,
Cornelia Turner and her mother Mrs. Boinville, and in 1814, Mary Godwin.
Shelley's emotional instability was marked during the early months of 1811.
He was in a state of constant emotional turmoil from this time until after the
climactic elopement with Mary in the summer of 1814. With each of the

---

[15] *Letters*, VIII, 98 [Roger Ingpen and W. E. Peck eds., *The Complete Works of Percy
Bysshe Shelley*, Julian edition, 10 vols., London, 1926–1930].

[16] *Shelley at Oxford*, p. 40. June 16, 1811. When Hogg printed this letter in his *Life of
Shelley*, he changed the pronoun "you" to "myself" in order to cover up the real situation.

[17] *Letters*, VIII, 117.

women the pattern was repeated until he met Mary: attraction, approach, involvement in the "pleasing delusion," and finally detachment or retreat. The determination to elope with Mary cost Shelley a great mental struggle, and only after the decision had been made, after the union had in fact been effected, did his emotions gradually settle back toward something approximating calm. Other excitants followed. Apparently the affair between Hogg and Mary in the early months of 1815 was the result of another attempt by Shelley to involve Hogg in the "pleasing delusion." Hogg was now sufficiently experienced to approach Mary only with considerable caution, so that his involvement was not especially spectacular.[18] But the mere existence of such a liaison must have been enough to keep the participants and the onlooker in an unusually active emotional state, which the premature birth and early death of Mary's child did nothing to mollify. Therefore the summer and early autumn of 1815, which saw the composition of *Alastor*, was the first period of reasonably complete emotional calm in four years' time. The point to be stressed here is that the psychological phenomenon which Shelley had early observed in Hogg recurred often enough in his own experience during the next four years so that he could call it, as he did in the preface to *Alastor*, "one of the most interesting situations of the human mind."

Shelley's most extensive and searching statement about this recurrent mental situation occurs in a letter to Hogg written in August 1815, about the time when, in calm of mind, all passion spent, he was beginning, or was about to begin, the composition of *Alastor*. The language here is so close to that used in the preface to the poem, and the theme he is discussing is so similar in its essentials to that of *Alastor*, that the paragraph ought probably be taken as a glossary to his intention.

It excites my wonder to consider the perverted energies of the human mind. That so much benevolence and talent, as the missionary who travelled with you seemed to possess, should be wasted in such profitless endeavours, nor serve to any other end than to expose its possessor to perpetual disappointments. Yet who is there that will not pursue phantoms, spend his choicest hours in hunting after dreams, and wake only to perceive his error and regret that Death is so near? One man there is, and he is a cold and calculating man, who knows better than to waste life; but who alas! cannot enjoy it. Even the men who hold dominion over nations fatigue themselves by the interminable pursuit of emptiest visions; the honour and power which they seek is enjoyed neither in acquirement, possession or retrospect; for what is the fame that attends the most skilful deceiver or destroyer? What the power which awakens not in its progression more wants than it can supply? [19]

[18] An account of this affair occurs in White, *Shelley*, I, 391–93, 400–402. The pertinent letters are reprinted in R. M. Smith, *The Shelley Legend*, pp. 148–53.

[19] *Letters*, IX, 116 (August, 1815).

The mind is energetic in the pursuit of illusions. One may, like Hogg's benevolent and talented missionary, cherish hopes for the reformation of the world through the influence of Christian doctrine. His doom is perpetual disappointment in the failure of his hopes. One may, like the statesman, go in search of honor, power, and fame. He will enjoy these neither in the getting, holding, nor remembering. One may, like the cold realist, entertain no illusions; yet by the same token he cuts himself off from the enjoyment of life. The paradox is that the pursuit of phantoms is necessary to human happiness but inevitably productive of despair, while one who refuses to admit illusions to his thinking at the same time dries up the springs of joy in life. Shelley's preface to *Alastor* indicates that he would side with the missionary as against the cold calculator. The most quixotic dreamer is preferable, if he hurls himself at a vision with passionate intensity, to those who wither up in loveless lethargy.

There is a strong hint in Shelley's remarks of a type of ethical hedonism, not unknown among the sentimental writers of the eighteenth century: the implication that it is man's duty to seek love; he can thus avoid moral desuetude, even though disappointment and disillusion are likely to ensue upon his efforts. This view would go far toward explaining the essential paradox of *Alastor*, where a blameless youth, in pursuit of an impossible ideal, comes to grief because of the very intensity of his search after perfection. It would also explain why Shelley felt that the poem was "not barren of instruction to actual men," and why Mary Shelley asserted that "the poem ought rather to be considered didactic than narrative." Didactic it is, though not in the usual sense of explicit moral preachment, for its truths, to follow for a moment the language of Wordsworth, are not "individual and local, but general, and operative; not standing upon external testimony, but carried alive into the heart by passion"—which was always Shelley's way in poetry after the time of *Queen Mab*.

It would thus appear that Brooke's generalization, while it helps to categorize Shelley's poetry as a whole, does not really inhere in this poem. Ostensibly, *Alastor* is a poem "inspired only by [Shelley's] ideas and regrets," written "without any ethical end, and absolutely apart from humanity." One may also catch hints of self-justification in Shelley's admiration for an essentially Shelleyan hero. But the buried movements of the poem have an ethical end, and against Brooke's belief that in works like *Alastor* Shelley stood apart from humanity one ought to place Shelley's own statement about his poem, which he called "my first serious attempt to interest the best feelings of the human heart."

III

Shelley's aim in *Alastor*, then, was to set forth as objectively as possible, and as an object lesson, a state of mind with which his own experiments and experiences had intimately acquainted him. The preoccupation with such problems has been distinguished as the "pan-erotic element" in Shelley.[20] At this stage of his career, however, he was only beginning to formulate the doctrine of love which came gradually to supersede the doctrine of necessity in his thinking.[21]

Although the work suffers from the conflict of motives under which it was written, *Alastor* was a key poem in Shelley's development as philosophical and psychological poet. For it was the first of the major poems to undertake an experiment with what may be called the psyche-epipsyche strategy, of which he was to make considerable use in the central story of *The Revolt of Islam*, which was to become one of the major interrelated themes in his first great poem, *Prometheus Unbound*, and which was to be used at the highest possible level in *Epipsychidion, Adonais,* and *The Triumph of Life.* The basic assumption of the psyche-epipsyche strategy may be found under explicit discussion in the *Symposium* and *Phaedrus* of Plato. Phaedrus himself calls it, in Lane Cooper's excellent rendering, "the emulous desire for what is fine," without which "it cannot be that either state or individual should accomplish any great and noble work." [22] Whether or not the mind is disciplined it wishes to possess that which it does not have. When the mind is reined in by discipline, its motivating or driving force (the eros of the *Symposium*) is directed toward the goal of what is fine: the good and the beautiful, or rather the best and the most beautiful. To put the matter in Shelleyan terms, the mind (psyche) imaginatively creates or envisions what it does not have (epipsyche), and then seeks to possess epipsyche, to move toward it as a goal. Therefore the psyche-epipsyche strategy in a nutshell is the evolution by the mind of an ideal pattern toward which it then aspires. Or, as Aristophanes puts the matter in the *Symposium* (in full awareness of its comic aspects): "Our species would be happy under these conditions, if every one achieved his love completely, and found his own true mate."[23]

Although the epipsyche terminology does not appear in Shelley until 1821, the notion of a search for a true mate, a complementary heroine for the

---

[20] J. Kooistra, *English Studies*, IV (July 1922), 171–76.

[21] See F. Stovall's valuable study of "Shelley's Doctrine of Love," *PMLA*, XLV (March 1930), 283–303.

[22] *Symposium*, p. 178. Lane Cooper, trans., *Plato: Phaedrus, Ion, Gorgias, and Symposium,* etc. (New York, 1938), p.224.

[23] *Ibid.*, p. 240.

Shelleyan hero, has been born by 1815 and is well developed by 1817. The relationship is always, at its highest level, a spiritual union. But it must be, as it were, supported from below by other unifications. The Spanish word *simpatico* expresses the whole notion with some precision. It includes not merely an idea of voluntary sympathy and empathy; it has also a psysio-logical aspect involving the sympathetic nervous system. The remarks which Shelley prefixed to *Alastor* specify a hierarchy of correspondences or levels of sympathy. As Shelley puts it there, the hero's

> mind is at length suddenly awakened and thirsts for intercourse with an intelli-gence similar to itself. He images to himself the Being whom he loves. . . . The vision in which he embodies his own imaginations unites all of the wonderful or wise or beautiful, which the poet, the philosopher or the lover could depicture. The intellectual faculties, the imagination, the functions of sense have their respective requisitions on the sympathy of corresponding powers in other human beings. The Poet [-Hero] is represented as uniting these requisitions and attach-ing them to a single image. He seeks in vain for a prototype of his conception.

This is not the straight supernaturalism of Keats in "La Belle Dame" or "Lamia"; nor is it that form of neurasthenic fixation which Byron sums up in his phrase, "The nympholepsy of some fond [i.e. foolish] despair." Rather it is a form of idealism, with its roots in the romantic psychology of aspiration, and its branches extending up toward the "light that never was on sea or land." Shelleyan nympholepsy appears to signify the fulfillment or rounding out of the unfinished self. It is a version of that longing for completeness which has been a constant theme in world literature from Dante to Henry James, and usually ends, as in Shelley's later work, by taking on religious connotations.

A possible inception for the epipsyche notion in Shelley may be his early conviction that he was dependent for complete self-realization upon "women of character," whom he tended to look up to and to lean on rather more than the facts ever warranted. Shelley's consciousness of this dependence is well shown in his statements to Elizabeth Hitchener and Mary Godwin. He told the former, "You are as my better genius—the judge of my reasonings, the guide of my actions, the influencer of my usefulness." [24] And again, a few months later, "You are to my fancy as a thunder-riven pinnacle of rock, firm amid the rushing tempest and the boiling surge." [25] In 1814, Miss Hitchener's place had been usurped by another female paragon.

> Your thoughts alone, [he told Mary,] can waken mine to energy; [my mind] without yours is dead and cold. . . . It seems as if you alone could shield me

[24] *Letters*, VIII, 206 (November 26, 1811).
[25] *Ibid.*, 320 (May 1, 1812).

from impurity and vice. If I were absent from you long I should shudder with horror at myself. My understanding becomes undisciplined without you.

Evidently Harriet had never been capable of performing this function. "I believe," says Shelley in the same letter, "I must become in Mary's hands what Harriet was in mine." [26] In the end, when all the evidence has been published, it will probably appear that the illusion of Mary's over-all superiority to Harriet, and the delusion that Mary was as superior to him as he was to Harriet, were prominent factors in Shelley's ultimate determination to leave his first wife and elope with Mary Godwin. But the biographical implications of Shelley's peculiar submissiveness to what he regarded as female superiority are less important for our purposes than the results as manifested in the poetry. The Shelleyan hero is very often somehow dependent upon the Shelleyan heroine. His spirit is often "girt round with weakness"; he is unable to cope with his environment effectively unless he is able to establish a connection with some epipsychological counterpart, through whom he is completed and strengthened, wakened to energy, shielded from impurity, disciplined, and directed. The pattern can be discerned in the Laon-Cythna relationship of *The Revolt of Islam*. In *Alastor*, the focus of these remarks, Shelley for the first time engages the theme. The separation of epipsyche from psyche produces death, whether actual or symbolic. The lamp is shattered, or at any rate is incapable of giving light because the energizing power is not there.

IV

One who has observed Shelley's preoccupation with Necessity, and his enthusiastic espousal of the doctrine at the time of *Queen Mab*, is naturally curious to discover what has happened to the doctrine by 1815. Since *Alastor* is primarily a picture of a state of mind, one would expect that, if necessitarianism is involved at all, it would be most likely to appear in the form of psychological determinism. *Alastor* pictures a superior and exemplary young man as subject to subliminal necessitarian drives: he cannot escape from pursuing an ideal, even though he may sometimes suspect that his ideal is an illusion, and never learn otherwise prior to death. In short, it may be fair to say that in accepting from Peacock the notion of *alastor* Shelley made certain reservations or perhaps alterations in the accepted view of the meaning of the term. Instead of regarding *alastor* as a spirit of evil he associated the word with a particular form of psychological determinism. The youthful

[26] *Letters,* IX, 103 (October 28, 1814).

poet of *Alastor* could not have chosen to act otherwise than he does act: The inevitability of his fate is indeed, as we have seen, the fundamental implication of the poem. Therefore a special kind of necessity is at work in the poem.

But the beautifully realized and majestic invocation to the poem recalls also the beneficent Daemon of the World as she appears in *Queen Mab*. In lines whose movement and texture are close to the caliber of Wordsworth, Shelley calls upon the "beloved brotherhood" of earth, ocean, and air, claiming a fraternal kinship with them which in turn presumes their and his common filial relationship to the "great mother." Shelley worships her with "natural piety," one of the several Wordsworthian phrases in the poem.[27] But the language in which he addresses the immanent spirit is strongly reminiscent of the "Necessity, thou mother of the world" phraseology for which he had caught the initial suggestion from Holbach.

> Mother of this unfathomable world!
> Favor my solemn song, for I have loved
> Thee ever, and thee only; I have watched
> Thy shadow, and the darkness of thy steps,
> And my heart ever gazes on the depth
> Of thy deep mysteries.

Although his mind's eye has never penetrated to the inmost sanctuary of the brooding maternal spirit, he is intuitively aware of an indwelling essence both in natural phenomena and the "deep heart of man," and serenely awaits the harmonizing powers of this spirit which he supposes will inform his verses. Some of this language may be discounted for what it is, conventional invocation. The tone also seems mimetically Wordsworthian, made Shelley's only by adoption, like the reworking of Gray in *Queen Mab*. But in addressing the "Great Parent" he uses language so reminiscent of that of the sixth canto of his earlier poem as to make it fairly clear that the maternal Necessity of *Queen Mab* and the immanent nature-and-mind essence of *Alastor* may be roughly equated.[28]

[27] Shelley quotes the *Excursion*, I, 503–505 at the end of his preface. Besides the phrase "natural piety" (from "My Heart Leaps Up," 9) Woodberry notices "obstinate questionings" (26) and "too deep for tears" (713), both from the "Ode on Intimations of Immortality," for which "My Heart Leaps Up" served as headnote. Shelley was evidently deeply struck by the great ode of Wordsworth, which affected his own great fragment, *The Triumph of Life*.

[28] Additional credence is lent to the equation of Necessity and the World-Mother of *Alastor* when it is recalled that Shelley rewrote parts of *Queen Mab* as "The Daemon of the World" and included it in the *Alastor* volume. At the other end, one notices a clear foreshadowing of "Hymn to Intellectual Beauty," Stanza V, in *Alastor*, 23–28. Stovall, who does not, I think, take Shelleyan necessitarianism into sufficient account, makes the rest of the equation. *Desire and Restraint in Shelley*, p. 144.

The long elegiac conclusion contains one curious episode which points up the full significance of necessitarian doctrine in *Alastor*, and its relation to the Epipsyche theme. After the poet's miraculous voyage, he seeks out a natural sepulcher in which to compose himself for death, and he comes, along the way, to a dark well, into whose mirror-like waters he pauses to gaze, seeing his reflection

> as the human heart,
> Gazing in dreams over the gloomy grave,
> Sees its own treacherous likeness there.

As he watches, less acutely conscious of his own image than filled with an intense awareness which is subliminally focused on that image

> A Spirit seemed
> To stand beside him—clothed in no bright robes
> Of shadowy silver or enshrining light,
> Borrowed from aught the visible world affords
> Of grace, or majesty, or mystery;
> But undulating woods, and silent well,
> And leaping rivulet, and evening gloom
> Now deepening the dark shades, for speech assuming,
> Held commune with him, as if he and it
> Were all that was; only—when his regard
> Was raised by intense pensiveness—two eyes,
> Two starry eyes, hung in the gloom of thought,
> And seemed with their serene and azure smiles
> To beckon him.

Then, "obedient to the light/ That shone within his soul" he goes on. Like the "fair fiend" passage discussed earlier in the chapter, this episode has been generally misinterpreted. Hoffman's reading of the lines may perhaps be taken as typical. He believes that the "Spirit" of line 479 is identical with the owner of the "two starry eyes." That is, the whole passage relates to the visionary maiden alone, except that she is now utterly without fleshly attributes, and has come to represent "the false lure of the soul's hope of survival beyond the grave." [29]

But this reading ignores the descriptive phrases applied to the "Spirit," phrases which make it plain that Shelley is alluding to Mother Nature, phenomenal nature, clothed in "undulating woods, and silent well,/ And leaping rivulet, and evening gloom." The spirit with whom the poet holds communion is the Spirit of Nature, that "all-sufficing power," Necessity, "the mother of the world," which Shelley had celebrated in *Queen Mab*. For

[29] Hoffman, *op. cit.*, pp. 48–49.

the poet is now in the very lap of nature, in the utter solitude of a mountain plateau where he is presently to die. He communes with that spirit as if it and he "were all that was." The "spirit" of line 479 is obviously not the visionary maiden. Hoffman's reading also ignores the crucial word *only* at line 488. When the poet's "regard" is "raised by intense pensiveness" (that is, when his imaginative powers are heightened by the very intensity of his concentration upon natural objects),[30] he sees "two starry eyes hung in the gloom of thought." He has at first considered the nature-spirit as if he and it were all that was—*only*, in the deep intensity of his communings, he becomes aware of the "two starry eyes" of the visionary maiden which beckon him onward in his quest.

It has been necessary to undertake this *explication de texte* in order to show that Shelley is not here speaking only of the visionary maiden. He intends rather to represent two visions in conflict. One is the vision of a beneficent nature-spirit with which the poet communes until that vision is superseded by a second vision. The "two starry eyes" of course symbolize the maiden he has loved and lost. The upshot of the matter is that the second vision draws him away from the consolations of inward calm which are tacitly offered by the first vision.

It may be asked what this very interesting episode signifies in the interpretation of the poem. The answer is simple enough: to commune in solitude with the spirit of nature will not suffice; man needs love. The poet of *Alastor*, driven on by his Faustian curiosity, had explored in solitude the world of phenomenal nature, attempting (though apparently not consciously) "to exist without human sympathy." But there was that in him which made such an existence impossible. He conceived an epipsyche whose sympathetic community with him was absolute, and in the end perished through the intensity of his search after an absolute he could not find again, either in the flesh or elsewhere.

Shelley inadvertently made the best commentary on his poem some three years later when, fresh from translating the *Symposium*, he was engaged in writing an essay on the arts and manners of the Athenians. The archetype of one's love, said he, "forever exists in the mind, which selects among those who resemble it that which most resembles it; and instinctively fills up the interstices of the imperfect image." Even in his most savage state, Shelley goes on, man is a social being. Civilization only quickens and enhances his sociality, producing a desire for "sympathies still more intimate and complete." Thence arises

[30] Wordsworth often observed a similar psychological phenomenon in his own experience. See the incident of the hooting owls in "There was a boy."

that profound and complicated sentiment, which we call love, which is rather the universal thirst for a communion not merely of the senses, but of our whole nature, intellectual, imaginative, and sensitive, and which, when individualised, becomes an imperious necessity, only to be satisfied by the complete or partial, actual or supposed, fulfillment of its claims.[31]

The precision with which these remarks bear on *Alastor* should be at once apparent. Man is not by nature a creature of solitude; he is a social being. The more civilized he is, the more he thirsts for communion of his whole nature with that of another. When his sentiment is individualized, it becomes an imperious necessity, and can be satisfied only by the fulfillment of its claims—whether partially, through sensual connections, or totally, through a communion involving one's whole nature.

The spirit of solitude therefore stands in opposition to what is human. The poet of *Alastor* is humanized (though also done to death) by the "imperious necessity" of love. The essential conflict is set forth in the crucial episode which we have examined in detail. The spirit of nature is the spirit of solitude; the poet is half in love with Necessity, the beneficent but inhuman law of the natural world. But his greater need, the need which draws him on with an intensity so great that it wastes and kills his body, is the unrequited need for human sympathy. In a very real sense the conflict in *Alastor* may be described as the love of necessity *versus* the necessity of love.

The principle of love gradually came to occupy the central position in Shelley's thought. Toward the end of his life he gathered up in terms of the concept all his deepest convictions about the aspiration and inspiration of the creative mind, about the immortality of thought, and about the reservoir of divine power which is available to all creatures according to their respective degrees of sensitivity, integrity, high seriousness, and perseverance. The process by which Shelley achieved this clarification of his vision was, however, gradual. As analyzed in *Alastor* and other documents of the 1815 period, love is a necessary concomitant of and motivating force in the individual mind, but it has not yet been purged of its fleshly attributes, nor has it passed beyond the sphere of imperious individual need. By 1817–1818, in *The Revolt of Islam* and *Prometheus Unbound*, love has broadened in Shelley's thought to an ethical principle: "the sole law which should govern the moral world." In the first of these poems love is still, in one of its aspects, an irresistible force making for the union of man and woman. But in both poems, and particularly in the *Prometheus*, love is seen also as the most important socializing, civilizing, and restorative power available to man. This development

[31] *Prose,* VII, 228.

is symbolically represented in the transfiguration of Asia. By 1821, love has undergone an apotheosis in Shelley's thinking and has become merged with the metaphysical concept of the "One"—that supreme power from which all that is good is born, and to which all that is best aspires to return.

"Mont Blanc"

by Earl R. Wasserman

I

Even as the reader begins his encounter with "Mont Blanc" he finds himself confronted with a set of strikingly paradoxical statements that call out for recognition of the order of things in which they are not paradoxical but accordant with the laws of that order. The universe, we are told, is "everlasting," and yet what is advanced about this everlasting universe is that it "Flows through" the mind. Apparently it is both ever-enduring and forever passing. It is, moreover, a unity ("universe") and yet a unity of multiformity ("things"), and it is alternately dark and bright. Most important, since it is the very first assertion of the poem, the "universe of things" is said to make its passage through mind. But, we might legitimately object—especially if we recall the persistent seventeenth- and eighteenth-century wrangle over epistemology—"things" belong to an external world and cannot, as things, have a mental existence. This last paradox is made even more vivid by Shelley's then describing the contents of mind as both "things" and "human thought," which we would normally assume to be entities belonging to wholly different categories.

Whatever else may appear obscure, it is perfectly clear that, like Denham in *Cooper's Hill* and Pope in *Windsor Forest*, Shelley is calling into being not a fragment of reality but a total cosmos. Like Windsor Forest and its governing law of *concordia discors*, the universe of things that flows through mind and is variously dark and bright has been created by poetic fiat that assumes no other reality exists—prior to the first creative Word of the poem there is only a void on the page—and that calls into being an organized world in which the poetic act may take place.

But what cosmic principles—what ontology and epistemology—we are driven to ask, might provide for the seeming inconsistencies and make them meaningful? The clue is found most easily, I think, in the opening account of the varying brilliance and darkness of the river of things. Manifestly the overt purpose is to specify the attributes of an objective world of things, which is the subject of the sentence and which has been cosmically imaged as a river; and the poet explicitly says it is "Now dark—now glittering" (3). Had he said no more, we could assume he posits an external matter whose attributes are truly those reported by the senses. But he then repeats his terms to redefine them, adding that the darkness is a "gloom" originating in mind and given back ("reflected") to it by the universe of things, and that the splendor is lent by things to the mind. Two opposing conceptions, therefore, are interwoven here, like warp and woof: on one hand, the river of things is itself dark and glittering; on the other, these qualities are located in the mind. Indeed, the ambiguity is further compounded, for if the glitter is a lent splendor it is the original property of things, not mind, and yet in the act of perception it is in the possession of mind, not the things which own it. Contrarily the darkness first assigned to things turns out not to be their true property; they are dark only as the agency for allowing the mind to perceive its own gloom. The agency that transmits the qualities is in each case the world of things, which lends and remits; but the center of reference is mind, since this is where the gloom and splendor reside in the act of perception.

Whatever the universe is, it clearly is not a self-existent reality possessing in itself the qualities of darkness and brilliance; and to describe it as now dark, now glittering is to understand it only partially by adopting the conventions built into the normal form of the English language. Nor, contrarily, is it a figment of the mind, since there obviously is an external something to lend the splendor and reflect the gloom. Nor is it quite Wordsworth's "mighty world/ Of eye, and ear,—both what they half create,/ And what perceive"; at any rate, it is not the meeting point between what the external world is in itself and what the mind contributes to it, a fusion of perception and creation. Rather, it is a reality provoked by (although not necessarily corresponding to) the objective, but existing in the subjective. To describe the splendor of things by saying that they lend their splendor to the mind is to dodge the question of the nature of an admittedly external world and to claim that man's knowledge of it is confined to his mental perceptions.

This philosophic paradox has shaped linguistically the paradoxical structure of the opening sentence of the poem. In making its subject the "everlasting universe of *things*," the poet adopts the normal materialistic bias of English that assumes the dualism of mind and matter, and the authenticity of what the senses record. But the assertion then made about the universe of things is that it is that which "Flows through the mind," and thereby reality has been defined in strictly subjective terms. We are not told that the flowing of the universe through the mind is only one of its characteristic acts; that is, the poem does not propose an autonomous world that can impress images of itself upon mind but whose reality is independent of this act. Nor do the lines reflect the subjective idealism which has often been mistaken for Berkeleyanism. That the universe flows and rolls its waves implies an independent and active world, not one that is constituted by the subjective mind and its various states. Rather, in defining the universe of things as that which passes through the mind, the opening lines carefully skirt both the materialistic and subjectively idealistic extremes. Both this definition and the description of the darkness and brilliance allude to an objective reality, but nevertheless what they both assert about that reality is its existence in the mind.

It is at this point that the temptation to fasten Shelley's thinking upon some one philosopher is greatest—and most treacherous. But actually the ontology and epistemology implied by the opening lines reflect the whole course of British empiricism, from Sir Kenelm Digby's "notional" philosophy and Hobbes's recognition of the disparity between sensible qualities and the nature of the object causing them, to Sir William Drummond's empirical scepticism, of which Shelley thought highly. Locke, for example, by dividing qualities into primary and secondary, posited a world partly objective and partly subjective; and by locating the primary qualities in what he confessed was an unknowable "substance," he left man convinced of the reality of his own mental experiences, but highly uncertain about the reality of an external world. Berkeley demonstrated that both primary and secondary qualities exist in mind only and, having thereby destroyed Locke's "substance," reduced the reality of the external world to the act of perception; but although this could reassure man of the real existence of his impressions it still left him puzzled as to what the source of his impressions might be, even though Berkeley answered, God. Hume agreed with Berkeley on the mental location of all qualities and, refusing to admit that the world is an idea, insisted that we cannot have any real knowledge of the source of our impressions[1] The entire tendency of empiricism was to encourage the psychologizing of reality by stripping it of material attributes and to leave man most unsure of what exists outside his own mind and yet stimulates it—a tendency that Shelley

---

[1] E.g.: "As to those *impressions*, which arise from the *senses*, their ultimate cause is, in my opinion, perfectly inexplicable by human reason, and 'twill always be impossible to decide with certainty, whether they arise immediately from the object, or are produced by the creative power of mind, or are derived from the author of our being. Nor is such a question any way material to our present purpose. We may draw inferences from the coherence of our perceptions, whether they be true or false; whether they represent nature justly, or be mere illusions of the senses." (*A Treatise of Human Nature*, I, iii, 5.)

reflects in naming reality a universe of things and then confining his definition of that reality to its activity in the mind; and in his alluding to the qualities of objects and then defining these qualities as purely sensible.

That Shelley was vividly aware of the ambiguous philosophic position he embodied in the opening lines of "Mont Blanc" is attested by some of his prose statements. With no sense of a contradiction, he wrote in his "Essay on Life" both that "the basis of all things cannot be . . . mind" and that "Nothing exists but as it is perceived." The first assertion excludes a purely subjective idealism that limits reality to a subject and its modes; the second excludes a pure materialism which reduces mind to a function of matter. But both positions are tenable if one assumes that the only knowable reality is the body of mental impressions and yet that an unknowable external something is responsible for these impressions. These assumptions, however, do not drive Shelley into a dualistic philosophy any more than they do Hume or Berkeley, and indeed one reason for his adoption of the assumptions is to avoid that dualism. In the "Essay" he rejects not only materialism and subjective idealism but also the dualism of "the popular philosophy of mind and matter" for what he calls the "Intellectual Philosophy." According to this doctrine the known data of the mind and their unknowable outer causes dissolve into a higher unity which can be defined discursively only by the double assertion that reality is that which is the source of our impressions and at the same time is those impressions aroused by an outer something. Neither definition is sufficient, for each independently is false; reality must be defined from both positions simultaneously. In other words, Shelley has adopted a fairly orthodox philosophic idealism that is close in its general outlines to Berkeley's. Subject and object have no real existence apart from their interdependence. Since all qualities are subjective, there is no "matter" or "substance," and therefore the reality of anything is dependent upon its being perceived; and yet the subjective mind has no thoughts, and therefore no reality, apart from the sensation of "things." Subject and object live in each other.

Shelley struggled repeatedly in the "Essay on Life" to capture in the unyielding dualistic language of discourse the paradox inherent in his monistic interpretation of the internal and external. "Each [life or being]," he wrote, "is at once the centre and the circumference, the point to which all things are referred, and the line in which all things are contained." The center of reality is the sentient self, and all the non–self outside it exists by virtue of the center and must be interpreted through it: the external world can be defined only by its being perceived. But at the same time, since the world must be translated into the realities of the mind, the self is the circle and contains all reality. In this geometry of the true reality, center and circumference contain each other, and the best that nonpoetic language can do is to state the paradox through a double perspective. Or, again, Shelley wrote that "Life and the world, or whatever we call that which we are and feel, is an astonishing thing." Apparently life (which he then identifies with mind) is what we are, and the world is what we feel: inner and outer are both referred to the center, the experiencing self. And I propose that in writing that life and the world "is," Shelley was not slipping into what has been called "Romantic grammar," but is denying the dualism of mind and world; life is also the line in which everything is contained as a unity. In yet a third effort Shelley struggled to define his complex metaphysical position: When we were children, what a

> distinct and intense apprehension had we of the world and of ourselves! . . . We less habitually distinguished all that we saw and felt, from ourselves. They seemed, as it were, to constitute one mass. . . . Those who are subject to the state called reverie feel as if their nature were dissolved into the surrounding universe, or as if the surrounding universe were absorbed into their being. They are conscious of no distinction. And these are states which precede, or accompany, or follow an unusually intense and vivid apprehension of life.

Since this unity of the opposing perspectives obliterates the distinction between subject and object, Shelley can claim that "The view of life presented by . . . the intellectual philosophy is that of unity. . . . The difference is merely nominal between those two classes of thought which are vulgarly distinguished by the names of ideas or of external objects." It imports little, he added in his "Essay on Morals,"

> whether thought be distinct from the object of thought. The use of the words *external* and *internal*, as applied to the establishment of this distinction, has been the symbol and the source of much dispute. This is merely an affair of words and as the dispute deserves, to say, that when speaking of the objects of thought, we indeed only describe one of the forms of thought—or that, speaking of thought, we only apprehend one of the operations of the universal system of beings.

Therefore on this basis Shelley can justify his conclusion that "By the word *things* is to be understood any object of thought—that is, any thought upon which any other thought is employed with an apprehension of distinction."

This extension of the empirical tradition, then, is the philosophic order into which the opening paradoxes of "Mont Blanc" fit and become meaningful. The ultimate doctrine of the Intellectual Philosophy is that reality is an undifferentiated unity, neither thought nor thing, and yet both. From one imperfect perspective this reality is called the "universe of things"; from another, it is the thoughts that flow through the mind. But the true unity of reality requires as a linguistic approximation that thing and thought be assimilated into each other by one constituting the subject and the other the predicate of the same sentence: "The everlasting universe of things/ Flows through the mind." It is at the very least a suggestive fact that in his first venture at an opening line Shelley wrote, not that the universe of *things* is now dark, now glittering, but, "In daylight *thoughts* bright or obscure." [2] And in the published version he will write that the "shapes" experienced in death and dream "the busy *thoughts* outnumber/ Of those who wake and live" (51–52), clearly meaning that shapes (or "things") and thoughts are interchangeable terms, since a thing is "any thought upon which any other thought is employed with an apprehension of distinction."

This philosophic pattern also provides a coherence for the poet's treatment of the qualities of things. From one perspective, as "things," they are themselves dark and glittering; as "thoughts" they are mental impressions—the lent splendor and the reflected gloom. Neither is right; only both are true. Of course this is the answer of the Intellectual Philosophy not only to the problem of the location of qualities but also to the problem raised by the customary empirical distinction between the two modes of sensory data, immediate and mediate. Our immediate sensations, being distinct and vivid, lend their splendor to the mind; as they persist in the mind, they become faint and indistinct. Or, as Shelley puts it, echoing the traditional philosophic metaphor, the darkness of the mind is reflected to the mind. Hume, for example, had distinguished between immediate and recalled sensations (impressions and ideas) in terms of brilliance and obscurity; and Locke explicitly called attention to his use of the metaphor of light to make the same distinction. But since in Shelley's idealism there is no essential difference between one thought and another, what Hume called impressions and ideas are only degrees of vividness.

Moreover, as Shelley had said, the "view of life" presented by the Intellectual Philosophy is that of unity; yet what characterizes the thought we call a "thing" is its distinctiveness. Hence reality must be both multiplicity and undifferentiated unity.

> A specific difference between every thought of the mind [he wrote in the "Essay on Morals"], is indeed a necessary consequence of that law by which it perceives diversity and number. . . . The principle of agreement and similarity of all thoughts is that they are all thoughts; the principle of their disagreement consists in the variety and irregularity of the occasions on which they arise in the mind. That in which they agree to that in which they differ is as everything to nothing.

But although this unity of all thoughts is the only final reality, the individual human mind, as distinct from the total Mind that comprehends all reality,

[2] [Manuscript in the Bodleian Library] MS Shelley adds. e 16.

cannot exist within its own unity of thought, shut off from the diversity of those thoughts called "things." The "diversities" of relationships to ourselves whereby we discover motion, time, and separate existence

> are events or objects and are essential, considered relatively to human identity, for the existence of the human mind. For if the inequalities produced by what has been termed the operations of the external universe were levelled by the perception of our being uniting and filling up their interstices, motion, and mensuration, and time, and space; the elements of the human mind being thus abstracted, sensation and imagination cease. Mind cannot be considered pure.

Although these inequalities are not in the universal Mind, the unity of thought in the individual mind, which is but part of the universal Mind, cannot exist without the diversity of these thoughts, for these diversities constitute the mind; yet diversity is meaningful only in the unity of thought. Both positions are necessary: the thoughts we experience as "things" must be discrete, and without them the human mind cannot be; but because they are all thoughts, they are all one. Or, as Shelley expresses it in the opening lines of "Mont Blanc," it is a "universe of things," constantly flowing "through" the mind as a multiplicity of discrete "things" and "everlasting" as a mental unity—that is, as a "universe," which Shelley elsewhere defined as our "mass of knowledge . . . including our own nature."

Finally, in describing the "human thought" (5) that flows as a tributary stream into the river of the universe of things, Shelley is distinguishing between an individual mind and the universal Mind through which the universal river flows in forming the universal Thought which is all reality. Just as for Berkeley all reality exists by being perceived by God, so for Shelley it exists by flowing through the One Mind. But it is at this point that it is necessary to separate Berkeley from Shelley lest other of Berkeley's doctrines falsify the poem. For although the One Mind is ontologically equivalent to Berkeley's God, Shelley certainly does not accept Berkeley's consequent orthodox theology. Nor is Shelley's One Mind God the Creator. Nor does Shelley assume, as Berkeley does, that the One Mind is the cause of man's experiences: the "secret springs" whence human thoughts flow are not the One Mind, nor is the One Mind the power that causes the universe of things to flow through it. Nor, most important at the moment, does Shelley make Berkeley's sharp distinction between the One Mind and the human mind. The churchman obviously could not in any way confuse God with man, but Shelley held that the individual mind is portion of the One Mind and that the particular assemblages of thought which distinguish one person from another are only different modifications of the One Mind ("Essay on Life"). Consequently the apparently tautological phrase "human thought" properly distinguishes that thought from those in the One Mind. It is only a portion of the thoughts in the One Mind, for through this flows the entire "universe of things," of which "human thought" is only one factor. But just as thought and thing are meaningless distinctions in the reality of the human mind, so they are in the total reality of the universal Mind. Since both "things" and "human thought" are expressed in the poem by similar and related water images—a mighty river and one of its tributary streams—they differ only in their early careers and magnitude, not in their essential nature; and ultimately they become the one universe. It is the confluence of these two bodies of thoughts, "things" and "*human* thought," that, flowing through Mind, constitutes the universe. Since human thought is not merely perception but the perception of something, the sound of the stream of human thought is "but half its own." And since, as Shelley wrote, all thoughts are to be included in the catalogue of existence ("Treatise on Morals"), the total reality is the perception by the One Mind of all things, including "human thought."

II

The occasion for "Mont Blanc" as that occasion is dramatized by the poem is not the poet's encounter with the Swiss scene, which does not make its appearance until the second stanza. We therefore cannot read back into the opening stanza the poet's later experience with an apparently external reality, but must confine its meaning to its own boundaries. More precisely, the poem is not lyric, but dramatic; not a static set of elaborations on a fixed theme, but a dynamic and consistently evolving course of discovery. Consequently each factor in it has no truly isolable meaning, but is a function of a forward progress: the total meaning resides in the entire course of the dramatic movement, and, conversely, the meaning of any passage is generated by both its presence and participation in the whole. In this dramatic development the primary duty of the first stanza is to establish the philosophic world in which the poem will take place. By means of a river, a stream of thought, the valley of the mind, and the attendant scenic images the poet calls into a symbolic form the Intellectual Philosophy, the essence of which is that mind and world, thought and thing, are meaningless distinctions, since they are only biased and partial versions of a unity, but that in order to give this unity linguistic form it is necessary to express it from both biases simultaneously.

Although an intricate contrivance of language allows a discursive account of this philosophic idealism, obviously there is no existing language that embodies it as the preconception of that language—no terms that name the paradoxical unity of reality as Shelley conceives of it or that name the features of that reality, and no syntax whose relational system is ordered by the Intellectual Philosophy. The poem is the product of the poet's urge so to reconstitute his available language that it will, not express, but inherently contain that philosophy and thereby open the otherwise closed doors to the dark corridors of thought that lie beyond ordinary conception. By creating the language of the Intellectual Philosophy the poet can think *with* it.

But the very fact that the paradoxical premise of the poem must be formed by the artificial linguistic fusion of the inner and the outer also means that it has a propensity to separate again into its contrary terms, the world of things and the world of thoughts. That is, the temporary interfusion of the antithetical worlds in the first poetic paragraph leads directly to the subject matter of the second, of which the first twenty-two lines depict a presumably real and independent external universe, and the last fifteen lines a self-existent mind. The initial ontology, however, is only the condition for this dissolution, not the dramatic power impelling it.

The forward and evolutionary drive is imparted to the poem by a set of successively more extreme hypothetical conditions that the poet supposes for himself—increasingly more visionary "scenes" that translate to progressively higher levels (figuratively and literally) the actions played against them. Of these the most obvious are the "trance sublime and strange" that permits him to view his own mind and its activities (35) and the visions of death and dream that reveal to him the symbolic meaning of the peak of Mont Blanc (49–57).

With this dramatic pattern in mind we can now return to the first stanza to fix more exactly the significance of its poetic movement. Because of the assumed identity of thought and thing, the opening metaphor—which decrees a cosmos by calling the contents of the mind a river of things and the total universe a river in the mind—is a mode of expression that the poet's philosophic position imposes upon him. Unlike the customary accessory metaphor, it does not imply a comparison, but is to be read literally as identifying objective things, such as a river, and the thoughts that flow through the mind. Any image that symbolically expresses the total outer world must, in the philosophy Shelley has adopted, also express the total substance of the mind. The use of the metaphoric mode, then, is both the formulation and the consequence of the Intellectual Philosophy, for if thoughts and things are merely nominal distinctions, then it is not only poetically but also ontologically valid to describe mental contents and activities in the language of supposedly outward things and to chart the topography of the mind by charting the topography of the world.

But this univocal metaphor is not sustained, and in the midst of its evolution it is diverted into a comparison of the sound of a feeble brook to that of the tributary stream of human thought. As Shelley moves from the river of things to its tributary stream of human thought, the water imagery remains consistent, but the figurative mode leaps from metaphor to simile—and a simile of an unusual character. The simile likening the stream of human thought to a brook has not developed from the disintegration of the metaphor: the thought-thing of the metaphor has not been fractured into the likeness of a thought to a thing. Instead, the already metaphoric stream of thought is likened to a strictly objective brook. Then, the original identity of thought and thing has not really been violated by the introduction of an apparently objective brook into the metaphoric scene, for the image has already been contained in the thought-stream to which it is compared, and the comparison, as comparison, is quite tautological. If it is philosophically permissible to identify the flow of thoughts with a stream, then the stream of thoughts may, it is only too obvious, be compared to a stream; and the simile only repeats what the metaphor had already said.

And yet, merely by means of the change of poetic mode, an independent external reality has been subtly led into the poem, for the feeble brook likened to the stream of thought is a separate term of a simile. Unlike a metaphor, whose function is to fuse its terms, a simile effects a relation between aspects of its terms while insisting that the terms are discrete. Here the very fact that the relationship is quite without meaning thrusts an unusual value upon the discreteness of the terms. This implication of an independent outer world is then intensified by the hurried accumulation of attendant images which, if they had no other purpose, would be merely accessory descriptive details too numerous and disproportionate to justify their presence: the offhand intrusion of the brook allows mountains, waterfalls, woods and winds, the vast river, and the rocks to insinuate themselves into the otherwise symbolic scene so as to give structure to the strictly external reality at which the brook only hinted. In effect, then, the simile proposes: while still holding that the distinction between thought and thing is meaningless, let us entertain the notion that the universe is an independent outer reality. This progression from the philosophic proposition of the metaphor to the supposition of the simile is symptomatic of, and preparatory to, the further evolution of the poem, and its logical extension would now be to isolate things and thoughts hypothetically for separate consideration. That is, while still insisting on the paradoxical ontology of the Intellectual Philosophy, the poet is shaping his artistry so as to make it possible at the same time to think *as though* it were not valid.

Continuing the progression of suppositions, the second paragraph then introduces another simile—"Thus thou, Ravine of Arve" (12)—as unorthodox as its predecessor. First, the simile is truncated: we are offered only the assertion of likeness and the second term of the likeness, for the duty of this simile is to concentrate attention upon and isolate this term—an external world. Second, just as the first simile tautologically draws a likeness between a thought-stream and a stream, so the first term of the second simile is all the topographical imagery of the opening stanza, part of which served as a metaphor for the thought-thing reality and part of which appeared in a simile likening external things to metaphoric thought-things. The movement is progressively away from the thought-thing world of the Intellectual Philosophy to an analogous outer world: the thought-river of the mind, and then the woods, mountains, and other features of the external world that had been likened to the thought-world are now likened to the completely external Ravine of Arve. By this gradual movement and by the reduplication of the same imagery in a different context, Shelley has, without destroying his initial thesis, succeeded artistically in reifying an external world. The full formulation of this emerging world has come at that point when in the overtly enacted drama the poet no longer explores the symbolic topography of the world of the Intellectual Philosophy but now confronts with his senses a particular, localized scene, the Ravine of Arve. It becomes fully hypostatized when he moves out of the symbolic thought-thing world of the first stanza and receives sensory impressions of a geographical scene that—behold!—is constituted in fact of the same images as those that had symbolized reality as formulated by the Intellectual Philosophy.

Denham, we have seen,[3] organized a meaningful universe, cosmic and political, around a composition of mountain, plain, and the river Thames; Shelley is building his cosmos of a similar scene, Europe's greatest mountain, its ravine, and the river Arve. But whereas Denham could invest his scenery with a system of significant relationships because that system was in the public domain and easily available, it is necessary for Shelley to generate, by means of his scenic construct, a cosmic order from which, in turn, that scene derives its symbolic significance. The two poets have chosen to work with almost the same stuff of images to build their poetic worlds; the difference between their poetic modes measures not so much the difference of individual genius as it does the disappearance of publicly accepted designs in nature, assumed to be prior to art, and the consequent additional creative act required of the modern artist, who must create nature and art in the same act.

There is remarkably close accord between the generalized scene of Shelley's first paragraph and the particularized scene of the Ravine in the second. Both consist of a mighty river, waterfalls, mountains, and interchange of woods and winds, and turbulent sounds; just as the mind-river is now dark, now glittering, so there pass over the Ravine "Fast cloud shadows and

[3] In an earlier chapter of the book. [ED.]

sunbeams" (15); and just as the source of human thought flows from "secret springs," so the Arve comes down from its "secret throne" (17). In the first stanza this structure of scenic images symbolized a total reality; and therefore the subtle and gradual disengagement of the scenic imagery as imagery, the eventual direct perception of the particular geographic scene, and the close parallelism of that scene with the symbolic scenery of the thought-thing world have not merely made possible the poetic supposition of an objective reality, but have also made the particular scene of the Ravine, like Denham's scene, synecdochic of the entire objective universe. The correspondence of the imagery of the two stanzas has acted out the conviction that "The difference is merely nominal between those two classes of thought which are vulgarly distinguished by the names of ideas and of external objects." Even though the obtrusion of a hypothetical external world seems to contradict the philosophic foundation of the poem, there is nevertheless a consistency with that premise in the poet's giving both the thought-thing world and the external world like forms and activities, and in expressing both in identical images. Poetically a total external world has emerged and been isolated within a system in which the world of things and the world of thoughts are not differentiable.

The poem, then, is proceeding by a series of suppositions. Having formulated the Intellectual Philosophy by means of the opening metaphor, Shelley has introduced a kind of supposition in the simile within the metaphor ("Such as a feeble brook . . .") preparatory to the full supposition in the next section. This second simile ("Thus thou, Ravine of Arve") completely filters out an external universe, which is then drawn in full through line 33. But the rest of the second stanza after line 33 considers in isolation the other side of reality, the individual mind. This, too, by the poet's hypothesis, has no true existence apart from those "diversities" called "events or objects" ("Mind cannot be considered pure"), and the poet's philosophy taught further that the individual mind, being a portion of the One Mind, which is the total undifferentiated reality, is not truly separable from it: "The words *I*, *you*, *they* are not signs of any actual difference subsisting between the assemblage of thoughts thus indicated, but are merely marks employed to denote the different modifications of the one mind" ("Essay on Life"). The poet therefore must call upon an even more extreme supposition, one that transcends normal experience. Gazing on the Ravine, the supposed objective reality, he *seems*, "as in a trance sublime and strange," to muse upon a distinct entity, his fantasy, his own "human mind" (35–37). Again the word "human" qualifies, distinguishing the hypothetically pure individual mind both from the external sources of its "thoughts" and from the universal mind, which Shelley in the "Essay on Life" equates with "exist-

ence." But even in the act of describing the results of the transcendent experience the poet is careful not to destroy the Intellectual Philosophy with
which he began. He does not claim that the vision of his mind is the product
of a trance; he merely *seems* to muse on his mind, he is *as though* in a trance,
and he explicitly differentiates his vision from a reality by calling it a
"fantasy." And thereby Shelley can record the results of the trance without
losing his hold on his empirical scheme. Throughout, the artistry works with
all the poetic intensity needed to achieve the paradox of yielding to the poet
the results of transcending the limits of his Intellectual Philosophy without
his ever really abandoning it.

III

The full significance of this complex poetic strategy which seems to have
provisionally divided the thought-thing universe of the first paragraph into
external world and individual mind in the second becomes clear when one
examines the imagery of the two stanzas comparatively.

1. Just as the thought-thing world of the first stanza is "now dark—now
glittering," so over the Ravine "sail/ Fast cloud shadows and sunbeams"
(14–15). The alternation in the mind of vivid sensory "impressions" and the
obscure "ideas" that these impressions become (to use Hume's terms) corresponds to the varying brilliance and darkness of the hypostatized external
world. For if, according to the Intellectual Philosophy, clarity and obscurity
are only modes of a thought-thing image—Berkeley and Hume having al-
located all qualities to the experiencing mind—then reference to cloud-
shadows and sunbeams is merely the materialist's causal way of attributing
the same modal difference to an external world and of assuming that cause
is a property of matter.

2. The Arve, which flows through the Ravine, is obviously the counterpart
of the river of the universe of things that flows through the mind. But the
Arve also shares the characteristics of the tributary of "human thought" in
the first stanza, for just as the "source of human thought" brings its tribute
from "secret"—that is, unknown and unknowable—springs, so the "Power"
which appears in the guise of the Arve comes down from its "secret throne"
(16–17).

Now, "Power" is one of the most recurrent terms in the poem, almost
casual at first, and then increasingly more insistent. We learn that the Arve
is a likeness of the Power, that the Power is inaccessible, and, at the climax,
that Power is symbolized by the summit of Mont Blanc and governs both
mind and matter. The word is being used in its traditional philosophic sense
of causation, and therefore there inheres in it the whole philosophical and

theological debate over the reality of causation and the nature of Ultimate Cause. If proof were needed for this interpretation of the term, it is to be found in the fact that in the poem the synonyms for "Power" are "secret springs," "source," "secret throne," "secret chasms," "secret Strength." The entire poem therefore is pervaded by this theme. For Shelley's day the problem of power, or causation, had been raised most provocatively by Hume, who denied the possibility of an empirical knowledge of power. Since we can experience only succession, it must be the imagination, he held, that converts the observation of succession into the notion of causation. True, Godwin and the French necessitarians also made the theme of causation central to their doctrines, but to them power is an attribute of matter, a view Shelley explicitly rejects by calling it "remote," "inaccessible," "secret." There is, moreover, indisputable evidence that Shelley repeatedly accepted Hume's conclusions. To cite a few instances: in a footnote to *Queen Mab* he wrote, " . . . the only idea we can form of causation is a constant conjunction of similar objects and the consequent inference of one from another"; in "a Refutation of Deism" he explicitly assented to Hume's sceptical definition of causation, or power; in the fragment "On Polytheism" he took Hume's position that our notion of cause is an "habitual conviction" arising from the repeated experience of the same succession of sensations; and in the "Essay on a Future Life" he wrote, " . . . when we use the words *principle, power, cause,* &c., we mean to express no real being, but only to class under those terms a certain series of co-existing phenomena."

But the statement that the source of human thought brings its waters from secret springs is a curious locution, since it seems to say that the source brings the waters from the source. Clearly Shelley must be distinguishing source from springs: the springs, being "secret," must be the unknown and unknowable cause, or Power, not to be experienced by man; and the "source" therefore must be apparent power, the point at which the unknown is experientially manifest as successiveness and is conceived of by man as cause. Obviously Shelley is, in general, adopting Hume's position: man cannot truly experience causation (and therefore the springs are "secret") but imaginatively converts the sensation of constant succession into the notion of cause (a notion that Shelley here calls "source"). And yet in a significant sense Shelley has exceeded Hume's thesis, for although he denies the possibility of experiencing Power, he allows no doubt of his own conviction of its real existence. When Shelley blended Hume's sceptical definition of cause with the Intellectual Philosophy it was inescapable that he admit the real, but unknowable, existence of Ultimate Cause:

   . . . the existence of a Power bearing the same relation to all that we perceive and are, as what we call a cause does to what we call effect, [was never the subject] of sensation, and yet the laws of mind almost universally suggest, according to the various dispositions of each, a conjecture, a persuasion, or a conviction of [its] existence. The reply is simple: these thoughts are also to be included in the catalogue of existence; they are modes in which thoughts are combined. . . .

("Essay on Morals")

Exactly the same distinction between unknowable springs and palpable source is drawn in the description of the Arve (16–17). The ultimate cause or origin of the river is unknowable ("secret throne"), but the Arve, being a "constant conjunction," is a "likeness" of the Power, a guise for it in the reified external world. Because the river is palpable, man falsely takes it to be the Power itself, confusing the sensory experience of successiveness with the inexperienceable Ultimate Cause; or, more precisely, when the Power does "come down" to man it does so only in the disguise of the Arve.

3. The contending of woods and winds in the symbolic world of the first stanza (10) foreshadows the coming of the "chainless winds" of the objective world to drink the odors of the pines and hear "their mighty swinging/ . . . —an old and solemn harmony" (20–24). The action described in these latter lines is significantly complex. The pines belong to continuous duration ("Children of elder time") and their harmony is "old"; but the winds that act upon them are characterized by continuity of flux and successiveness ("chainless winds [that] come and ever came"). Moreover, the harmony that the winds come to hear belongs to the pines, and yet it comes into existence by the winds' swinging the pines: the winds must make the harmony upon the pines in order to gain possession of the harmony that belongs to the pines. The action symbolizes in the outward world a cosmic order—a "harmony"—born of the interaction of the continually transient and the continually enduring; and an energy (the winds) that brings into being for itself what already inherently exists in something else (the pines).

Again the symbolic action in this objective world answers precisely to the account of the thought-thing reality symbolized in the first stanza. Like the children of elder time, the universe of things is "everlasting," but it exists in perception as a continuity of flux: it "flows" through the mind, and its rapid waves, being an ever-changing sameness, correspond to the chainless winds that come and ever came. To describe the universe as "everlasting" would be inadequate, since this would imply its autonomy; to describe it only as flowing would be partial, since this would imply it is wholly mental. The reality of the world of the Intellectual System is its transient everness, its enduring transiency—the eternal passing of the winds over the enduring pines.

Moreover, the interaction of the winds and pines, echoing the contending of woods and winds (10), corresponds perfectly with the linguistic fusion of subject and predicate that, in the opening sentence, conveyed the paradoxical nature of the ontology taught by the Intellectual Philosophy. To say that the winds come to hear the harmony of the pines postulates an external world available to perception. But of course there is no harmony to be heard by the winds unless, by stirring the pines, they bring into being the harmony of the pines. That the harmony is not the original property of the winds corresponds to the rejection of subjective idealism ("the basis of all things cannot be mind"); that the harmony does not come into being until the winds swing the pines corresponds to the rejection of materialism ("nothing exists but as it is perceived"). In the terms of the Intellectual Philosophy the harmony of the pines is a reality that can be heard by the winds, and yet its existence depends upon its being "heard" by the winds, just as the initial lines of the poem named an outer universe of things and then located those things in the percipient mind. The symbolic action of the hypothetically objective world turns out to be in exact accord with the assumptions concerning the thought-thing reality in which the poem is rooted. Even though the independent existence of an objective world has been only pretended, that world insists upon acting out symbolically the ontology of the Intellectual System and thereby denies its own exclusive reality.

4. In the second section the poet's seeming trance opens to him the fantasy of an independent and individual mind that passively renders and receives fast influencings in its unremitting interchange with an independent, "clear" (i.e., not darkened by its presence in mind) universe of things (37–40). The rendering and receiving of the human mind repeat the river's lending splendor to the mind and reflecting its gloom, the contending of woods and winds, and the curiously complex rendering and receiving of the winds and pines. The reality Shelley has accepted can be grasped only by his simultaneously adopting the perspectives of the object perceived and the perceiving subject: just as the harmony is received from the pines by the winds and yet is brought into existence by the winds' act, so reality is what the mind receives in sensation and yet what comes into existence by being experienced. The pattern of reality remains constant whether Shelley views it in terms of the Intellectual Philosophy, or in the fictitious terms of an outer universe, or in the equally fictitious terms of mind as a distinct individual entity. The first is truth; and, being true, it imposes upon its purely suppositive variants its own pattern.

This interaction that takes place in cognition is attended by an interplay of light and darkness. In the first stanza the characteristic of the universal Mind, through which the universe flows, is its darkness; the characteristic of things is their brilliance. And in shaping the universe as it truly exists the two contend and play upon each other. Similarly, in the account of the individual human mind in the second paragraph the universe of things that interacts with the mind is "clear," and its container, the Ravine, is a "darkness" (40, 42). But when Shelley writes that the wings of wild thoughts "Now float above thy darkness" (41–42), the antecedent of "thy" is, indifferently, the human mind and the Ravine, which the seeming trance has transmuted into a vision of the poet's own mind, since each is a darkness through which the brilliance of things passes. The ambiguous reference calls us back to the fact that in the description of the supposedly autonomous outer world in the first half of the paragraph this same interplay of light and darkness had been enacted, but by outward things serving a symbolic role. Even if we delete the mind from our ontology we find that the container of the external world is a "dark, deep Ravine" (12) and that the mountains forming this container are "dark" (18). But the Arve, which is a guise for the Power and therefore a surrogate for the activity perceptible in the world of things, corresponds to the "*clear* universe of things" (40) and the glittering river of things flowing through the mind (3–4), for it bursts "like the flame/ Of lightning" through the "dark mountains" (18–19). The image is especially precise in symbolizing in outer reality the dynamic relation of sensation to mind, for it presents not merely light and darkness, but a flash that bursts through the darkness of the container and momentarily permeates it, and darkness that quickly recovers its power to roll back and press out that sudden illumination. The description of the Ravine, then, continues to assert—as though unwittingly, and in a set of substituted materialistic terms —the ontology of the opening stanza: reality is an interchange of light and darkness whether that reality is the world of the Intellectual System, the world of the mind, or an objective thing. It is as though the poet were proving his own postulates, for even when he denies them in fact and imagines an external world, that world insists upon transmuting itself from palpable imagery into symbols that act out the truth of the premise that has been temporarily abrogated.

5. In his seeming trance the poet finds that the consequence of the interchange of his mind and the clear universe is a "legion of wild thoughts" (41) endowed with two opposite capacities. One of these is to seek among the shadows passing in the "cave of the witch Poesy" for a "faint image" that corresponds to the Ravine (43–46). There is no justification, I think, for severely restricting the meaning of "Poesy" here; undoubtedly the form of the word is chosen to evoke the Greek meaning of "making," or "forming," rather than the limited sense we give to the word "poetry." This cave is explicitly not "above" the "darkness," but in the dark experiential world below, just as the corresponding caverns that echo the Arve (30) are at the base of the Ravine, the symbol of the external world that the poet's trance

has made analogous to the human mind. Now, the legion of wild thoughts is the consequence of the human mind's "passively" rendering and receiving influencings in its encounter with the hypothesized external world. They are, therefore, the discrete, unorganized, and limited thoughts resulting from perception by any individual mind. And the mind is passive in such experience because, just as one passively experiences by exposing his senses to a stimulus, so in Shelley's philosophical idealism some force outside the mind exerts itself through both subject and object to effect perception. These disordered and fragmentary thoughts are all the mind has to work with in the act that is customarily called thinking. When this legion of wild thoughts examines further perceptions by the individual mind it regards them as shadows passing on the walls of the cave. It cannot know directly the objects outside the cave casting their shadows on the walls and, since the mind is now assumed to be distinct from the objective world, can only examine the shadows. As the entire universe in its multiplicity moves before the mind, the legion of wild thoughts surveys the shadows: the "Ghosts of *all* things that are" (46), but ghosts nevertheless. Each is a "phantom" (47), the mere show of a thing. Indeed, in naming the shadow in the cave a "faint image" Shelley is pointing back to its symbolic analogue in the hypostatized outer world: the "unsculptured image" veiled by the ethereal waterfall (26–27); and the sense of darkness implicit in the words "shadows" and "shade" reminds us again of the darkness of the mind through which the glittering universe flows to become obscure ideas, "unsculptured" images.

But how, then, are we to conceive of the total reality if we assume temporarily the dualism of mind and external object? For in seeking among the shadows that pass in the mind, or among the ghosts of all discrete things that are, for some "shade" of the Ravine, the disordered and fragmentary thoughts that have been formed in the passive mind are now wilfully attempting to formulate the total and ordered reality that the Ravine symbolizes. Never able to know directly the objects of its thoughts, the mind knows only the shadows passing within itself; and therefore it cannot be said that man exists in a universe outside himself. On the other hand, Shelley cannot say that the shadows are indeed the universe we live in; thoughts are not mind-born but derive from some unknowable object. What he actually says is that in wilfully attempting to realize the ordered universe the wild thoughts only *seek*—and of course seek in vain—for the "faint image" that answers to the unknowable objective universe (45), just as in the reified world the echo of the caverns answers to "the Arve's commotion" (30) but obviously is not the same as the sound of the Arve.

Only by defining reality as the *searching* for the correspondence can Shelley grasp both the subjective and objective poles of his ontological paradox—the paradox already insisted upon in the lending and reflecting of light and darkness, in the interaction of the fluid and the permanent, in the rendering and receiving of mind and universe, of woods and winds, of winds and pines, sound and echo. Reality, then, is neither a thing nor a place, but an act; it is not in the mind nor outside it, but in the very act of searching. It is for this reason that neither the legion of thoughts ("that") nor the objective universe ("thou"—the Ravine) is an "unbidden guest" in the cave of the mind (43). Being a guest, reality is not resident in the mind—reality is not mental. On the other hand, it must be invited into the mind to be a reality, and this very bidding, like the searching, constitutes the reality. Since reality resides in neither subject nor object, but in both simultaneously, it truly resides in the verb, which implicates both subject and object; in the searching, which contains both the searcher and the sought. Since neither thoughts nor reality is native to the cave of the mind, since they are only guests and transients, reality can exist only while the thoughts seek. And it is for this reason also that the searching which constitutes the total universe takes place in the cave of Poesy, in the sense of the place of making, shaping, and formulating. But the wild thoughts are not native to the individual, "separate" human mind, for they are portion of the total Thought in the universal Mind; only as a modification of the universal Mind do they exist in what is termed an individual mind. Therefore only so long as the modification exists ("till the breast/ From which they fled recalls them," (47–48), reality, the Ravine, exists in a human mind by virtue of the search to correlate with an objective universe some faint image in the successive array of the shadows of all things.

IV

To summarize briefly to this point. The inner logic of the first two verse paragraphs has divulged that even if one imaginatively and falsely isolates an external world or the human mind, both errors revert to the paradox that Shelley called the "Intellectual Philosophy," for both insist upon acting out symbolically the relationships belonging to that philosophy. All three ontological positions reveal that Power, or Ultimate Cause, is unknowable, although man ascribes causation to the first perceptible item in a chain of succession. And all equally reveal that reality must be defined paradoxically: it is both thing and thought; it is marked by the interplay of the glittering dynamic world of "things" and its dark container; it is born of the mind's passively rendering and receiving influencings in its encounter with the universe, as the Power works through both subject and object and fuses their data; it is the paradoxical co-presence of a fixed sameness and a sameness of change; it is known by an energy that brings into being what already exists; it is that tension which is the mind's searching to identify its own data with an unknowable externality. No matter which philosophic position is assumed, these truths of the Intellectual Philosophy emerge. The strategy whereby even the false conceptions have been made to body forth this truth has consisted in the fact that every detail in the description of the supposed external world, imaged as the Ravine of Arve, is a symbolic parallel of some detail in the thought-thing world of the first paragraph or in the world of the supposedly distinct mind and universe described at the end of the second.

With one exception. Of all the characteristics of the Ravine of Arve one alone has no analogue in the paragraph that precedes or the lines that immediately follow: when in the external world supposedly distinct from mind the "voices of the desert fail," a strange sleep "Wraps all in its own deep eternity" (27–29). Although the carefully guarded supposition of an autonomous external reality has only reaffirmed the original ontology that it theoretically violates, nevertheless it has also given access to a truth outside the limits of that system. Quite casually there has been deposited in the poem the fact that if there were a self-sustaining reality wholly independent of mind, if all were only substance and motion, any pause in its activities could be only a vacuum, and such a reality would be meaningless in its recurrent moments of inaction. Later, in the fourth section, when the poet again will consider reality as only matter and motion, he will speak of the "feeble dreams" or "dreamless sleep" that "Holds every future leaf and flower" (88–90)—a pause in nature that is only emptiness. One of the manuscript readings of the lines, "no human dreams," makes even more vivid the distinction Shelley is drawing between matter and the human mind. Moreover, in the same passage he will describe this dreamless sleep as a "detested trance" from which vegetative nature leaps with a bound (90–91). But when the poet himself experienced a seeming trance (35) it was neither detested, nor dreamless, nor empty; on the contrary, it was filled with a vision of his own mind. An empty pause in a merely external reality, therefore, is a condition that exists only in the materialistic philosophy—a revelation the poet has gained by causing his Intellectual Philosophy to parade as materialism.

We have already noticed that the legion of wild thoughts can perform two acts, one of which, the search for the mental shadow of reality, is a representation in mental symbols of the ontological premise that governs the poem. But the other capacity of thoughts, to float above the darkness of the Ravine of reality, like the vacancy possible in matter, does not echo any factor in the description of the Ravine or in the symbolic outline of the Intellectual Philosophy in the first paragraph. By pretending the possibility that Mind is an independent entity the poet discovers the otherwise unknowable capacity of thoughts to transcend the universe. Since the trance explicitly causes the Ravine to become an emblem of the human mind, it matters little in which way we read the "darkness": if we choose to think materialistically, it is the darkness of the Ravine, which contains the objective universe of things; if we accept the vision of the trance, it is the darkness of the human mind, which casts a gloom over all its sensory data; and if we recognize the meaningful ambiguity whereby both Ravine and the mind are inextricably present in the words "thy darkness," it is the darkness of reality as defined by the Intellectual Philosophy. At any rate, it is the darkness of the reality in which man exists and experiences; and thought can transcend it.

Grounding his reality in philosophic idealism, Shelley has, with organically perfect poetic motivation, twice pretended its falsity. Paradoxically these pretenses have only proved the validity of that philosophy, and yet at the same time they have opened to him two truths that not only would be unavailable to that system but would be meaningless within the confines of its terms. By penetrating beyond what is philosophically true, the poet has also unveiled what is imaginatively true. Out of the convergence of these two special revelations of the imagination the next movement of the poem will grow.

V

The movement that begins with the third section receives its impetus from, and is made possible by, the poet's last and most extreme imaginative supposition: that he has entered the region of death and dreams. Yet, just as the suppositions of the simile and the trance were carefully counterstated so that even in unfolding imaginative truth they did not deny the premise of the poem, so now the poet seeks the revelations of death and dream without really abandoning his empirical ontology. He had not claimed to have a vision of his own mind through trance: he only *seemed as if* in a trance; now he only *asks* whether he is in the "mightier world" of dream (54–55). Nor does he even assert that dream is surely entry into the "remoter world": *"Some say that gleams of a remoter world/ Visit the soul in sleep"* (49–50). By not committing himself Shelley can have the data of his imaginative experience and yet keep his empirically grounded philosophy. But that he is grasping for the transcendent he makes abundantly clear: the realm that perhaps is entered in sleep is not the world defined by the Intellectual Philosophy, but a "remoter world"; there the "shapes" outnumber the thoughts of "those who wake and live" (49, 51–52); and this "mightier world" radiates infinitely out from the human world, spreading "far around and inaccessibly/ Its circles" (56–57). It contains not only the world of human experience but also the infinitude beyond it.

This transcendence is also acted out dramatically. In the continuity of dramatic gestures the poet has progressed from abstract contemplation of the unlocalized thought-thing world to a sensory examination of the Ravine symbolizing an external world, and, while still gazing at the Ravine, has dreamily envisioned his own mind. Now, leaping in thought above the experiential world, he also suddenly lifts his glance from the Ravine-world to the farthest heights: "I look on high/ . . . Far, far above, piercing the infinite sky,/ Mont Blanc appears" (52, 60–61). Consequently, just as in the topographical structure the Ravine at the base of the mountain symbolizes the world of ordinary experience, so the peak of Europe's highest mountain symbolizes the transcendent; and since Mont Blanc gives its name to the title of the poem, we might well expect that the essence of the poem will be the revelation handed down from those heights.

In this final act of transcendence the two special revelations of the imagination come together into a meaningful relationship. In the putative external world devoid of mind the silence of its voices produces a sleep that "Wraps all in its own deep eternity": inaction in the purely objective world is only a vacancy. But to the mind sleep opens access to the "mightier world," whose "shapes" are more numerous than those of the waking mind: far from a vacancy, sleep is plenitude, embracing the infinity that surrounds the sensory world. This discovery is made coincidentally with the other special revelation, the power of thought to float above the "darkness"; for it occurs because of the poet's power to lift both his glance and his thought above the dark Ravine-world, perceive the gleaming heights of Mont Blanc, and feel his spirit, aspiring to the transcendent, "Driven like a homeless cloud from steep to steep/ That vanishes among the viewless gales!" (58–59).

With this achievement one of the two motivating forces in the drama of the poem, the series of increasingly more extreme suppositions, has come to its end, since it has fully accomplished its function and reached the limits of its potentialities. The other directing, or drama-making, force is the route traced by the poet's glance. This has already been a subordinate factor as the poet moves from the symbolic scenery of the thought-thing world, to a sensation of an outer world, to a glimpse of the peak of Mont Blanc. Now that the course of his attention has been fully energized by impulses from the successive suppositions, it assumes complete control over the further development of the poem. In particular, the third and fourth paragraphs will derive their shape and meaning from the gradual lowering of the poet's gaze until he once again watches the flow of the River Arve through the Ravine.

Upon this transfer of dramatic control the poem enters upon its central theme: the nature of the Power, or Cause, and its relation to the meaning of human experience. This, and not merely the nature of reality, is the governing concern of the poem. Should we wish to think in terms of philosophic systems we might say, loosely, that having accepted Berkeley's ontology, Shelley now raises Hume's question of causation. But not only, as we have seen, do such terms introduce confusion by raising irrelevant systematic problems, they also are untrue. Most significantly, unlike Berkeley's God, who is both the universal Mind and cause, Shelley's Power is independent of the universal Mind: for example, the wild thoughts in the poet's mind were not caused by the universal Mind; they "fled" from its "breast," and it can only recall them. And whereas Hume sceptically abandons causation as mysteriously unknowable, Shelley is intent upon gaining imaginative insight into it. Rather, having accepted as true the reality defined by philosophical idealism and having acknowledged that man's empirically grounded thoughts are limited by that definition, Shelley nevertheless strives to break free from those limitations, not by empirical thought, but by that other capacity of thought, imagination. By means of successive imaginative insights —through simile, trance, the death-like dream of sleep—he strives to free himself from what exists to discover what, outside it, moves and energizes it.

The theme of Power has already been touched on in the first two units of the poem in the references to "secret springs," "source," "secret throne," and the "Power in likeness of the Arve," but the first two stanzas are mainly preparatory, making possible the insight into the Power within a system that denies the possibility of knowing its real existence. Now the third and fourth paragraphs will each unfold two essential truths about the Power: although the poet catches symbolic glimmerings of it in dream, it is beyond the experiential knowledge of man; and it is its own end, active only because to act is its essence.

Glancing at the "subject mountains" about Mont Blanc, Shelley proposes his own variants of the two current theories of the origin of mountains, the Neptunian and the Catastrophic:

> Is this the scene
> Where the old Earthquake-daemon taught her young
> Ruin? Were these their toys? or did a sea
> Of fire, envelope once this silent snow?
>
> (71–74)

But the efficient Cause is unknowable to man: "None can reply—all seems eternal now" (75). Similarly in the next unit Power is described as dwelling "apart in its tranquillity/ Remote, serene, and inaccessible" (96–97). This knowledge of its inaccessibility, moreover, has been taught *even* by the "primaeval mountains" (99). Since they belong to the earliest of time ("primaeval"), and since man thinks of causation as a chronological process initiated by some first impulse, presumably the primaeval mountains should

hint at the event immediately prior to their creation, and therefore at Cause
itself. But instead the mountains only reveal that Cause is infinitely remote
from its first palpable manifestation; that the timeless is entirely "apart" from
the first in time. The relation of the Power to the primaeval mountains is
identical with the relation in the first two sections between the "secret
springs" and the "source" of thought and between the "secret throne" of
Power and the Power "in likeness of the Arve."

But although the Power is inaccessible to man, its character is discoverable
in its consequences. As the poet lowers his gaze from the summit of Mont
Blanc, he encounters the region of the glaciers. Lying between the peak and
the Ravine, it is between the Power and the human world and therefore
symbolizes the extra-human workings of the Power. Here the mountains
are "unearthly" (62); the glaciers are a "desert peopled by the storms alone"
(67); its shapes are hideous, "Ghastly, and scarred, and riven" (71); and
man is destroyed when he ventures here. But it would be wholly wrong to
read this as an evaluation: the poet is merely discovering that the universe
is not homocentric. The Power is neither benevolent nor hostile; it is self-
contained and indifferent to everything but its own need to act. The horror
that permeates the description is simply the consequence of the bias inherent
in man's partial view.

Therefore, in revealing that the Power, unlike the Christian God, has no
human concerns, the extra-human region of the glaciers (the "wilderness,"
76) is capable of teaching man to doubt—that is, in the sceptical sense, to
recognize that the Power is neither good nor evil, neither benevolent nor
vicious, but only amoral, serenely indifferent. Or—what amounts to the
same thing—it teaches the necessitarian doctrine that the Power is an inexorable force man cannot command or control and that he must therefore
passively yield himself to it: should man have faith in this Power, this faith
alone ("But for such faith," 79) would reconcile him to the workings of
nature. As Shelley was to state the necessitarian theme in *Prometheus Unbound*
(II, iii, 94–99),

> Resist not the weakness,
> Such strength is in meekness
> That the Eternal, the Immortal,
> Must unloose through life's portal
> The snake-like Doom coiled underneath his throne
> By that alone.

But, in accordance with the whole sceptical milieu of the poem, this is not
constructive knowledge. Of the Intellectual Philosophy, Shelley had written
that it "establishes no new truth, it gives us no additional insight into our

hidden nature, neither its action nor itself. . . . It makes one step towards this object: it destroys error and the root of error." The sceptical doubt and the submission to the Power lead to no further truth, but merely destroy man's false conceptions of Power, expressed in the institutions man has constructed and called ultimate and compelling truths: the mountain has a voice "to repeal/ Large codes of fraud and woe" (80–81).

In the next paragraph again, as the poet moves his glance down the mountainside, the unconcern of the Power is forced upon him. The glaciers, a region within the universe but outside the human, are marked by their destructiveness. Deriving from the Power—"their far fountains" (101)—they move irresistibly, crushing everything before them. Indeed, the poet observes, it is false to call this a "city of death," since this suggests the human, which has no relevance here; it is, instead, "a flood of ruin" (105–107) extending death inside the borders of the living and forever claiming this newly won region of the inhuman. "So much of life and joy is lost" (117). But this is no more an evaluation of the workings of the Power than is the description of the subject mountains as hideous, "ghastly." It is but a truth that man must face and passively accept, for the Power acts "in scorn of *mortal power*" (103), which by working against the Power can only institute the "codes of fraud and woe."

This amorality of the Power is then brilliantly dramatized by the abruptness with which the description pivots. Continuing his downward glance through the area of the destructive glaciers, Shelley gradually moves to the border between the extra-human and the human:

> The race
> Of man, flies far in dread; his work and dwelling
> Vanish, like smoke before the tempest's stream,
> And their place is not known.
>
> (117–20)

With this last, drably monosyllabic line the process of devastation has come to its hollow end and left only a dull vacancy. But now, suddenly and without transition, the poet's glance plunges down into the world of human existence, the Ravine that had been the subject of the first two stanzas:

> Below, vast caves
> Shine in the rushing torrent's restless gleam,
> Which from those secret chasms in tumult welling
> Meet in the vale, and one majestic River,
> The breath and blood of distant lands, for ever
> Rolls its loud waters to the ocean waves,
> Breathes its swift vapours to the circling air.
>
> (120–26)

With this dramatically violent shift in tone the horror and devastation of the preceding scene have been abruptly displaced by a rich and boundlessly vital energy. And yet the poet has merely been tracing one continuous succession: the peak of Mont Blanc—the glaciers—the River Arve. Destruction and animation therefore do not distinguish two different forces, one good, the other evil; it is because the river and its source, the glacier, are essentially one that the poet has described the glacier in terms of a river, a "flood of ruin" that "Rolls its perpetual stream" (107–109). For the glaciers, which create a waste and crush life, themselves become the one majestic river. The energy which, in the form of the flood of ruin, eats into the living world, is the same energy which, in the form of the Arve, is both animate (*breathing* its "swift vapours to the circling air," 126) and animating ("The breath and blood of distant lands," 124). The abruptness of the tonal transformation, then, is a dramatic presentation of the indifference, the serenity of the Power. In its successive manifestations the Power acts in different contexts, glacier and river, and man mistakenly defines good and evil in terms of those contexts; but the Power within itself is neither, having as its nature only the inexorable necessity of acting in a fixed pattern manifested to man as succession.

For in the necessitarian ethics Shelley is developing here, Power alone is the ground of reality, and therefore it alone is the ethical center. If the first two verse sections have been devoted to unfolding the nature of what is, the rest of the poem is concerned with the ground of that existence. For the Power bears "the same relation to all that we perceive and are, as what we call a cause does to what we call effect" ("Treatise on Morals"). All reality is the One Thought within the One Mind, but within the One Thought is the possibility of infinite diversity: the universe is "everlasting," but it flows through the One Mind as "things." It is, therefore, only the ground of the universe, the Power, that is immutable and eternal. For what the poet has learned is that the universe he experiences is wholly different in kind from the Power. Although the palpable universe also manifests energy, all the turbulence in that hypostatized outer world—its persistent energy perceived as motion and sound, and its vigorous but vain resistance to emptiness—is indicative, not of its eternity, but, contrarily, of its mutability:

> All things that move and breathe with toil and sound
> Are born and die; revolve, subside and swell.
>
> (94–95)

The only immutability is transcendent, completely apart from the universe it causes and sustains; and, unlike the turbulent, noisy, fluid world, it is without qualities. It is the noiseless power of sound, the motionless power of activity, the unmoved mover:

> Power dwells apart in its tranquillity
> Remote, serene, and inaccessible.
>
> (96–97)

VI

It must by now be obvious that the summit of Mont Blanc is the symbol of Power. The transcending capacity of dream has granted insight into that transcendent Power, unknowable in normal experience or in terms of the idealistic definition of existence. By spreading "far around and inaccessibly/ Its circles" the "mightier world of sleep" has allowed the poet to see the symbolic meaning of Mont Blanc "Far, far above, piercing the infinite sky . . . still, snowy, and serene." In a letter to Peacock (June 24, 1816) describing his visit to Mont Blanc, Shelley wrote at nearly the very time he composed the poem:

Within this last year, these glaciers have advanced three hundred feet into the valley. Saussure, the naturalist, says, that they have their periods of increase and decay: the people of the country hold an opinion entirely different; but as I judge, more probable. It is agreed by all, that the snow on the summit of Mont Blanc and the neighbouring mountains perpetually augments, and that ice, in the form of glaciers, subsists without melting in the valley of Chamouni during its transient and variable summer. If the snow which produces this glacier must augment, and the heat of the valley is no obstacle to the perpetual existence of such masses of ice as have already descended into it, the consequence is obvious; the glaciers must augment and will subsist, at least until they have overflowed this vale.

It is, therefore, the perpetual falling of the snow that leads Shelley to conceive of the mountain peak as symbolic of the Power, a timeless, invariable, and self-existing energy. At all times, in both "the calm darkness of the moonless nights" and "the lone glare of day, the snows descend/ Upon that Mountain" (130–32). And this symbol produces the perfect symbolic pattern of the poem, for the snow is at an inaccessible height, but even as it perpetually renews its own existence it becomes the destructive glaciers, which in turn become the vital and vivifying river.

In effect, "Mont Blanc" is a religious poem, and the Power is Shelley's transcendent deity. The Power cannot be experienced: the snows perpetually fall, but "none beholds them there" (132). Yet it works through reality by a series of consequences stemming from itself. It is, indeed, a *"secret* strength" and yet the "strength of things/ Which governs thought, and to the infinite dome/ Of heaven is as a law" (139–41). Though it governs both thought and things (and hence the human passivity in the rendering and receiving of mind and world that produce the legion of wild thoughts), it can come down only "in *likeness* of the Arve."

Moreover, by reason of its transcendence, it can, like the Christian God, be characterized by none of the attributes of sensory reality, but is the ineffable essence of these qualities. Throughout the poem experiential reality has been vividly and persistently marked by its turbulence and its boisterous sounds, and the tone that pervades the entire poem is that of powerful energy: the universe of things flows and rolls its rapid waves; waterfalls leap for ever; woods and winds contend; the river bursts and raves; the Arve bursts through the mountain; the winds stir up the sounds of the pines; caverns echo the Arve's commotion. These are sensory attributes of reality as it is experienced and are stages in a chain of succession that leads back to the Power. But the Power, being infinitely remote from these consequences, is the essence of these qualities, and therefore is inaccessible to sensory experience, although not completely to the imagination. It is "still, snowy, and serene" (61); it "dwells apart in its tranquillity/ Remote, serene, and inaccessible" (96–97); it is the "still and solemn power of many sights,/ And many sounds, and much of life and death" (128–29). The final paragraph especially underscores the fact that, although it is the source of the incessant clamor in the world below, the Power is soundless: unlike the winds that contend with the woods and evoke the harmonious music of the pines,

> Winds contend
> *Silently* there, and heap the snow with breath
> Rapid and strong, but *silently!*
>
> (134–36)

And there the lightning is "voiceless" (137). This theme of silence most skilfully pivots about an ironic opposition that distinguishes the experiential from the transcendent. Since the very existence of the experiential world is dependent upon its sensory qualities, such as sound, the absence of sound wraps that world in an empty and meaningless sleep from which nature is eager to escape; but at the transcendent level silence is the totality of all possible sound, since it is the essence, just as sleep, although a vacancy in the external world, admits the human mind into the reality of the Power itself.

But the most pervasive preparation for the revelation that the Power is the inaccessible essence is the strategic handling of the images of light and darkness. That the universe of things is varyingly dark and bright is an expression in terms of the Intellectual Philosophy, we have already noted, of the customary distinction between immediate and mediate sensations. But more particularly Shelley has attributed the brilliance to the consequences of the Power—to the flowing universe of things, to the River Arve bursting through the mountains; and he has attributed the darkness to the earthly and human context through which the Power works—the mind, the Ravine. Since, then, the brilliance derives from the Power, when the poet aspires to a transcendent knowledge, he recalls that some say sleep divulges *"gleams* of a remoter world" (49). The word "gleams" has not only its metaphoric sense of "intimations," but also its literal meaning: the vision of the infinite is the vision of Light—the Light that Shelley was later to describe as kindling the universe. The gleams of the remoter world are, of course, symbolically imaged by the snow at the summit of the mountain, and the poet prepares for this conjunction by describing Mont Blanc as "still, *snowy,* and serene" (61). When he then traces the successive stages of the work of the Power down the mountainside, he also sees the successive stages of the brilliance: the glacier forms a "wall impregnable of *beaming* ice" (106), and "Below, vast caves/ *Shine* in the rushing torrent's *restless gleam*" (120–21). But it is the unqualified "gleam" that is the term for the unrealizable essence of light, and "glittering," "splendour," "flame of lightning," "beaming," and "shine" are words that describe the "gleam" in its experienceable and hence inessential, or accidental, modes. The preparation for the final value of the ideal term is made by the poet's telling us that perhaps *"gleams* of a remoter world/ Visit the *soul* in sleep" (49–50) and by his qualifying the gleam of the rushing torrents as "restless," since the palpable manifestation of the transcendent can be only a mutable and inconstant realization of the unchangeable essence. For the "gleam" of the Power is beyond and distinct from what man calls "light." Consequently, when, through the ability of thought to float above the "darkness," the poet once again looks up to the snow on the mountain he is struck by the discovery that "Mont Blanc *yet gleams* on high" (127), since it is an eternity of light in contradistinction to the "restless" gleam perceived in the mutable sensory world. Even in the midst of all mutability, even in the fluctuating vividness and obscurity of the world man calls reality, even

> In the calm darkness of the moonless nights,
> In the lone glare of day, the snows descend.
> (130–31)

And so they do "when the flakes burn in the sinking sun,/ Or the star-beams dart through them" (133–34). Man's light is to the characterless transcendent light as "glare" is to "gleam."

VII

The mystery of the final lines of the poem, then, is not the muddle of philosophic confusion, but the mystery of religion itself. For the religious paradox of a God who is not experienceable and is different in kind from the world we experience, and yet who directs its activities and makes them meaningful by His being, is of the same order as the paradox of an inaccessible Power whose nature is the essence of experiential qualities and yet who governs, although without concern and by fixed law, both mind and matter. But how this paradox is made possible in the poem and is given significance must be arrived at through a consideration of the evolving gestures.

Throughout the third and fourth sections the poet had been recalling his gaze from his transcendent vision of the mountain peak, down through the extra-human, back into the world of man; and thereby he had learned the inaccessibility of the Power and the need of man's submission to its amoral and necessary laws. But the pattern of this gesture is a succession acted out in time. The only questions the gesture can answer are, Where is the Power? and How does it manifest itself here? not *What* is the Power in its absolute self? In order that this be answered the poet has abruptly glanced back to the mountain height so that he might know that the factor of time involved in the successiveness of his downward glance, as snow became glacier, and glacier river, is irrelevant to the ground of being. The Power itself is outside time and infinitely greater than the mere process of governing mind and matter: "Mont Blanc *yet* gleams on high:—the power is there" (127). The significance of the abruptly repeated upward glance is that, having perceived Power as *becoming* in a spatial and temporal context, he wishes now to know it in its pure *being*, since in itself the Power remains "Through time and change unquenchably the same." In religious terms we might say that Shelley has found it insufficient to know God's earthly and human economy; he seeks to grasp God's timeless being and the significance of that being to man. It is in this sense that his suddenly renewed vision of the heights divulges that the Power is the quality-less essence of experiential qualities: still, gleaming, silent, innocent, solitary. It is all that Shelley meant by the words, "the intense inane": a vacancy that nevertheless holds in itself the potentiality of all that is.

But still another gesture is required in order that the poem may fulfill itself. The first gesture revealed the spatial and temporal continuity in which the transcendent Power manifests itself in the human world; the second revealed the self-contained nature of that Power and therefore its absolute difference from the phenomenal world. What remains in order that the poet's experience be meaningful is that he conjoin his imaginative knowledge of the noumenal with his experiential knowledge of the phenomenal, not through the unreal process of becoming, as he did with his first gesture, but absolutely, now that his second gesture has grasped for him the absolute nature of the Power. It is this remaining gesture of a timeless and spaceless conjunction of noumenal and phenomenal that is implicit in the closing lines and gives them their significance as the climax and consummation of the poetic experience.

We must recall that the poem has been an extensive elaboration of oppositions: the experiential and the transcendent, which is not experienceable; the immediate and the inaccessible; qualities and essence; cause and effect; the actual and the suppositive; thought and thing. Since the elaboration has continued up to the final lines we might reasonably expect that here we shall find the oppositions resolved. We have already observed that in the hypostatized objective world a pause in sound is a sleep of vacancy, a vacuum that nature abhors; but that to the hypostatized mind sleep opens up the plenitude of the "mightier world." Now it has also been learned that the Power, the ultimate Cause, is a silence—not a vacancy, but the essence of all sound. Moreover, in nature the region of the glaciers has revealed itself as a solitude, empty of man: it is a "desert peopled by the storms alone," and man cannot survive there. But the residence of the Power is also a solitude: "none beholds" the snows there "in these solitudes"—solitudes that, paradoxically, are absolute fullness, since they are the source of all things. Silence and solitude, therefore, are decidedly not a vacancy either in the Power or in the "human mind's imaginings" (143). What is an emptiness in the objective world is the mind's entry into the absolute, since the absolute is silent (and therefore the essence of sound), solitary (and therefore the essence of fullness).

The sense of the final lines, then, is that although in the objective world experienced as qualities the absence of all qualities can be only nonentity, to the mind in its act of imagining (not of experiencing), the absence of qualities is the vision of the ultimate Cause, the quality-less essence of everything. And what the total rhetorical question at the end of the poem implies is that if the mind did not have this imaginative capacity, the objects of human experience—mountain, earth, stars, and sea—could have neither meaning nor value to man. Man's wild thoughts can enter the cave of Poesy and, by seeking, shape an ordered universe, or they can float above the "darkness" of that universe and perceive on high the "gleam" of the Power; but it is the combination of these acts that makes the universe meaningful to man. What Shelley is finally concerned with is the potential worth of human experience, and again the religious analogy is pertinent. The mere thought-thing universe can have, in itself, no value, and yet it is meaningful to the mind because the mind brings to it a knowledge of the transcendent Power, an atemporal and aspatial conjunction that is the gesture inherent in the closing lines. In Christian terms it is man's supernatural knowledge of a transcendent Deity that gives meaning to his existence in a world of mutability. And Shelley's term "imaginings," which refers to his transcendent intuitings in the successive suppositions of the simile, the trance, and the dream, is his secular correlative for Christian "faith," faith in the supernatural revelations of the unknowable God who is essence.

Indeed, the word "imaginings" embodies an ironic inversion of values that characterizes the relation of the position from which the poem begins to the position it finally attains. We have already observed that one of the two acts of the mind's thoughts is the striving to correlate the mind's faint images with an unknown externality, and that in this act the universe comes into being for man. The other act of thought, therefore, is of a precisely parallel nature: it conjoins the reality we call mountain, earth, stars, and sea, with the imaginatively intuited truth of the transcendent and thereby invests the universe with value. Valued reality, therefore, is as much the result of an act as the universe is, an acting that is implied by the participial forms "seeking" and "imaginings." But the act that brings the universe into the mind also involves images, since it is conducted by thoughts which are "things" and is their effort to find faint images in the mind that correspond to the unknown externality. Shelley therefore is not assigning valued reality to the purely intuitive mind: we can think of nothing, he always insisted, which we have not perceived. The imagining that makes reality meaningful is simply a higher form of the imaging that constitutes reality. The conjecture, persuasion, or conviction of the existence of the Power, Shelley wrote, is a thought "to be included in the catalogue of existence"; it is one of the modes "in which thoughts are combined," and is proof that "beyond the limits of perception and thought nothing can exist" ("Treatise on Morals").

This transfiguration in the poem of imaging into imagining parallels the ironic inversion involved in the discovery that the restless activity, turbulent sound, and destruction and vitality of the phenomenal world are, at the noumenal level, silence, stillness, and innocence. Similarly, because of the transfiguration of the phenomenal world that the poem brings about, the splendor and brilliance that at the beginning of the poem appear as the characteristics of sensory perception become the "gleam" of the Power. Most important, the quasi-religious experience that is at the core of the poem effects an inversion of the ratio of human mind to universe. When, in the opening stanza, the poet constructs the universe in terms of the Intellectual Philosophy, he finds that the human mind contributes little to the mighty sum of things: its sound is "but half of its own,/ Such as a feeble brook will oft assume" (6–7). This ratio will not be repudiated in the poem; it is indeed true if one is merely defining the universe. But when at last the poet seeks the meaningfulness of reality he discovers that the elements of the universe would be negligible were it not for the power of the human mind to invest them with values by conjoining them through the mind's imagination with the ground of being.

However, if these are the discoveries of the poem, why does the poet so severely understate them by the mere negative intimation that silence and solitude are not vacancy to the human mind?

> And what were thou, and earth, and stars, and sea,
> If to the human mind's imaginings
> Silence and solitude were vacancy?

And why does he merely hint obliquely through a rhetorical question the meaningfulness that earthly experience gains through the transcendent vision, instead of affirming it directly? For my paraphrase of the closing lines claims more than they actually state. It must be recalled that the sceptical philosophy in which the poem is firmly rooted denies not only that Power may be directly known as one knows "things," but also that "thought" and "thing" are separable terms. At no point has this assumption really been denied. Even the successive suppositions, although they make it possible to imagine that mind and universe are separable in order that a transcendent knowledge may be gained, have actually only confirmed the original premise. And yet, the putative division of mind and things that took place in the second paragraph has persisted up to the closing lines. It is the supposedly autonomous mind that seems in dream to view the mountain peak. In the fourth section Shelley explicitly says that the knowledge of the mutability of animate entities and the infinite remoteness of the Power are taught by "the *naked* countenance of earth" (i.e., the self-existing objectivity) to the "adverting mind" (i.e., the autonomous mind that attentively turns to this objective world). What the rhetorical mode of the final lines recognizes is that these suppositions lie outside the limits of the ontology of the Intellectual Philosophy that everywhere controls the poem, and that therefore the contents of the final lines cannot be directly asserted. That they are in the form of a question is an admission of the purely suppositive, or imaginative, progress of the poem; they have been arrived at by moving outside reality as defined by the Intellectual Philosophy and by knowing imaginatively the Power, which is unknowable. And yet by shaping the conclusion into the form of a rhetorical question Shelley has indeed incorporated in his world his transcendent discovery without overtly doing so.

By this means the empirical and the suppositive come together: the experiential and the transcendent, qualities and essence. That the mode of the lines is a rhetorical question returns us to the ontology with which the poem began: "the difference is purely nominal between those two classes of thought. . . ." Yet the rhetorical question obviously has an answer: "Nothing of any worth." The thoughts we call "things" would be meaningless if thought did not have the imaginative power to float above the darkness of the universe and, in dreams, bring to those "things" a knowledge of a supernal, immutable essence that is the ground and Power of everything.

Shelley's Theory of Evil

by Melvin M. Rader

I

Shelley's theory of evil has been frequently interpreted after a fashion that expresses only a portion of the truth. Walter Bagehot long ago formulated the prevailing view:

> All the world is evil and will be evil, until some unknown conqueror shall appear—a teacher by rhapsody and a conqueror by words—who shall at once reform all evil. Mathematicians place great reliance on the unknown symbol, great X. Shelley did more; he expected it would take life and reform our race.[1]

> The essential feelings he hoped to change; the eternal facts he struggled to remove. Nothing in human life to him was inevitable or fixed; he fancied he could alter it all. His sphere is the "unconditioned;" he floats away into an imaginary Elysium or an expected Utopia; beautiful and excellent, of course, but having nothing in common with the absolute laws of the present world.[2]

These strictures have been revoiced by contemporary scholars. Mr. H. N. Brailsford, for example, declares that Shelley thought of evil as "something factitious and unessential." [3] Likewise Professor S. F. Gingerich maintains that the poet's belief in the perfectibility of man was "based on the more fundamental belief in the essential unreality of evil." [4] Mr. A. Clutton-Brock believes that

> Shelley had no knowledge either of the nature of evil, or of the means by which evil can be abolished; therefore he could not represent either.[5]

Again, Professor W. E. Peck advances the charge of superficial understanding:

"Shelley's Theory of Evil" (Original title: "Shelley's Theory of Evil Misunderstood"), From Western Reserve Studies, A Miscellany, pp. 25–32 (*Western Reserve University Bulletin*. n. s. vol. 23 (Sept. 15, 1930), No. 16). Copyright 1930 by the *Western Reserve University Bulletin*. Reprinted by permission of the Press of Western Reserve University and the author. The author has made minor changes for this reprinting.

[1] *Literary Studies* (London, 1884), Vol. I, p. 83.

[2] *Ibid.*, p. 116.

[3] H. N. Brailsford, *Shelley, Godwin, and Their Circle* (New York, no date), p. 240.

[4] S. F. Gingerich, *Essays in the Romantic Poets* (New York, 1924), p. 229.

[5] A. Clutton-Brock, *Shelley, the Man and the Poet* (New York, 1909), p. 183.

Whatever evil there was in the world, he believed, grew out of the blight of government and church and law. He could not perceive that these organisms of society, with all of their good and evil, were but reflections of the mixed warp and woof that are the hearts and minds of the persons who create these institutions.[6]

Such critics agree that Shelley regarded evil as externalistic and temporary: that his grasp of the entire problem was weak.

Opinions to this effect do Shelley less than justice; they are substantiated by his early poems, but are partially negated by his later works. The youthful poet, aghast at the world's iniquity, conceived wrong as a scourge that has been imposed from without. In *Queen Mab*, the kings, priests, and statesmen, dabblers in "gold and blood," dictate slavery to the mob. Likewise in *Laon and Cythna*, the tyrant Othman and his blackhearted priests strangle the good impulses of a people who are inwardly incorruptible. Even in Shelley's mature works, the thick fumes of evil drift in from the stew-pots of church and state. The poet soon outgrew the belief, however, that the iniquitous few have clamped misery upon the innocent multitudes. In his *Speculations on Morals*, probably written about the year 1815, he asserted that evil is deep, pervasive, and endogenous. He maintained that there is a class of actions which

flow from a profounder source than the series of our habitual conduct, which . . . derives from without. These are the actions, and such as these, which make human life what it is, and are the fountains of all the good and evil with which its entire surface is so widely and impartially spread.[7]

Shelley's later writings testify to this same conviction: that much evil has a profound inward source which is deeper than villainy. In *The Cenci*, for example, the sharp antithesis between good and evil has been abolished; the virtuous Beatrice wreaks vengeance;[8] the diabolical father is courageous and superbly rebellious. The evil-doers in *Hellas* are not wilfully malevolent; Mahmud grasps madly for light, and Hassan, the altruist, is ready to die for "one God, one King, one Hope, one Law." [9] In the last of Shelley's works, *Charles the First* and *The Triumph of Life*, he has risen to a modern view of life's tragedy. Charles is the reverse of the villainous tyrant; he feels himself the trustee of a sacred commission; he is being ruined by his own fatal conception of righteousness. In *The Triumph of Life*, the idealistic Rousseau is undone by a cause inward and unextinguishable:

[6] W. E. Peck, *Shelley, His Life and Work* (Boston and New York, 1927), p. 507.

[7] *Works*, ed. by H. B. Forman (London, 1880), Vol. VI, p. 318.

[8] In his preface to *The Cenci*, Shelley states: "Revenge, retaliation, atonement, are pernicious mistakes. If Beatrice had thought in this manner she would have been wiser and better. . . ."

[9] L. 333.

> "I was overcome
> By my own heart alone, which neither age
> Nor tears, nor infamy, nor now the tomb,
> Could temper to its object." [10]

Thus Shelley not only abandoned the idea of melodramatic villainy, but minimized the notion of "sin," conceiving the essential tragedy of life as the struggle of man against the heavy bars of that cage which his own spirit has constructed blindly.

II

In *Prometheus Unbound*, which has furnished much ammunition to the critics initially quoted, Shelley again expresses his mature viewpoint. He distinguishes, in this work, between two types of evil: one sort is ineradicable and objectively grounded; the other sort is subjective but deeply based. After that grand metamorphosis in which souls and stars cast off their timeworn husks, the race is still confronted by "chance, and death, and mutability." [11] Although "labour, and pain, and grief" [12] have been tamed, they have not been obliterated. Concerning the origin of such inescapable evil, the poet remains silent. If he had been questioned, very likely he would have confessed ignorance. In *Hellas*, indeed, after contrasting the mutability of matter with the eternity of mind, he added in a note: [13]

> Let it not be supposed that I mean to dogmatize upon a subject, concerning which all men are equally ignorant, or that I think the Gordian knot of the origin of evil can be disentangled by that or any similar assertions . . . That there is a true solution of the riddle, and that in our present state that solution is unattainable by us, are propositions which may be regarded as equally certain. . . .

Shelley here refers to those troubles which root in the necessitous order of nature. But there is a type of evil, on the other hand, whose origin we know and whose quietus we ultimately can obtain. In the "smithy of his soul," man beats out his own calamities. Jupiter, the enslaver, has been invested with Power by Prometheus, the spirit of man:[14]

[10] Ll. 240–43.

[11] Act III, scene iv, l. 201.

[12] Act IV, l. 404.

[13] To line 197 *et seq.*

[14] Although there is considerable disagreement among the critics concerning the significance of the characters, there is substantial accord in identifying Prometheus with human life. To W. M. Rossetti (*Proceedings of the Shelley Society*, Series I, Part I), Prometheus is the "Mind of Man"; John Addington Symonds (*Shelley* in *English Men of Letters Series*) agrees with Mr. Rossetti; John Todhunter (*A Study of Shelley*) believes that Prometheus is the "genius of Humanity"; Miss Vida D. Scudder (Introduction to her edition of *Prometheus Unbound*) calls Prometheus "Humanity"; H. S. Salt (*A Shelley Primer*) identifies Prometheus with the "Human Mind"; Allen R. Benham ("An Interpretation of Shelley's *Prometheus*

> Then Prometheus
> Gave wisdom, which is strength, to Jupiter,
> And with this law alone, "Let man be free,"
> Clothed him with the dominion of wide Heaven.
> To know nor faith, nor love, nor law; to be
> Omnipotent but friendless is to reign;
> And Jove now reigned.[15]

Whatever specific interpretation we give to the character of Jove, we must recognize that he represents the reign of evil. The above passage, therefore, must mean that the mind or soul of man, without prevision of the tragic consequences, has made the knout and appointed the castigator for the laceration of humanity.

This mind-created evil is so radical that even the consciousness of time must be fundamentally altered before man can be altogether freed. Consequently, in the last Act of *Prometheus Unbound*, time is carried to his tomb in eternity. The mind is transformed to its deepest foundations. Shelley means by this symbolism, as we shall try to make clear, that the mind learns to see reality *sub specie aeternitatis;* that it rends aside the veil of the temporal order. Thus the poet suggests the profundity, the drastic tenacity of human affliction.

Since evil is so firmly intrenched, it can only be expelled after a vast number of assaults. Even in his boyish production, *Queen Mab*, Shelley anticipated no abrupt conversion of the malefactors: "Slow and gradual dawned the morn of love." [16] In *Laon and Cythna*, it is true, he compressed the "Revolutions of the Golden City" into a brief period; but it is reasonable to believe that he thus foreshortened time to gain dramatic unity. He indicated his real attitude in the Preface:

> Can he who the day before was a trampled slave, suddenly become liberalminded, forbearing, and independent? This is the consequence of the habits of a state of society to be produced by resolute perseverance and indefatigable hope, and long-suffering and long-believing courage, and the systematic efforts of generations of men of intellect and virtue.

The liberation of man does not approach swiftly in *Prometheus Unbound;* "an hundred ages" elapse before the regeneration of the world.[17] Since Shelley could never be content with less than a complete reconstitution of society,

---

Unbound," *The Personalist*, April 1923) makes the Titan represent "the Soul of Man." Even Newman I. White, who objects to the allegorical interpretation of the poem ("Shelley's *Prometheus Unbound*, or Every Man his Own Allegorist," *PMLA*, XL, 172–184), recognizes that the drama represents "the struggle of humanity against oppression" (p. 179), and is willing to recognize in Prometheus the leading opponent of oppression.

[15] Act II, scene iv, ll. 43–49.   [16] IX, i, 38.
[17] Act IV, i, 61.

he based his hopes upon no sanguine expectation of immediate redemption but upon a faith which outsped despair:

> The system of society as it exists at present must be overthrown from the foundations with all its superstructure of maxims and of forms before we shall find anything but disappointment in our intercourse with any but a few select spirits. This remedy does not seem to be one of the easiest. But the generous few are not the less held to tend with all their efforts towards it. If faith is a virtue in any case it is so in politics rather than religion; as having a power of producing a belief in that which is at once a prophecy, and a cause.[18]

Although his works are prophetic of revolution, he advocated a most gradual reform. In 1817, he wrote:

> Nothing can less consist with reason, or afford smaller hopes of any beneficial issue, than the plan which should abolish the regal and aristocratical branches of our constitution, before the public mind, through many graduations of improvement, shall have arrived at the maturity which can disregard these symbols of its childhood.[19]

Three years later, he still counseled moderation:

> Any sudden attempt at universal suffrage would produce an immature attempt at a Republic. It is better that an object so inexpressibly great should never have been attempted than that it should be attempted and fail.[20]

III

These quotations are in contradiction to the summary of Shelley's doctrines advanced by such a representative critic as Professor S. F. Gingerich:

> Thus it requires but a small amount of self-assertion to get rid of an accident or a mere error and to attain to perfectibility. There is no purifying, developing, and enriching of the personality in the process. In fact, it can hardly be spoken of as a process, but rather as a mere instantaneous change.[21]

This mistaken conception gains plausibility from Mary Shelley's note to *Prometheus Unbound:*

> The prominent feature of Shelley's theory of the destiny of the human species was that evil is not inherent in the system of creation, but an accident that might be expelled. . . . Shelley believed that mankind had only to will that there would be no evil, and there would be none. . . . That man could be so perfectionized as to be able to expel evil from his own nature, and from the greater part of the creation, was the cardinal point of his system.

[18] Letter to Leigh Hunt, May 1, 1820. *Letters*, ed. Ingpen (London, 1915).

[19] "Proposal for Putting Reform to the Vote Throughout the Kingdom," *Works,* VI, 96.

[20] *A Philosophical View of Reform*, ed. by T. W. Rolletson (Oxford, 1920), p. 72.

[21] *Op. cit.*, p. 229.

We might suppose that this testimony was not merely the overstatement it is, but altogether false, if Shelley had not expressed himself to nearly the same effect in *Julian and Maddalo:*

> ". . . It is our will
> That thus enchains us to permitted ill—
> We might be otherwise—we might be all
> We dream of—happy, high, majestical.
>   . . . those who try may find
> How strong the chains are which our spirit bind;
> Brittle perchance as straw. We are assured
> Much may be conquered, much may be endured,
> Of what degrades and comforts us. We know
> That we have power over ourselves to do
> And suffer—what, we know not till we try." [22]

   In view of the poet's other pronouncements quoted previously, we are bound to place upon his words and Mrs. Shelley's note a construction which is consonant with the main tenor of his thought. We must remember that he gave a Platonic formulation to the doctrine that evil is partially subjective. We compose the darkness in which we are immersed, he believed, while the rays that issue from "Heaven's light," "the burning fountain," are consumed in the gloom thus fabricated:

> For love, and beauty, and delight,
> There is no death nor change: their might
> Exceeds our organs, which endure
> No light, being themselves obscure. [23]

All things present to sense, since they are shut off from this light, delude men with their false appearance. Concrete perceptions are but the apparitions of their immutable archetypes. They are phantoms, shadows cast by a hidden sun, the "white radiance of Eternity." In comparison with the pure form, evil is no more than an accident, an appearance:

> The One remains, the many change and pass;
> Heaven's light forever shines, Earth's shadows fly. [24]

Decay and sorrow are fleeting; truth, beauty, and love are fixed beyond the "firmament of time." Thus evil belongs to the shifting time stream, good to the eternal order; but "the troubles of our proud and angry dust" are none the less grave:

[22] Cf. ll. 161–91. Note that certain evils must be "endured," "suffered." This passage thus recognizes a certain inescapable and objective residuum of evil.

[23] Conclusion of *The Sensitive Plant*. Cf. *Adonais*, LIII.

[24] *Adonais*, LII.

> What is this world's delight?
> Lightning that mocks the night,
> Brief even as bright.[25]

The remainder of Mrs. Shelley's testimony need not greatly trouble us. Prometheus or the Human Soul, in the play, redeems life by willing with the profoundest intensity that evil shall be no more. In other words, he excludes from his heart all hatred and malice. The fundamental problem in reform is thus to change men's hearts. The revolution must be inward; when all men are reborn, the outer renovation may quickly be consummated. "Seek ye first the Kingdom of Heaven," said Christ, "and all these things shall be added unto you." To make the vast mass of men *willing* is supremely difficult; it requires "resolute perseverance and indefatigable hope, and long-suffering and long-believing courage, and the systematic efforts of generations of men of intellect and virtue."

To banish almost completely the apparent contradictions in Shelley's theory of perfectibility, we must remember that he was an assiduous student of Spinoza.[26] The cardinal principle of Spinoza's ethical system is the belief that the mind, by conceiving existence *sub specie aeternitatis*, can be liberated from bondage to time. "Eternity," declares the philosopher cannot

> . . . be defined in terms of time, or have any relation to time. But, notwithstanding, we feel and know that we are eternal. For the mind feels those things that it conceives by understanding, no less than those things that it remembers. For the eyes of the mind, whereby it sees and observes things, are none other than proofs. Thus, although we do not remember that we existed before the body, yet we feel that our mind, in so far as it involves the essence of the body, under the form of eternity, is eternal, and that thus its existence cannot be defined in terms of time, or be explained through duration. Thus our mind can only be said to endure, and its existence can only be defined by a fixed time, insofar as it involves the actual existence of the body. Thus far only has it the power of determining the existence of things by time, and conceiving them under the category of duration.[27]

That Shelley was profoundly impressed by this doctrine, and its expression in the "intellectual love of God," we may infer from his study of Spinoza, from the mystical trend of his mind, and from the embodiment of this teaching in his poetry. Ahaseurus, the Wandering Jew of *Hellas*, is the incarnation

---

[25] "Mutability."

[26] Cf. Olwen Ward Campbell, *Shelley and the Unromantics* (London, 1924), p. 146 fn.; Allen R. Benham, "Shelley and Spinoza," *Nation*, CII, sup. 16–17, F. 10 (1916); Adolf Droop, *Die Belensenheit Percy Bysshe Shelleys nach den direkten zeungnissen und den bisherigen Ferschungenen;* Sophie Bernthsen, *Der Spinozismus in Shelleys Weltanschauung* (Heidelberg, 1900).

[27] *Ethics,* trans. by R. H. M. Elwes (London, 1906), Part V, Prop. XXIII.

of Spinoza's ethical ideal.[28] He dwells in the temple of the mind, reared above the wrecks of time. In *Prometheus Unbound*, we also seem to find Spinozistic doctrines. The bearing of time to his tomb cannot possibly mean that duration in its literal meaning will perish, for death, chance, and mutability still overarch the life of man. It can only mean that the mind, intoxicated with Eternity, will leap beyond the "Category of duration." [29]

Hence, when we discover Shelley speaking as if the thinnest veil separates us from an unmythical Golden Age, we should realize that he is voicing a conviction which bears the impress of Spinoza. Confronted by hostile forces, he was exultant to discover that the mind could draw into itself, and subjectively transmute that heavy weight of centuries which separates the soul from its adored object. Undismayed by the empire of time, he could anticipate and ideally dwell in the age of dawn.

This interpretation of Shelley avoids the misconstructions that some critics have placed upon his theory of evil. It recognizes, to be sure, that, in a sense, evil to the poet was an appearance and an accident, since imperfection was attributed to the time barrier that hides the Absolute, the ultimately real. If this belief is an indication of shallow-mindedness, then a host of Idealists and Platonists stand convicted. The poet's speculations, however, could scarcely be called shallow: he distinguished between two types of evil, one kind, objective and ineradicable, another kind, subjective and profound; and he regarded the subjective evil as in large measure to be escaped by minds freed from all hatred, all superstition, minds that conceived of existence under the form of eternity, which Plato and Spinoza had revealed to the wise. This metamorphosis, however, requires so profound a transformation in man's nature that a "hundred ages" must elapse before its enactment. But to the poet who has learned the secret of Spinoza, who instructed men to overstep the "category of duration," the ideal Republic can even now be actualized in the mind.

[28] See especially ll. 762–85. Also cf. Shelley's translation from Spinoza's *Tractatus Theologico-Politicus*, in *Works*, VII, pp. 314–18.
[29] Cf. Benham, *Personalist, op. cit.*, for a significant discussion of the poet's adaptation of Spinoza's doctrines in *Prometheus Unbound*. I am merely endeavoring to advance to one further stage Professor Benham's interpretation.

A Volcano's Voice in Shelley

by G. M. Matthews

I

During the mutual exchange of dreams in Act II, scene i [of *Prometheus Unbound*], Asia and Panthea discover the command to "follow" explicit in nature and in each other's eyes. Invisible echoes then invite them

> Through the caverns hollow,
> Where the forest spreadeth. . . .
> (II, i, 175-76)

We need not hesitate to recognize these caverns as volcanic, since the Echoes definitely tell us they are: the nymphs are urged to follow

> Through the many-folded mountains;
> To the rents, and gulfs, and chasms,
> Where the Earth reposed from spasms,
> On the day when He and thou
> Parted, to commingle now. . . .
> (II, i, 201-5)

Without doubt Shelley had the 1794 eruption of Vesuvius—the last before his own visit—in mind when depicting the path of the ocean nymphs. The mountains above Torre del Greco (a village obliterated in this eruption) he described in language closely similar to that of the poem as

> covered with the rare and divine vegetation of this climate, with many-folding vales, and deep dark recesses, which the fancy scarcely could penetrate. . . .[1]

The forcible separation of Asia and Prometheus, therefore, either caused, or resulted from, volcanic upheavals—presumably caused, since Earth recalls

"A Volcano's Voice in Shelley." From *ELH*, XXIV (1957), 191–228 (sections i–iv omitted; sections and notes renumbered). Copyright 1957 by the Johns Hopkins Press. Reprinted by permission of the author and the Johns Hopkins Press.

[1] Letter of February 25, 1819.

the outbreak of "new fire From earthquake-rifted mountains of bright snow" when Prometheus was first enchained (I, 166–67).[2]

As the pair approach these mountains, they enter "A Forest, intermingled with Rocks and Caverns"; here the lush exuberance of the flora and fauna, the interwoven bowers and voluptuous nightingales, have been criticized as excessive, but the lushness is neither fanciful nor gratuitous. Asia and her companion have reached an area of volcanic fall-out, long famous for extreme fertility. Since classical times observers had recognized that "the Campania Felice . . . owes its exuberant fertility to frequent showers of volcanic ashes," [3] and those of Shelley's letters which describe this area show that the passage was by no means exaggerated. Shelley's scene is, of course, overdetermined: the mention of Silenus (II, ii, 90) suggests that Etna and Sicily were also in his mind; but the clearest influence—and, indeed, the clearest scenic influence on the whole of *Prometheus* apart from Act I—is not Rome, but the area around Naples which Shelley explored with such delight in late 1818 and early 1819, especially the Phlegraean Fields, where, by some accounts, the Titans and Giants had fought their vain risings against Jupiter. Lake Agnano and the Astroni crater had particularly impressed him: they were the first places he mentioned after telling Peacock that the scenery surrounding Naples was "more delightful than any within the immediate reach of civilized man." [4] The prose and the verse must be compared at some length to establish this more precise connection. "They are both the craters of extinguished volcanos," Shelley wrote,

> and Nature has thrown forth forests of oak and ilex, and spread mossy lawns and clear lakes over the dead or sleeping fire. . . . [The Astroni crater] is a royal chace, and is surrounded by steep and lofty hills, and only accessible through a wide gate of mossy oak. . . . The hills are covered with thick woods of ilex, myrtle, and laurustinus. . . . The plain so surrounded is at most three miles in circumference. It is occupied partly by a lake, with bold shores wooded by evergreens, and interrupted by a sylvan promontory of the wild forest, whose mossy boughs overhang its expanse, of a silent and purple darkness, like an Italian midnight; and partly by the forest itself, of all gigantic trees, but the oak especially, whose jagged boughs, now leafless, are hoary with thick lichens, and loaded with the massy and deep foliage of the ivy.[5]

[2] Some incidental support may be given to the contention of C. E. Pulos (*PMLA* [March 1952]) that Malthusianism is adverted to in *Prometheus Unbound*, by a passage in *A Philosophical View of Reform* (1819), where Malthus is represented as saying: ". . . after the frost has bitten their defenceless limbs, and the cramp has wrung like a disease within their bones . . . the last tie by which Nature holds them to benignant earth whose plenty is garnered up in the strongholds of their tyrants, is to be divided." Prometheus is precisely so divided from Asia, while Jupiter and Thetis beget an ironically "fatal child."

[3] *Edinburgh Review* (April 1804), 27.   [4] Letter of February 25, 1819.
[5] *Ibid.*

The effect, he added, was "of an enchanting solemnity." Here is part of the verse:

> The path through which that lovely twain
> Have passed, by cedar, pine, and yew,
> And each dark tree that ever grew,
> Is curtained out from Heaven's wide blue;
> Nor sun, nor moon, nor wind, nor rain
> Can pierce its interwoven bowers,
> Nor aught, save where some cloud of dew,
> Drifted along the earth-creeping breeze,
> Between the trunks of the hoar trees,
> Hangs each a pearl in the pale flowers
> Of the green laurel, blown anew . . .
> And the gloom divine is all around,
> And underneath is the mossy ground.
>
> (II, ii, 1–23)

Shelley's cedars and pines may be Roman (or Spenserian) imports; but the ivy, evergreens, and hoar trees of the poem, the mossy ground, the gloom divine, the green laurel, all have counterparts in the letter.[6]

The "clear lakes" of the Second Faun also derive from the scene of the letter. For this rich forest harbors the echoes (or exhalations) which draw (or drive) those destined to be agents of historical change toward the "fatal" mountain of Demogorgon. In it dwell nightingales, the "poets" or imaginative thinkers: among others, Spenser (in echoes of the opening canto of the *Faerie Queene*); Shakespeare (the opening of *Twelfth Night*); Milton (the opening of the "Nightingale" sonnet); probably Gray, whose "Progress of Poesy" had adopted the same idea of successive schools of poetry; perhaps the "frail form" of Shelley himself (the anemone). It is difficult to share the enthusiasm of Professor Grabo and more recent commentators for the scientific knowledge displayed in the dialogue of the Fauns, where it is suggested that the spirits causing these echoes live in bubbles sucked up from lakes by the sun and return to the earth on shooting stars. For one thing, what the sun raised from *live* conferva in *clear* water, according to Priestley and Darwin, was not hydrogen, but oxygen.[7] And for another thing, it was a mere poetic fancy by 1819 to suppose that hydrogen, raised from the earth and ignited, was the cause of meteors; Humphrey Davy had indeed proved this to be impossible before the Shelleys left England.[8] Like

[6] There are other undoubted details of this visit in *Prometheus*: for instance, the "budding . . . blooms Which star the wind with points of coloured light" (III, iii, 137–38) recall the willow-buds in the Astroni crater which "gleamed like points of lambent fire" in the forest. The visit was made earlier in spring than the season described in the poem.

[7] ". . . pure dephlogisticated air" (Erasmus Darwin, *The Botanic Garden*, IV, 195 note).

[8] *Philosophical Transactions*, CVII Pt. I (1817), 75–76.

much of Shelley's science, therefore, it did not intend to be scientific; and the passage was in any case interpolated so as to give time for Asia and Panthea to reach their destination.[9] But it is true that in popular folklore all kinds of similar exhalations continued to ignite into meteors, and were particularly common in volcanic country. Hamilton was told by the 1794 survivors of Torre del Greco that

> they often see a vapour issue from the body of the lava, and taking fire in air, fall like those meteors vulgarly called falling stars.[10]

Shelley would have seen gases liberated under water or mud in the Burning Fields, and possibly at Matlock Bath (which he must have visited on about October 7, 1813), and the passage is overdetermined.

The volcanic tract through which the ocean-nymphs pass, then, corresponds broadly to the country near Naples, where, as a contemporary journal put it,

> we find . . . the whole territory . . . rough with craters, and fuming with exhalations; and near these half-extinct remains, we find the formidable Vesuvius resting from the work of desolation, and concentrating his energies for another overwhelming explosion.[11]

This association points a way through the complexities of the third Semichorus:

> . . . And first there comes a gentle sound
> To those in talk or slumber bound,
> And wakes the destined: soft emotion
> Attracts, impels them: those who saw
> Say from the breathing earth behind
> There steams a plume-uplifting wind
> Which drives them on their path, while they
> Believe their own swift wings and feet
> The sweet desires within obey. . . .
>   (II, ii, 48–63. Locock's punctuation)

Sleep, in Shelley, is another overdetermined concept which awaits investigation. It may imply what is now known as hibernation, an artificial state of cold insensibility, or a "detested trance" like that of winter; but *winter* is also "the winter of the world," an era of bondage or of apathy in the face of social injustice. This is why the West Wind wakened the Mediterranean

---

[9] See C. D. Locock's note to line 64 in his edition of *The Poems of Percy Bysshe Shelley* (London, 1911), I, 610. The episode seems to have been suggested by the dialogue of the Shepherds in Leigh Hunt's *The Descent of Liberty* (1815), Sc. I.

[10] *Phil. Trans.*, XVII, abr. ed. (1809), 502.

[11] *Edinburgh Review* (April 1804), 28.

from dreams of Roman grandeur and oppression; why the news of Peterloo (that "tremendous storm") roused Shelley as he "lay asleep in Italy" to write "The Mask of Anarchy," and why in the same poem the workingmen were summoned to "Rise like lions after slumber." "Those in talk or slumber bound" therefore means something like "those who are too shallow or insensible to heed the summons of history." I have tried earlier[12] to indicate the heavy overdetermination of the "plume-uplifting wind" that blows the destined along their path. Volcanoes had always been thought to contain caves, and to generate underground winds; where else could the lava come from, and how else was combustion to be maintained? "Omnibus est porro in speluncis ventus et aer," Lucretius remarked of Etna,[13] and the moderns supported him: "The immense quantities of such matter [as] we see above ground must necessarily suppose very great hollows underneath." [14] Hamilton had investigated the *ventaroli* near the base of Etna; possibly Shelley, too, had felt an underground wind in what is now called the Great Rutland Cavern at Matlock Bath. He certainly introduces volcanic winds and caves into his address to Athens in the "Ode to Liberty" (1820):

> The voices of thy bards and sages thunder
> With an earth-awakening blast
> Through the caverns of the past. . . .
> (80–82)

Of course, the "plume-uplifting wind" not only lifts the wings of the chosen and wafts them onward, but involves other volcanic associations: the *mofette*, like that of the Solfatara (illustrated with "plumes" in Plate XXVII of Hamilton's *Campi Phlegraei*); the geyser (illustrated in Mackenzie's book); the steam from hot springs (Bladud's springs at Bath), and so on. Fumaroles were commonly described as emitting "plumes," for instance in Captain Tillard's striking account of the birth of Sabrina Island in 1811, when the sea erupted jets of vapor like "innumerable plumes of black and white ostrich feathers." [15] Other determining factors such as the tricolored plumes worn by the French revolutionaries are important but irrelevant to this inquiry. The point is that the "destined" think they are doing as they choose, while they are really doing as Demogorgon chooses. This is a hard nut to crack for those who think Shelley abandoned his belief in "Necessity" as applied to the individual will; but he stated repeatedly, throughout his life, that "poets" are subject to coercive forces which they are powerless to evade,

---

[12] *Essays in Criticism* (July 1954).   [13] *De Rerum Natura*, VI, 684.
[14] Sir William Hamilton, *Observations on Mount Vesuvius, Mount Etna, and other Volcanos.* 2nd ed., 1773, p. 67.
[15] *Phil. Trans.*, CII, Pt. I, 154.

although they themselves form part of those forces. In the Preface to *The Revolt of Islam* (1818), he put it like this:

> . . . there must be a resemblance, which does not depend upon their own will, between all the writers of any particular age. They cannot escape from subjection to a common influence which arises out of an infinite combination of circumstances belonging to the times in which they live; though each is in a degree the author of the very influence by which his being is thus pervaded.

All artists, he said again two years later in the preface to *Prometheus* itself, being companions and prophets of social change, "are, in one sense, the creators, and, in another, the creations of their age. From this subjection the loftiest do not escape." And in *A Defence of Poetry* (1821), almost the last piece of prose he wrote, he reiterated that "Poets are the hierophants of an unapprehended inspiration" (i.e. the servants of an unconscious influence), that "even while they deny and abjure, they are yet compelled to serve the power which is seated upon the throne of their own soul . . . it is less their spirit than the spirit of the age."

It is an influence of the same sort that surrounds Asia and Panthea as they approach the realm of Demogorgon. Swept along by the movement of change, they are borne like clouds to the fatal mountain. For it was observed of volcanoes that they not only generated their own "clouds of fire," but attracted more orthodox clouds from elsewhere. Breislak watched the 1794 eruption of Vesuvius from June to July, "and during that period," he declared, "every cloud that appeared on the horizon was attracted to Vesuvius." [16] In the same way the sound bears the sea-nymphs

> to the realm
> Of Demogorgon, and the mighty portal
> Like a volcano's meteor-breathing chasm,
> Whence the oracular vapour is hurled up
> Which lonely men drink wandering in their youth,
> And call truth, virtue, love, genius, or joy. . . .
>   (II, iii, 1–6)

It is hard to see why, in order to undertake what C. S. Lewis has eloquently called "this descent into hell, this return to the womb, this death," [17] the two sisters should have done so much climbing. *Facilis descensus Averno.* And why seek a return to the womb on a dizzy "Pinnacle of Rock among Mountains"? To make the real position clear it is helpful to recall Shelley's letter to Peacock describing Vesuvius:

> On the summit is a kind of irregular plain . . . riven into ghastly chasms. . . . In the midst stands the conical hill from which volumes of smoke, and the foun-

[16] *Edinburgh Review* (April 1804), 31.   [17] *Rehabilitations* (1939), 32.

tains of liquid fire, are rolled forth forever. The mountain is at present in a slight state of eruption; and a thick heavy white smoke is perpetually rolled out, interrupted by enormous columns of an impenetrable black bituminous vapour, which is hurled up, fold after fold, into the sky. . . .[18]

We may note in passing that what alarms Jupiter, at the opening of Act III, is that the soul of man ("like unextinguished fire") is busy "Hurling up insurrection," just as the vapor is "hurled up" from Demogorgon's spiraculum and from Vesuvius itself. But the objective setting seems unchallengeable: the nymphs have been attracted (impelled) to the terminal cone of a colossal volcano.[19] The pinnacle of rock corresponds to the "conical hill" of Vesuvius, and the "oracular vapour," like the earlier "plume-uplifting wind," patently flies the same flag as the militant volcanic exhalation which, Shelley said, forced him to write the "Ode to Naples":

> From that Typhaean mount, Inarime,[20]
> There streamed a sunbright vapour, like the standard
> Of some aetherial host;
> Whilst from all the coast,
> Louder and louder, gathering round, there wandered
> Over the oracular woods and divine sea
> Prophesyings which grew articulate—
> They seize me—I must speak them!—be they fate!
>
> (44–51)

Later, in Demogorgon's presence, Asia's tongue will be loosened by these *venti loquaces*. "When this divine inspiration has been conceived in the virgin's breast," according to Lucan, ". . . it re-echoes, and opens the mouth of the prophetess, just as the Sicilian peaks undulate when the flames press upon Aetna; or as Typhoeus, buried beneath the everlasting mass of Inarime, roaring aloud, heats the Campanian rocks." [21] Before becoming drugged by inspiration, however, Asia bids her companion admire the view ("ere the vapour dim thy brain"); and the description which follows has been recognized as deriving from the Alps, where the poem was first conceived. Nevertheless, Alpine as it is, Asia's description confirms the poet's intentions. "Beneath is a wide plain of billowy mist," she says, "islanding the peak

[18] Letter of December 22, 1818.

[19] It is no objection to this reading that Panthea describes the realm of Demogorgon as *"Like* a volcano's meteor-breathing chasm." Panthea has not been there before, and does not know whether it is a volcano or not; in the same way, Ione compares the moon to itself before identifying it in IV, 206–13.

[20] Inarime was an old name for the island of Ischia in the Bay of Naples, under whose volcano, Epomeo, the Earth-born Typhon, or Typhoeus, was said to have been imprisoned after rebelling against Jupiter.

[21] *Pharsalia*, V, 97–101 (Bohn translation).

whereon we stand"—a peak that is naked at the top (if we take the make-
shift adverbs "midway, around" as qualifying "encinctured"), but belted
lower down by the forest through which they had come. All round them
and "far on high" stand mountains, in such a way that "The vale is girdled
with their walls"—the idea of a *circle* being insistently enforced by the
vocabulary: *islanding* the peak, *around, encinctured, girdled.* A familiar picture
emerges: a cone of rock in the centre of a luxuriant elevated valley, encircled
by a mountainous wall. One remembers the "circular vale" "surrounded
by steep and lofty hills" of the Astroni crater. There is little doubt that Asia
and Panthea are conceived as standing in a gigantic *caldera*, the bowl-shaped
crater of a quiescent volcano with a tall cinder-cone in the middle. Both
Astroni (splendidly illustrated in Plate XX of Hamilton, *op. cit.*) and
Vesuvius are calderas, and although the latter was "the most horrible chaos
that can be imagined" in 1818, Shelley had probably seen Bracini's description of it as it had been prior to the eruption of 1631, when boars were
hunted and cattle grazed in the wooded crater. He is known to have read
a guide-book which states—following Bracini—that at this time the summit,
"and even the hollow of the crater, was covered with verdure and forest
trees, as *Astroni,* a long extinguished volcano, is at present." [22] Other regions
may well have contributed to the scene: Las Faldas on Teneriffe,[23] for
example, or Morne Garou in the Canaries, which is said to have had a
moss-lined circular crater, with a conical hill in the center and a terminal
cone of granite-like rock on top, the apex emitting smoke.[24] The Alpine
associations reinforce as well as modify the volcanic. The "sun-awakened
avalanche," compared by Asia to the accumulation of thoughts in a great
mind,

> till some great truth
> Is loosened, and the nations echo round,
> Shaken to their roots, as do the mountains now,—
>   (II, iii, 40–42)

no doubt owes its existence to the avalanche Shelley witnessed in Switzerland,
but the shaking of the nations round must refer to the collapse of Mont
d'Anterne, which in 1751 had sent people "from Turin to investigate
whether a volcano had not burst from among the Alps." [25] Shelley himself
saw the fallen mountain the day after writing the letter.

Meanwhile Asia and Panthea are urged downward by a "Song of Spirits,"

[22] J. C. Eustace, *A Classical Tour through Italy* (1812), 1818 ed., III, 40 note. Mary's
Journal notes that Shelley read this work August 3–5, 1818.
[23] *Geological Transactions,* II (1814), 293.   [24] *Phil. Trans.,* XIII, abr. ed., 636–37.
[25] Letter of July 25, 1816.

one of which has burning "An azure fire within its golden locks." Grabo
thinks, not unexpectedly, that this Spirit must be some kind of electricity,
but it is more likely to be gaseous oxide of carbon, described by Davy as
burning blue at the base of yellow flames, which—together with what the
old mineralogists called "the inflammable breath of the pyrites"—was
sometimes suggested among the causes of volcanic activity. Asia is now told
that she must

> Resist not the weakness—
> Such strength is in meekness
> That the Eternal, the Immortal,
> Must unloose through life's portal
> The snake-like Doom coiled underneath his throne,
> > By that alone.
>
> > > (II, iii, 93–98)

Earlier analysis has shown that Locock's interpretation of these lines must
be correct: it is only by submitting to the wind of doctrine that the ocean-
nymphs can assist the desired change. A reasonably close modern equivalent
would be the Hegelian "freedom is the consciousness of necessity." The
nymphs are guided, "As steel obeys the spirit of the stone," as the needle
follows the magnet, but their submission to the influence is conscious and
cooperative. A note to *Mab* had observed that "In the only true sense of
the word power, it applies with equal force to the lodestone as to the human
will." [26]

The "Cave of Demogorgon" is attained at last. In his metaphysical study
"The Motivation of Shelley's *Prometheus Unbound*," B. Rajan observes at this
point, with sudden disconcerting facetiousness, that "Demogorgon lives in
a cave, because a cave is dramatically more appropriate than Bayswater." [27]
But if Demogorgon inhabits a quiescent volcano, a cave is not only appropriate but unavoidable. Shelley had visited the Solfatara, Strabo's *forum
Vulcani*, and had doubtless heard the guide thump with his stick on the
hollow ground "thrown like a vault over an abyss of fire," and listened where
"the workings of the furnace beneath are heard distinctly through it." [28]
In this cave, Panthea senses Demogorgon as he sits enthroned:

> I see a mighty darkness
> Filling the seat of power, and rays of gloom
> Dart round, as light from the meridian sun.
>
> > (II, iv, 2–4)

---

[26] Note to VI, 198.   [27] *Review of English Studies* (July 1943), 299.
[28] Eustace, *op. cit.*, II, 495.

The reference to the infrared rays discovered in 1800 was first detected by Grabo; but as unluckily often happens with Shelley's scientific allusions, no one has troubled to explain its relevance to the scene it occurs in. *Why* should Demogorgon emit infrared rays? There is naturally only one answer—because he is extremely hot; too hot to be visible. It was known, in Herschel's own words on the solar spectrum, that "the full red falls still short of the maximum of heat; which perhaps lies even beyond visible refraction." [29] Demogorgon is, in fact, realized in terms of molten magma, the obscure and terrible volcanic agent hidden in the depths of the earth. His further connections with Milton's Satan, and with the Snake in Canto I of *Islam*, lie outside the scope of this article.

It is now time to inquire what caused the magmatic reservoirs to explode and discharge their contents, in the opinions of Shelley's contemporaries. Here the explanation of the ancients seems to have survived modern scepticism. Strabo and Pliny declared that volcanoes erupted when their caves were invaded by sea water; and this theory was applied to Etna by Lucretius, whose influence on *Prometheus* is appreciable:

> Ex hoc usque mari speluncae montis ad altas
> perveniunt subter fauces, hac ire fatendumst
> et penetrare maris penitus percocta in apertum
> atque efflare foras, ideoque extollere flammam
> saxaque suiectare et arenae tollere nimbos. [30]

Shelley had read an article in which Breislak (a Plutonist) was quoted as stating that "the access of the waters of the sea" contributed to volcanic activity. [31] There were doubters, admittedly, Humboldt among them; and it was hard to conceive how sea water could provoke an effusion of lava; but the theory was generally accepted, and indeed, according to *Chambers' Encyclopedia*, Breislak's cautious statement would still have been acceptable in 1950. After the great eruption of Vesuvius in 1794, Hamilton found

[29] *Phil. Trans.*, XVIII, abr. ed., 683.

[30] *Op. cit.*, VI, 696–700. "From this sea subterranean caverns penetrate all the way to the depth of its throat. It cannot be doubted that by this channel a blend of wind and water from the open sea is forced into the heart of the mountain. From here it spouts out, shooting up flame, volleying stones and disgorging clouds of sand" (R. E. Latham's Penguin Books translation [London, 1951]).

[31] *Edinburgh Review* (September 1816), 161. The *Quarterly Review* (January 1816), 382, refuting Humboldt, pointed out that "All the volcanoes known in the world are either on islands or within no great distance of the sea coast . . . and it is a fact, well known to mariners and sufficiently remarkable, that, in the neighbourhood of insular volcanoes in a state of activity, a constant current or indraught sets towards the island or group of islands."

that the majority of the people here were convinced that the torrents of mud and water, that had done them so much mischief, came out of the crater of Vesuvius, and that it was sea-water.[32]

Shelley himself believed that Pompeii had been overwhelmed by "torrents of boiling water" from Vesuvius.

It is clear what was to be expected, scientifically speaking, if children of Ocean were drawn into contact with the magma of a volcanic cavern— a violent eruption, accompanied by the classic symptoms: earthquakes; mephitic vapors; the familiar pine-tree cloud; the bursting of a storm, with *ferilli* or volcanic lightning; and of course destruction—in this case final destruction of the heavenly dictatorship which Demogorgon tells Jupiter.

> none may retain,
> Or reassume, or hold, succeeding thee.
> (III, i, 57–58)

All these symptoms occur. First Asia breathes the divine vapor and is inspired to be her own oracle,[33] until her ultimate question: "When shall the destined hour arrive?" And at this point she is answered by a volcanic explosion. The rocks are cloven; blackening the night, that terrible shadow, Demogorgon, floats

> Up from its throne, as may the lurid smoke
> Of earthquake-ruined cities o'er the sea.
> (II, iv, 150–52)

[32] *Phil. Trans.*, XVII, abr. ed., 502. Miss Porden's poem *The Veils: or the Triumph of Constancy* (1815), of which Sir Humphrey Davy's presentation copy is in the Bodleian Library, explains (citing geysers in evidence) that "Volcanic eruptions are known to be connected with the flowing of water into subterranean caverns, and therefore probably owe their origin to the contention of fire and water, and the expansive force of steam" (Canto III, 355 note). This remarkable work, ludicrous as it is, merits much of the admiration bestowed on the Newton among Poets; it anticipates the infrared rays of Shelley's Demogorgon, and the ultraviolet rays of Shelley's moon (*Prometheus Unbound*, IV, 219–230); it is much better informed about meteors than Shelley's Fauns; and it borrows from Southey's *Thalaba* the same X-ray carbuncle as Shelley used in *Prometheus Unbound* (IV, 270–287). Its hero, clad in insulators, fights the chief of the Gnomes with electricity, and (more pertinent here) one of its heroines, Leonora, descends into the crater of Stromboli in order to visit Pyros (Fire). The poem has been overlooked by students of Shelley's science.

[33] Asia's exasperating "dialogue" with Demogorgon only makes sense, and becomes dramatically satisfying, if it is realized that she is talking to herself. She is made to interrogate her own soul; and Demogorgon can supply no answer that she cannot supply herself at this moment of supreme prophetic consciousness, or for which she has insufficient knowledge even to frame the question meaningfully. Demogorgon is described by Lucan as a god "qui mundum cogere, quidquid Cogitur ipse, potest" (*Pharsalia*, VI, 496–99).

Any of a dozen accounts of major eruptions would serve to gloss this scene.
I select one from Hamilton (Vesuvius, 1767) which Shelley may have read:

> . . . the mountain split; and, with much noise, from this new mouth, a fountain
> of liquid fire shot up many feet high, and then, like a torrent, rolled on directly
> towards us. The earth shook, at the same time that a volley of pumice stones fell
> thick upon us; in an instant, clouds of black smoak and ashes caused almost a
> total darkness; the explosions from the top of the mountain were much louder
> than any thunder I ever heard. . . . the pumice-stones, falling upon us like hail,
> were of such a size as to cause a disagreeable sensation upon the part where they
> fell.[34]

Shelley himself had seen identical "fountains of liquid fire" rolled forth
from Vesuvius; and the Earth, who might be presumed to know a good deal
of geology, was right to warn the Spirit of the Hour that the flight of its
horses "must be swifter than fire." It would not do to be caught in the
"bursting cloud" that overwhelmed Jupiter, like an eagle blinded by lightning and struck down by hail.

Apollo is held in heaven by wonder: the "sun will rise not until noon."
The reason for the apparent anachronism initiated by this statement is that
hinted at (but dismissed) by "B. V." in his amusing summary of the time-
problems in *Prometheus*,[35] as anyone interested in volcanoes would assume
at once. The sun is eclipsed by the eruption, and day "dawns" only at noon,
when Jupiter has been overthrown. Pliny, Cicero, Seneca, and other classical
authors read by Shelley had described a similar volcanic darkness. Breislak,
a witness of the 1794 outburst of Vesuvius, wrote that

> At Caserta, more than ten miles from Vesuvius, torches were obliged to be used
> at mid-day, and the gloom was only broken by the frequent flashes of lightning
> which partially displayed the mountain. . . .[36]

Hamilton had shared this experience at Somma, where "the darkness was
such, though it was mid-day, that even with the help of torches it was
scarcely possible to keep in the high road.[37] Artificial night was an expected
result of eruptions. In 1768 "the quantity of ashes ejected by the mouth of
Cotopaxi was so great, that, in the towns of Hambato and Tacunga, day
broke only at three in the afternoon. . . ."[38] Shelley had no first-hand
knowledge of this phenomenon; but his night view of Vesuvius on December
16, 1818, perhaps contributed to his picture of the defeated Jupiter illumining

---

[34] *Observations, op. cit.*, 26–28.
[35] *Shelley, a Poem: with other writings relating to Shelley, by the late James Thomson* ("*B.V.*"),
privately printed (London, 1884), 56.
[36] Quoted by the *Edinburgh Review* (April 1804), 31.
[37] *Phil. Trans.*, XVII, abr. ed., Pt. I, 502.
[38] Humboldt's *Researches, op. cit.*, quoted by the *Quarterly Review* (July 1816), 461.

heaven with "sanguine light" through the "thick ragged skirts" of the victorious darkness.[39]

With astounding unanimity, critics have contrived to find that Jupiter's overthrow is an essentially peaceful process. "Tyranny always falls without a struggle";[40] "no real conflict is possible";[41] "Jupiter simply falls." [42] No doubt in these days of nuclear intimidation, respect for merely volcanic power may seem a little naive. Nevertheless, it must be allowed that a dispute which eclipses the sun and shakes the planets (possibly even the Milky Way) has its claim to seriousness. A hotter war could hardly have been imagined with the resources of 1819, though for the normal Aristotelian reasons its climax is not staged but reported. Perhaps the root of the error still lies in the old fallacy that determinism exempts its adherents from the need to act. In fact, Shelley's bloodless revolutionism existed more in his hopes than in his expectations, which were less optimistic; both his major pictures of social revolution involve catastrophic violence. "So dear is power," he believed at the time of writing *Prometheus*, "that the tyrants themselves neither then, nor now, nor ever, left or leave a path to freedom but through their own blood." [43] Nothing could be more explicit than that. A conflict was inescapable because the "tyrants" were habitually the first to resort to force.

The fall of Jupiter under a "bursting cloud" brings the concept of *volcanic activity* into close relation with that of the *storm*. Violent rains mixed with black ash, hail, and lightning, commonly accompanied volcanic eruptions. In that of 1794 Hamilton said:

> . . . the discharge of the electrical matter from the volcanic clouds during this eruption . . . caused explosions like those of the loudest thunder; and indeed the storms raised evidently by the sole power of the volcano, resembled in every respect all other thunder storms; the lightning falling and destroying every thing in its course.[44]

Jupiter's thunderbolts thus provided a metaphorical connection between the concepts. "Sceptred curse," Earth cries later in the poem,

[39] "We were, as it were, surrounded by streams and cataracts of the red and radiant fire; and in the midst, from the column of bituminous smoke shot up into the air, fell the vast masses of rock, white with the light of their intense heat, leaving behind them through the dark vapour trains of splendour" (Letter of December 22, 1818).

[40] Crane Brinton, *Political Ideas of the English Romanticists* (1926), 169.

[41] C. M. Bowra, *The Romantic Imagination* (1950), 122.

[42] Graham Hough, *The Romantic Poets* (1953), 137.

[43] *A Philosophical View of Reform*, 1819.

[44] *Phil. Trans.*, XVII, abr. ed., 495–96. Grabo has noted (*A Newton Among Poets* [1930], 183–85) the volcanic reference in this passage, but treats the "thunder-stones" of eighteenth-century "philosophy" and nineteenth-century folklore, volcanic debris, and meteorites, as interchangeable, which no responsible scientist could have done in 1818. Shelley's "thunder-stones" describe in metaphor the products of a metaphorical eruption.

> Who all our green and azure universe
> Threatenedst to muffle round with black destruction, sending
> A solid cloud to rain hot thunder-stones,
> And splinter and knead down my children's bones. . . .
>
>   (IV, 337–41)

Again the origin of these lines is likely to have been Hamilton and the 1794 eruption; his report for June 18th includes this sentence:

> One cloud heaped on another, and succeeding each other incessantly, formed in a few hours such a gigantic and elevated column of the darkest hue over the mountain, as seemed to threaten Naples with immediate destruction, having at one time been bent over the city, and appearing to be much too massive and ponderous to remain long suspended in the air.[45]

The following day, "thunder-stones" fell near Siena during a storm, the biggest weighing over five pounds.[46] The affinities of these phenomena with the congregated might of vapors, solid atmosphere, black rain, and fire and hail of the "Ode to the West Wind" make it patent that the sepulchral "dome" in that poem—a favorite word of Humboldt's for the cones of the Cordillera—has its strong volcanic overtones as well as its share of starlight.

II

Who or what, then, is Demogorgon, and what underlies this volcanic symbolism, these "characters and mechanism of a kind yet unattempted"[47] of *Prometheus*? He can scarcely be literally what he pretends, "Eternity," though some have accepted the paragram at its face value. This is rather as if an arrested rioter gave his name as "Swing," and saw it solemnly inscribed on the indictment. We must expect him, naturally, to be an over-determined, not an allegorical figure, and his interpretation is therefore limited to the aspects isolated in this study. Several critics have felt Demogorgon to be uncomfortably alien among the classical *personae* of the poem; D. G. James even says—almost incredibly—that "at least, through him Shelley was able to fill up his second Act."[48] But Demogorgon in his volcanic capacity is, in typical Shelley fashion, at once a denizen of the Jupiter-Prometheus cosmos and an intruder into it. His close affinity with Earth's "prostrate sons," who had revolted against Jupiter over the Burning Fields, is sufficiently evident. Like these, Demogorgon is located at the bottom of a volcano; according to one of Shelley's most admired authorities, his name

---

[45] *Phil. Trans.*, XVII, abr. ed., 498–99.   [46] *Ibid.*, 503.
[47] Letter of April 6, 1819.   [48] *The Romantic Comedy* (1948), 130.

cannot be mentioned without causing an earthquake;[49] and Jupiter himself, in Act III, hoped to use the "earthquake" of his arrival for destructive purposes, unless indeed this metaphor represents the irony of ignorance (contrary to traditional teaching, *Prometheus* contains brilliant and savage irony). Demogorgon is accurately described in terms of shapeless molten magma or lava; he erupts in order to overthrow Jupiter; and Jupiter's impulse, when he sees the danger, is to deal with him exactly as he had dealt with the Titans and the Giants—that is, to attack him with lightning and incarcerate him underground:

> Detested prodigy!
> Even thus beneath the deep Titanian prisons
> I trample thee!
>
> (III, i, 61–63)

Demogorgon's novelty consists in the fact that, unlike earlier rebels, he genuinely possesses the power to overthrow Jupiter, so that no figure named by Hesiod could have served Shelley's purpose. Shelley thought that his own contemporary society contained a force which was familiar and alien in the same way. He believed that since 1688 a new social class and ideology had been acquiring separate existence, destined ultimately to give the death-blow to political oppression, and he expressed this belief on many occasions, notably in the suppressed paragraph of the preface to *Hellas* (1821), and in *A Philosophical View of Reform*, from which, as it was written with the same impulse as *Prometheus*, my quotations are taken. After William III's accession, Shelley said, the number of "hands" increased greatly in proportion to that of the upper classes.

> A fourth class therefore appeared in the nation, the unrepresented multitude. . . . the nation universally became multiplied into a denomination which had no constitutional presence in the state. This denomination had not existed before—

or, at least, had not been conscious of having independent interests. But as the growth of a middle class came to impose a "double aristocracy," intensified exploitation impoverished it and drove it to seek redress in an after-life, yet to its members

> The gleams of hope which speak of Paradise seem like the flames in Milton's hell only to make darkness visible. . . .

Shelley knew that in 1818–19 this class had few enlightened leaders, little organization, and no common plan of action, that it was, in fact, shapeless,

---

[49] "Quo nunquam terra vocato Non concussa tremit" (Lucan, *Pharsalia*, VI, 745–46).

with neither limb, nor form, nor outline; but he felt passionately that it was a living Spirit. "He believed that a clash between the two classes of society was inevitable, and he eagerly ranged himself on the people's side," Mary wrote in her note to his 1819 poems. It is likely, therefore, that scholars were wasting their time in pursuing the name "Demogorgon" to its unilluminating origins in Lactantius and Hyginus. Shelley was of the school of Peacock in his etymologies, as *Swellfoot* demonstrates, and it is impossible that the combination δῆμος-γοργώ did not commend itself as one reason for the choice of name. To take the physical significance of Demogorgon any further within the limits set is hardly practicable.

The basis of much of the volcanic imagery in Shelley's mature poetry must now be clear. This is the perception of revolutionary activity in the external world and in the human mind—of irrepressible collective energy contained by repressive power. (Such a usage, it will be remembered, by no means prohibits others, including its opposite, that which implies despotic energy exerted against the oppressed). The Naples area presented a perfect mythological background. The classical tales of the risings of Earth's sons against Jupiter clearly record the volcanic upheavals that shaped the land-scape in this part of Italy. Hamilton quotes an earlier witness as writing, during the 1538 eruption of Monte Nuovo,

> "It appeared to me as if Typheus and Enceladus from Ischia and Etna with innumerable giants, of those from the Campi Phlegrei (which, according to the opinions of some, were situated in this neighbourhood), were come to wage war again with Jupiter." [50]

Hamilton used the comparison himself when his powers of description failed;[51] and the same tradition is to be found in many authors read by Shelley.[52] With his volcanoes, Shelley was really making use of a myth or "symbol" at least as old as *Exodus*, which has survived with formidable vitality into quite recent times.[53] There are, in fact, grounds for regarding the volcano as an archetypal image; which poses an interesting question for followers of Jung: how Collective is the Collective Unconscious?

It is understandable that the literature of the French Revolution should

[50] *Observations, op. cit.*, 131.

[51] *Phil. Trans.*, XIV, abr. ed., 618:—"It may have been from a scene of this kind, that the ancient poets took their ideas of the giants waging war with Jupiter" (August 11, 1779).

[52] E.g. in Pindar, "1st Pythian Ode"; and Bacon, *De Sapientia Veterum*, under "Typhon, sive rebellis." Shelley speaks of "many-headed Insurrection" in *Hellas*, 334.

[53] The first line of the English version of the *Internationale*, "Arise, ye starvelings, from your slumbers!" was directly influenced by Shelley; the French original continues:

> "La raison tonne en sa cratère,
> C'est l'éruption de la fin!"
> (Pottier, 1871)

exploit this inviting analogy between social upheaval and the highly topical science of geology. Shelley must have met it early, in the Abbé Barruel's *Memoirs Illustrating the History of Jacobinism*, "a favourite book at college," according to Hogg, of which "he went through the four volumes again and again." [54] To Barruel, subversion appeared "to arise from the bowels of the earth";[55] the disaffected hid their purposes under "the black cloud . . . round the summit of the volcano," [56] but "at length the erruption denotes the abyss where so great a convulsion was generated." [57] After the suppression of the Jacobins, warned Barruel,

> The sect, weakened, may slumber for a while, but such a sleep is the calm preceding the irruption of the volcano. It no longer sends forth its curling flames; but the subterraneous fire winds its course, penetrates, and preparing many vents, suddenly bursts forth and carries misery and devastation wherever its fiery torrent rolls.
>
> (I, xix)

Shelley's prose establishes beyond doubt that these associations were deliberate. When in 1821 the Holy Alliance mandated Austria to intervene against the rebels of southern Italy, Shelley declared that notwithstanding the soldierly advantages of the invaders,

> all these things, if the Spirit of Regeneration is abroad, are chaff before the storm, the very elements and events will fight against them, indignation and shameful repulse will burn after them to the valleys of the Alps.[58]

The image of the pursuing lava would perhaps go unnoticed but for the letter to Peacock a month later, employing less indefinite terms:

> We are surrounded here at Pisa by revolutionary volcanoes which as yet give more light than heat: the lava has not yet reached Tuscany.[59]

It is useful to find the importance of Demogorgon's heat confirmed by this remark. Nor are these the only confirmatory passages in the prose. In weighing the chances of an Irish rising in 1821, for example, Shelley lamented that "there are no regular bodies of men in opposition to the government, nor have the people any leaders. In England," he continued, "all bears for the moment the aspect of a sleeping volcano." [60] Shelley's description of the vegetation spread "over the dead or sleeping fire" in the Astroni crater will be remembered. Some of the associations he attached to the

---

[54] Hogg, *op. cit.*, I, 376. The English translation in four volumes was published in 1797. Shelley was reading it again in 1814 (see Mary's *Journal* for August 23, 25 and October 9, 11, 1814).

[55] Barruel, *Memoirs, op. cit.*, I, x.

[57] *Ibid.*, IV, 356–57.

[59] Letter of March 20, 1821.

[56] *Ibid.*, IV, 3.

[58] Letter of February 18, 1821.

[60] Letter of December 31, 1821.

concept *sleep* have already been pointed out; and a sleeping volcano carried a double significance. Demogorgon remained quiescent until visited by the sea-sisters. "In the world unknown," the Echoes had told Asia,

> Sleeps a voice unspoken;
> By thy step alone
> Can its rest be broken;
> Child of Ocean!
>   (II, i, 190–94)

In other contexts the "sleep" of a nation or people might be broken by the summons or the inspiring example of a neighbor; and this idea, much cherished by Shelley, commonly involves imagery drawn from a related geological discovery:

> England yet sleeps: was she not called of old?
> Spain calls her now, as with its thrilling thunder
> Vesuvius wakens Aetna, and the cold
> Snow-crags by its reply are cloven in sunder:
> O'er the lit waves every Aeolian isle
> From Pithecusa to Pelorus
> Howls, and leaps, and glares in chorus. . . .[61]

These lines, with their pounding rhetoric and comically inappropriate visual evocation ("Volcanoes of the World, Unite!"), are scarcely among Shelley's best, but for contemporary readers the comedy would not be quite so apparent. Only since Michell's impressive essay of 1760 had it been fully realized that the volcanic regions of the globe were interconnected, and could and did communicate at enormous distances.[62] The Lisbon earthquake had been felt in the mines of Derbyshire. Humboldt remarked in his *Personal Narrative* that in Chile and Guatamala "the active volcanoes are grouped in rows," [63] and noted that those of Mexico, too, "are ranged in a line from east to west." [64] These and other facts led to a disturbing conviction

> that the subterranean fire has pierced through an enormous crevice, which exists in the bowels of the Earth . . . and stretches from the Pacific to the Atlantic Ocean.[65]

[61] "Ode to Liberty" (1820), xiii. The Aeolian or Lipari Islands contain Vulcano and Stromboli; Pithecusa was another early name for volcanic Ischia.

[62] John Michell, *Phil. Trans.*, abr. ed., XI, 447–72.

[63] Alexandre de Humboldt and Bonpland, *Personal Narrative of travels to the equinoctial regions of the New Continent during the years 1799–1804*, trans. H. M. Williams, London, 1818, I, 200.

[64] Humboldt and Bonpland, *Researches concerning the institutions and monuments of the ancient inhabitants of America*, etc., trans. H. M. Williams, London, 1814, II, 103.

[65] *Ibid.*

Some thought with Humboldt that the world's volcanoes were ganged together along isolated crevices; others that they penetrated direct to the central fires;[66] but in either case the recognition permitted an alarming analogy to be drawn between international political subversion and volcanic activity.[67] It was this consciousness of interconnection that enabled Barruel to say of Jacobinism that "the subterraneous fire winds its course," and Shelley to write of the "contagious" fires of revolutionary sentiment; it explains why the curses of Laone's fellow-captives could be compared to "the voice of flames far underneath";[68] and why the Greek Captive Women in *Hellas* long to hear

> The words which, like secret fire, shall flow
> Through the veins of the frozen earth,
>
> (32–33)

until, as a messenger announces later in the same poem,

> Crete and Cyprus,
> Like mountain-twins that from each other's veins
> Catch the volcano-fire and earthquake-spasm,
> Shake in the general fever.
>
> (587–90)

Readers should be wary of referring every outbreak of "fire" in Shelley's poetry to the electrical fire of Beccaria or the occult fire of Ficinus: even his purest flame is apt to have some relish of damnation in it. Again it will be noted that his "tingling joy" extends equally to the earthquake and the eruption. For both, in his symbolic usage, represent an essentially preservative and creative force as well as a destructive one. On a social and political level they connote reform, liberation,[69] the indomitable and united energies of oppressed mankind, besides the destructiveness and destruction of Jupiter. On a physical level they involve, as we have seen, the fertility of nature. More, they involve the creation or renewal of the earth. It is unquestionable

---

[66] Erasmus Darwin held the latter view. See *The Botanic Garden* (1791), I, 141–42, and *The Temple of Nature, or The Origin of Society* (1803), I, 321.

[67] "If we consider a burning crater only as an isolated phenomenon . . . the volcanic action at the surface of the Globe will appear neither very powerful, nor very extensive. But the image of this action swells in the mind, when we study the relations that link together volcanoes of the same group; for instance those of Naples and Sicily, of the Canary islands, of the Azores . . . or the distance to which, by subterranean communications, they at the same moment shake the Earth" (Humboldt, *Personal Narrative, op. cit.,* IV, 31–32.

[68] *The Revolt of Islam*, VII, vii.

[69] Cf. *A Philosophical View of Reform:* "The great monarchies of Asia cannot, let us confidently hope, remain unshaken by the earthquake which shatters to dust the 'mountainous strongholds' of the tyrants of the western world."

that the "bright garden-isles" of *Queen Mab* and the "fortunate isles" of *Prometheus Unbound*, like the pumice-isles and *faraglioni* which Shelley had seen off the coast of Naples, are to be imagined as rising from the wastes of the sea by volcanic action.[70] Contemporary records of the birth of new islands, from Iceland to the Aleutians, are too common to enumerate, but the *Quarterly Review* justly observed that they constituted "the most recent act of creation in the western world." [71] Of the Naples region, Sir William Hamilton roundly declared:

> The more opportunities I have of examining this volcanic country, the more I am convinced of the truth of what I have already ventured to advance, which is, that volcanoes should be considered in a creative rather than a destructive light. . . .[72]

This attitude, it should be added, was thoroughly in accord with the most advanced geogenic theory of Shelley's day, that of Hutton, who thought that the continents and islands of the globe, worn continually down into the sea by attrition, were continually replaced by subaqueous material thrust up by volcanic fire.[73] One might say that according to the Huttonian Hypothesis, the renaissance of the earth depended on volcanic change, and it would not be surprising if Shelley accepted this hypothesis in a literal as he incontestably did in a metaphorical sense.

III

"It is a mistake," Shelley wrote in his preface to *Prometheus*, "to suppose that I dedicate my poetical compositions solely to the direct enforcement of reform." Present-day critics are perhaps less liable to this particular mistake than the writer anticipated; yet it *must* be inferred from Shelley's words that the poem is at least partly so dedicated. The pursuit of "symbols" can become an evasion of reality. Some of the poet's most energetic concepts have never been allowed their full significance in his work, and others have been examined too exclusively from a mystical point of view. The eruption, the earthquake, the volcanic dome, cloud, cavern, and fire, the burning fountain

---

[70] "Like rocks which fire lifts out of the flat deep" ("Ode to Liberty," ix, 125). The name 'fortunate isles' itself derives from Plutarch's name for the volcanic Canaries.

[71] April 1814, 194.   [72] *Phil. Trans.*, XVI, abr. ed., 134.

[73] James Hutton's *A Theory of the Earth* was first published in 1785, and elaborated in 1795 and 1799. Professor Playfair's *Illustrations of the Huttonian Theory of the Earth* appeared in 1802. After initial hesitation, the theory was consistently championed by the *Edinburgh Review*, which hailed Playfair's popularization as "perhaps the most eloquent work on science in our language" in Feb. 1816, 157. Writers as widely known as Mackenzie, Humboldt, and Erasmus Darwin accepted it (see esp. *The Temple of Nature, op. cit.*, IV. 431–442).

or *girandole*, the storm, the spark blown from the metallurgical "hearth" (a technical word probably picked up from Henry Reveley)—all these, and others, contribute to a meaning which has been more and more attenuated by specialized metaphysical assumptions. It would be falling into an equal error to claim that the volcano is the "key-symbol" of *Prometheus Unbound*, or that its recognition in the imagery and structure of the work exhausts the significance of the scenes discussed. Obviously many problems set by the poem are outside the present terms of reference, while others have been raised as a result of them. What is the relation of Demogorgon to Prometheus? Of volcanic to electrical energy? What is the purport on a social level of Asia's part in the drama? What modifications are necessary in the orthodox "moral myth" view, which presupposes a forgiveness of Jupiter which is demonstrably absent? These questions remain to be answered. What is obviously wrong, however, is to acknowledge on the one hand Shelley's passionate and lifelong interest in the progress of social relations, and on the other hand to study his major poetry as if its symbolism had no bearing except on the progress of the individual soul. Shelley's boyhood recognition of Intellectual Beauty was a simultaneous recognition of the social and political principles which, in his opinion, illustrated and indeed constituted that Beauty. Whatever full reading may be given to the great poems of 1818–19, it must, I am sure, remain constantly attentive to the principles Shelley regarded as central: the beauty and grandeur (to redistribute his own words) of the doctrines of equality and liberty and disinterestedness, which first determined him to devote his life to the inculcation of them.

The Role of Asia in the Dramatic Action
of Shelley's *Prometheus Unbound*

by Frederick A. Pottle

Since it is a myth, *Prometheus Unbound* is capable of endless allegorization. Some readers like to work out a detailed and particular allegory for it, others prefer to keep the allegory vague and general. Some even deprecate any attempt to formulate a "second meaning." All readers ought to agree that one should understand the myth as dramatic action on its own terms before one starts allegorizing. It may be legitimate to conclude that Demogorgon is Necessity because he says so-and-so, but until we despair of making dramatic sense out of him, we should not conclude that he says so-and-so because he is Necessity. What *happens* in *Prometheus Unbound*?

Though the opposition counts distinguished names, majority opinion seems agreed that there is only one action in the whole so-called drama, and that that action is completed before the First Act has hardly got under way. Prometheus announces at line 53 that he pities Jupiter; the remaining 2557 lines, it is maintained, consist merely of the unrolling necessary consequences of that action, and of jubilation over those consequences. This does not at all accord with what I find the text saying.

What has happened by the end of Act I? Prometheus, who cursed Jupiter three thousand years ago and has remained till at least very recently in a state of passionate enmity toward him, discovers that he no longer hates his persecutor and repents of his curse. This discovery by no means ends his sufferings or brings any alleviation of them; on the contrary, it precipitates a visitation of the Furies and a particularly horrible train of tortures. His state is then cheered by a chorus of prophetic spirits who announce that the hope, the prophecy they bear begins and ends in him (I, 690–91, 706–7). Two things are to be noted about these spirits and their songs. First, it is not intimated that they are now putting in an appearance for the first time as a result of Prometheus's change of heart. On the contrary, one would infer that they have been consoling him all along, just as the Furies have been torment-ing him. Secondly, their songs are by no means expressions of unmixed joy and hope: they are as sad as they are sweet.[1] No portion of *Prometheus Unbound* has been so generally ignored as the songs of the Fifth and Sixth Spirits (I, 763–79). Ione (I, 756–57) characterizes their voices as despair mingled with love, and surely despair is not too strong a word for the sentiments these beautiful beings utter. "Yes," says the Fifth Spirit, "Love exists, I have seen him. But he was closely followed by Ruin." "Ah," rejoins the Sixth Spirit, "it is worse than that. Ruin—or Pain—masquerades as Love to betray the best and gentlest." [2] The Chorus, speaking after Prometheus's recantation, does not deny that this is a true description of things as they still stand, but announces confidently that Prometheus will overcome Ruin: they know it as herdsmen know that the hawthorn will blow when they feel the winds of spring. The winds they have felt breathe from Prometheus:

> Wisdom, Justice, Love, and Peace,
> When they struggle to increase,
> Are to us as soft winds be.
>   (I, 796–98)

Undoubtedly Prometheus begins the action and will end it; we are told so explicitly. But one can begin and end an action without being able to per-form all the middle parts of it. At the end of the First Act Prometheus has realized that only through Love can he be freed. All he can do now is to endure and willingly accept his destiny as "the saviour and the strength of suffering man" (I, 816–17). He has passed beyond agony and solace (I, 819), and is just as firmly pinned to the crag as he was when he cursed Jupiter. Only love can help, and his beloved is far from him (I, 808). And the proph-ecy of his triumph, though the seasonal metaphor makes it seem more im-mediate than his own bleak vision of victory after an agony of literally innumerable years (I, 424), is actually conditional and ambiguous. Wisdom, Justice, Love, and Peace must go on struggling to increase; even if spring comes, there may be delays and setbacks. Frost may blast the young blossoms.

The First Act is the action of Prometheus, the Second is devoted entirely to

---

[1] *Panthea.* 'Tis something sadder, sweeter far than all.
                                      (I, 671)
   Ione.   And, hark! their sweet, sad voices!
                                      (I, 756)
Lines 86–90 of "To a Skylark" are the obvious commentary.
   [2] One may well ask what there is consoling in these utterances, since they repeat pretty much what the Furies had said. Vida Scudder gives the answer: the Furies gloat over the evil in experience, the Spirits lament it (*Prometheus Unbound*, 1892).

the action of Asia. She goes to her spouse in response to a summons—not *his* summons, for he has not consciously issued one, but a summons conveyed in two dreams which Panthea has dreamed at his feet. The first presents Prometheus freed, unscarred and rejuvenated, an ardent bridegroom awaiting his bride. But Asia is not summoned to go to her husband by the direct route that Panthea travels. Panthea's second dream was ostensibly another vision of things as they are, a vision of Ruin dogging the steps of Love. She saw a blasted almond-tree bloom, and the miraculous flowers were immediately thrown down by frost. But the fallen petals in this case bore no message of despair; they were stamped with the hopeful directive FOLLOW. And Asia then remembers that she too had had a dream in which FOLLOW was written across the mountain shadows and the leaves of the plants, and the wind in the pines had taken up the message. Echo-songs in the air now repeat the summons and indicate what is to be followed, whither, and why. Asia is to follow the aerial voices through caverns and forest, by lakes and fountains, through mountains growing ever more rugged, to rents, gulfs, and chasms in the earth (II, i, 175–202). She is to do it because

> In the world unknown
> Sleeps a voice unspoken;
> By thy step alone
> Can its rest be broken;
> Child of Ocean!
> (II, i, 190–94)

She accordingly sets out, hand in hand with Panthea. The eddies of echoes, we are informed, are actually much more than the mere guide they appear to her to be. They are a positive force attracting and impelling her, and they grow steadily stronger as she yields to their impetus; she half walks, half floats on her way, thinking her motion due to her own limbs (II, ii, 41–63) She and Panthea pass through a shady damp forest thronged with nightingales, and are finally borne to the top of a pinnacle of rock among the mountains which they recognize as marking the portal to the abode of Demogorgon, a mysterious power already identified as directing the stream of sound (II, ii, 43). As they stand admiring the Alpine landscape, which moves Asia to overt theologizing, the spirits, now for the first time become visible, urge her to put herself utterly into their hands and allow herself to be borne unresisting down to the throne of Demogorgon in an abyss below all natural caverns. A spell is treasured there for her alone (II, iii, 88), but she can exert it only by utter surrender:

> We have bound thee, we guide thee;
> Down, down!

> With the bright form beside thee;
> Resist not the weakness,
> Such strength is in meekness
> That the Eternal, the Immortal,
> Must unloose through life's portal
> The snake-like Doom coiled underneath his throne
> By that alone.
>
> (II, iii, 90–98)

The lyric (there are five stanzas in all) is apparently not merely an invitation to the descent but accompanies it. At any rate, when the next scene opens, Asia and Panthea are in the Cave of Demogorgon, and there is no reason to doubt that they got there on the Spirits' terms.

The statements that only Asia can rouse Demogorgon to action, that in Demogorgon's cave is treasured a spell for Asia alone, are as express as the earlier statement that the prophecy of regeneration begins and ends in Prometheus. Why then the critics' reluctance to grant that Asia performs an independent and essential part of the action? Undoubtedly because of her seeming passivity in the first three scenes of the Second Act. She follows, she is borne, she does not resist an invading weakness. Significant action, the critics seem to feel, needs to be embodied in language like that of the First Act, language that testifies to a struggle against resistance, language that asserts difficulty. Now, one very important critic, C. S. Lewis, of course does maintain that difficulty is precisely the subject of these scenes,[3] but I do not see any evidence for thinking that the journey was meant to seem physically arduous. We might take as the norm of a really arduous journey that portion of the Second Book of *Paradise Lost* which deals with Satan's ascent from the gates of Hell up through Chaos. If the Second Act of *Prometheus Unbound* were presenting external or physical difficulty, as the Second Book of *Paradise Lost* is, we should hear of lacerating, almost impenetrable, undergrowth in the forest, of rough stones that draw blood from clinging hands and clambering knees, of abysses that the giddy traveler must hang over with inadequate support, of tunnels and chimneys that narrow and threaten to hold him fast. The forest in *Prometheus Unbound* is damp and very shady, but it has the open pathways between the tree trunks that one would expect in a stand of large evergreens (II, ii, 1–2). If the poet had wished us to feel that passage through it was physically difficult, he would not have

---

[3] "The whole of the next act, in story, is occupied with the difficult efforts of Asia to apprehend and follow a dream dreamed in the shadow of Prometheus: the difficult journey which it leads her; her difficult descent to the depths of the earth. . . . Difficulty is, so to speak, the subject of this act" ("Shelley, Dryden, and Mr. Eliot," in *Rehabilitations and Other Essays* [1939], p. 31).

called its gloom "divine" (II, ii, 22), and he would not have devoted seventeen lines to a description of the songs of the nightingales. If Asia and Panthea encounter any physical difficulties in the ascent to the pinnacle, they are not reported or alluded to, while the help they are getting from the stream of sound is insisted on.

Yet no careful reader can feel that Asia is an automaton or even that she is naturally impassive. When we first meet her, she is displaying extreme impatience for Panthea's return. She does not instantly follow the echo guide, but ponders her action and takes time to make up her mind (II, i, 188–89, 207–8). She says nothing further to indicate that she is on the alert, but the spirits, in everything *they* say, assume that her assent is not irrevocable, that she might balk at any moment. In short, she wills to follow, she wills to continue to follow, and that constitutes her action in these scenes. *Pace* Professor Lewis, her progress is not physically difficult but rather the opposite: it is so easy and pleasant as to raise doubts whether it can possibly conduct to an heroic goal. Asia's difficulty in these scenes is to overcome the scruples that would keep her from surrendering herself to a duty which is disquietingly pleasant. And this difficulty, which I feel to be real, is expressed only indirectly.

This may be considered too subtle for drama. Drama is the most primitive of all literary forms, and our own dramatic tradition is especially committed to physical violence. It has, indeed, often been stated as a truism that physical non-resistance is essentially undramatic. That seems to me simply not true. Willing, not muscular action, is the essential of drama. A physical non-resistance which we see to be gravely and consciously willed, though not the usual stuff of drama in our tradition, will function dramatically in our experience if we will allow it to.

Difficulty in the Fourth Scene is of a more obvious sort, and is expressed directly in Asia's speeches. In the Cave of Demogorgon she performs an action parallel to and of equal importance with that of Prometheus in the First Act. He forgave Jupiter, she works her way to the word that will topple Jupiter from Olympus. In a way, the action is more difficult than his. He had to struggle with excruciating pain, both physical and mental, but it does not appear that he had to struggle with his hatred in order to overcome it. Reaching for it one day, he found it evaporated (I, 53). On the other hand, we see her in the agony of struggling through and out of some of her most passionately held attitudes.

One should not speak too confidently of "understanding" this pregnant and subtle colloquy, but two remarks concerning it seem warranted. Demogorgon, though definitely a mighty power who can tell Asia all she dares ask

(II, iv, 7),[4] always in fact answers her in her own terminology and at the level of her own understanding. We are not to assume that she is merely talking to herself, but she certainly gets no answers she has not herself thought her way to. Secondly, because Demogorgon adapts his answers to her understanding, his oracular utterances must be taken as provisional and progressive.[5] They are not coordinate articles of a creed, but a progress through dogma to the utterly undogmatic faith which will unloose the Doom sleeping under Demogorgon's throne:

> So much I asked before, and my heart gave
> The response thou hast given; and of such truths
> Each to itself must be the oracle.
>
> (II, iv, 121–23)

Prometheus, the god-defier, engages in no theological speculation whatever. To him Jupiter is god and all but omnipotent; Jupiter is wicked, cruel, ungrateful, and unjust; Jupiter will ultimately fall. Until he falls, Prometheus expects to be tortured. To Prometheus evil is a fact of experience. He never asks why evil should exist, or if Jupiter comprehends all the evil there is in the cosmos.

Asia, on the other hand, is a passionate theologian, or to be precise is passionately interested in the problem of evil. On the pinnacle, before descending to the Cave of Demogorgon, she had tentatively suggested that the glories and shortcomings of the physical universe might be explained by assuming that it was the work of some beautiful spirit too weak to prevent evil from invading and staining its work. She says she could worship that kind of Creator (II, iii, 11–16). Her cast of mind, we see, leads her to posit creation and a Creator with human attributes, and to repel any suggestion that the Creator of the physical universe may be responsible for evil.

But she is not so sure as to other possible creators, and in the Cave of Demogorgon she at once begins putting the questions that trouble her profoundly. Who made the *living* world, the world of Mind? Who made thought, passion, reason, will, imagination? Who made the sense of love? Demogorgon, in the tersest possible fashion, replies God, Almighty God, Merciful God.

---

[4] It has frequently been objected that Demogorgon contradicts himself in II, iv, 114–19, but the objection is literalist. A problem (say a mathematical problem) is "answered" when somebody demonstrates that it is incapable of solution. It would have been intolerably prosaic of Demogorgon to add the saving clause, "so far as the limitations of language permit."

[5] See Shelley's second note to *Hellas*, where he explains that his Chorus of captive Greek women has been allowed to represent "the popular notions of Christianity . . . as true in their relation to the worship they superseded [Greek polytheism], and that which in all probability they will supersede [Islam], without considering their merits in a relation more universal."

He will later suggest that she relinquish this terminology and some of the concepts associated with it, but the important thing at this stage is to give emphatic confirmation, in such terms as possess reality for her, to her intuition that the world of mind is fundamentally divine, or is like divinity, beneficent divinity. Who then, she continues, made terror, madness, crime, remorse, hate, self-contempt, all the varieties of pain? Demogorgon again uses her implied references, but to cover the facts this time he has to resort to ambiguity. "He reigns" may be taken as a virtual repetition of his previous answer, "Almighty God," or it may mean that the Maker of Evil is a usurper. Actually, it means both things at the same time. "Almighty God," the Primal Power, did not make Evil, but if one is to use this kind of language, he "made" the "evil things" which the malignancy of Jupiter converted into positive evil. Demogorgon at this stage wishes to give emphatic confirmation to Asia's intuition that the world of mind is dominated by an Evil Power which it is possible and proper to dethrone, but also to prepare the ground for his next and final position, which will be that when the usurper goes and the Primal Power alone "reigns," the means or occasion of evil, relative to man, will still inhere in the universe.

Asia not unnaturally takes him to be referring solely to a Usurper, and passionately demands the Usurper's name. The world asks but his name, she says; curses shall drag him down. She of course knows Jupiter's name, though she has not yet spoken it, but she confidently expects a curse already uttered to drag *him* down. Before ever she entered the Cave of Demogorgon she had come to the conclusion that the evil of Jupiter, real and horrible as it is, cannot cover all the evil in the universe. There is, she feels sure, an Evil more radical; Jupiter is only a front man. And Demogorgon, by saying "He reigns" rather than "Jupiter" has told that she is so far on the right track.

Well, who *does* reign? Demogorgon's first three utterances might make us think that we had left Greek theology for the Judaeo-Christian, but that would be too hasty. We are still within the Greek system, and in that system the question is highly pertinent. Greek myth records a succession of reigning deities, none of them omnipotent. Jupiter (Zeus) had dethroned Saturn (Kronos), just as Saturn had dethroned Uranus, but Jupiter himself was held to be subject to Fate or Necessity. He took over a created universe, and (in Shelley's version) had made nothing but evil. But he was not the originator of evil. So far as Asia could make out, evil entered the world in the reign of Saturn, when Time first appeared.[6] Evil under Saturn had been negative or

---

[6] It must seem odd that Shelley did not make this point by using the Greek name Kronos rather than the Roman Saturn. Perhaps he wished to obviate allegorizing of a merely reductive sort. But the fact that Keats in *Hyperion* used a similarly mixed nomenclature rather suggests that both followed contemporary fashion.

privative: men lived in joy but in a calm vegetable joy, denied the knowledge that was their birthright. Positive evil—famine, heat, cold, toil, disease, war, violent death, raging and lacerating passions—arrived with Jupiter, and increased in direct proportion as men received knowledge and skill from Prometheus.[7] Prometheus's gifts were obviously not in themselves evil but glorious. Who then rains down evil? Surely not Jupiter. Prometheus pretty much set him up in business, and he is obviously afraid of Prometheus. He does not act like the Creator of Evil, he acts like some one who takes orders. Who is his hidden master? Is his master perhaps a slave too? Where does it all end?

My paraphrase, though highly speculative in its inferences, has so far been content to base itself on what is explicitly provided by Shelley's text. I want now, however, not merely to read *into* the dialogue, but to read *in* some dialogue, and I shall not be deterred if the result sounds more like Shaw than like Shelley.

Asia. Who is his master? Is he too a slave?

Demogorgon. All spirits who serve evil things are enslaved. You are right in thinking Jupiter enslaved.

Asia. But how about the Being you called God some lines back? If he made the living world, if he is almighty, must *he* not be the hidden master of Jupiter? If he is using evil, is he not enslaved by it?

Demogorgon. I employed the terminology and the concepts you gave me, and am glad to note that you now see some difficulties in them. If you load your questions concerning the Primal Power with demands that that Power be a personal, omnipotent Creator, you are going to run into irresolvable contradictions. And "God" is not a very good term either. I suggest that it had better be left to Jupiter.

Asia. Very well, I give up those demands, holding on only to your assurance that the universe of mind is god-like and beneficent. But is it not possible to carry Jupiter any farther back? If he is a slave, who is his master?

Demogorgon. I said that spirits who serve evil *things* are enslaved; I did not say that Jupiter serves the Evil One. I grant that "slave" implies "master"; all figures from the world of human experience are misleading when applied to ultimates. *The deep truth is imageless.* Would it be at all helpful if I told you that the evil Jupiter serves is not personal, that it is, as you yourself hinted, Time? Time, relative to man, is evil, and Time is a mystery. Everything on earth is subject to Time, but not because of malignancy in the will of some Power superior to Jupiter. The Ultimate Power wishes man well and can and does get through to him. Love is not subject to Time.

Asia. I have asked these questions before, and you have now confirmed the answers

---

[7] What Asia says in II, iv, 59–99 needs to be reinforced by recollection of the speeches of the Furies in Act I, especially ll. 542–45.

that my heart gave me. These truths must not be elaborated, systematized, institutionalized. In such matters each heart must be its own oracle. One question more, a question I would not ask if I had the answer anywhere within my own being. Prometheus will be freed, but when?

Demogorgon. Now.

Prometheus's action was to repent of his curse, to stop hating the manifested evil he continued unyieldingly to resist. Asia's action is to give up her demand for an ultimate Personal Evil, to combine an unshakable faith that the universe is sound at the core with a realization that, as regards man, Time is radically and incurably evil. That action is now finished. Demogorgon ascends the car to dethrone Jupiter, Asia rises from the abyss transfigured by the pouring in of that Eternal Love which is not subject to Time and Change.[8]

Allegorization of myth has exactly the same values and is subject to the same dangers as any other kind of paraphrase of poetry. A paraphrase that is substituted for or imported into a poem is reductive, but a paraphrase that is annotative or exploratory may lead us deeper into the poem's concreteness. My allegorization of *Prometheus Unbound* will be justified if it backs up my reading of the action.

Shelley's Prometheus has too often been taken to represent the human mind, Asia to represent Eternal Love or Intellectual Beauty, and Jupiter to be the embodiment of merely external evil. Though in one aspect (an important one) Prometheus does seem to symbolize human mind and Asia Nature, a more profound and consistent reading would regard human mind as divided between Prometheus, Asia, and Jupiter. Prometheus (whose name in Greek means "forethought") symbolizes intellect, understanding, the inventive, rational faculties of mankind. Asia is the affective side of mind: emotion, passion, imagination. The separation of Asia from Prometheus is a "fall" of the Blakean sort which produced Urizen and Ahania, Los and Enitharmon. Asia is not Intellectual Beauty or Eternal Love, for she dwells in, and is wholly subject to, the world of Time and Change, but she is the chief conduit of Eternal Love into that world. Jupiter does not represent all the evil of human experience. He is subjective or man-made evil: custom, reaction, tyranny, superstition, outworn creeds. Man's intellect gave this kind of evil all its strength and has then been confined and tortured by it.

---

[8] Though, as I have said, Shelley keeps more closely within the bounds of Greek myth than is commonly supposed, his parallels to Christian dogma are too numerous to be fortuitous. *Prometheus Unbound* contains a Crucifixion, a Descent into Hell, and a Transfiguration which is also a Resurrection.

Intellect of itself is capable of realizing that we make our own mental tortures by hating what we should merely resist, but knowledge alone will not bring reform or regeneration. Prometheus will never get free without help from Asia. "Until," Shelley says in his Preface to *Prometheus Unbound*, "the mind can love, and admire, and trust, and hope, . . . reasoned principles of moral conduct are seeds cast upon the high-way of life." Or again, in *A Defence of Poetry*, "The great instrument of moral good is the imagination" (paragraph 13).

But not the unregenerate Imagination. Asia must go down to the Cave of Demogorgon, the affections must sink back on themselves down into the unconscious depths of being and be made over. Specifically, the affections must exorcize the demons of infancy, whether personal or of the race, and must rebuild themselves in accord with a mature theology. But is not this to turn matters precisely upside down? Surely it is the function of the heart to forgive and of the head to construct theologies? No, would certainly be Shelley's firm rejoinder. The head must sincerely forgive, must willingly eschew hatred on purely experimental grounds. "Revenge, retaliation, atonement, are pernicious *mistakes*"; intellect must "discover the *wisdom* of universal love." [9] And since the evidence on which all religions are founded is revealed to the heart and does not have the character of experimental verifiability which the intellect demands for its operations, intellect, to be true to itself, must remain scrupulously agnostic. If it does apply the operations of logic to the content of revelation, it produces precisely Jupiter. Theology, in the form of concrete poetic speculation, is the domain and the duty of the imagination.[10]

The Imagination will not get a mature theology and a right religion until, as I have said, it is able to reconcile an unshakable but unelaborated faith that the universe is good and radically beneficent with a calm acceptance of the fact that when all man-made evil is cast off, men will still be confronted by chance and death and mutability.

And a right religion is essential for the overthrow of man-made evil. *Prometheus Unbound* is not humanist in its implications. The power we need to help ourselves is not our own but comes from on high, and will be granted if we make ourselves receptive of it. Eternal Love will stream with increasing power through us to reform the world, not merely the world of mind but also the world of matter. Human intellect thus empowered will build a new

---

[9] Preface to *The Cenci;* "Essay on Christianity" (*Shelley's Prose*, ed. D. L. Clark [1954], p. 209); emphasis mine.

[10] See especially the second note to *Hellas*, already cited (n. 5 above).

heaven and a new earth. The action which began in Prometheus will end in him.[11]

[11] The method of developing an argument by expressing one's adherence to or dissent from positions taken by one's predecessors is tedious, and in this case is rendered unnecessary by Professor L. J. Zillman's very comprehensive variorum edition of *Prometheus Unbound* (1959). The readings of the poem which I find most satisfactory are those of C. S. Lewis (see above, n. 3) and J. W. Beach (*A Romantic View of Poetry* [1944], pp. 110–22), but I think I had arrived at my own views before I read theirs. The works from which I learned the most seem to me now to have been Ellsworth Barnard's *Shelley's Religion* (1937), A. M. D. Hughes's *Shelley, Poems Published in 1820* (1910), and especially the very important article by M. M. Rader included in the present collection.

The Witch of Atlas

by G. Wilson Knight

The poem is very compact. Its phrases, like Panthea's, compress the intangible into concrete forms:

> She took her spindle
> And twined three threads of fleecy mist, and three
> Long lines of light. . . .
>
> $(13)^1$

Again, there are "intertangled lines of light" (25). The poem's lady "kneaded fire and snow together" (35) for her purpose. There is, too, a wonder and splendor burning through greenness as in *Prometheus*, and the word "emerald" occurs often. "Emerald" crags "glowed in her beauty's glance" and deep water is a "green splendour" (28). The poem is remarkable for carefully housed and concretely projected fire-variations:

> Their spirits shook within them, as a flame
> Stirred by the air under a cavern gaunt.
>
> (11)

The *still* flame is seen to flicker. In a marvelous cave there are

> Carved lamps and chalices, and vials which shone
> In their own golden beams—each like a flower,
> Out of whose depth a fire-fly shakes his light
> Under a cypress in a starless night.
>
> (20)

"Shakes his light": light burns from metal solids, which are also flowers, itself felt as living. Elsewhere the Witch "shakes" light out of funeral lamps (70). We might recall the similar splendor falling "like flakes" in *Prometheus*. Such "green and glowing light" (39) is one with the "living spirit" (34)

"The Witch of Atlas." From *The Starlit Dome: Studies in the Poetry of Vision* by G. Wilson Knight. Copyright 1941 by Methuen & Co., Ltd. Reprinted by permission of Methuen & Co., Ltd.

[1] Numbers in parentheses refer to stanzas in Shelley's *The Witch of Atlas*. [ED.]

within all manifestations whether of nature, man, or, as with our last phrase, a magic boat; and the fire-solidification marks a sense of spiritual *substance*, that fiery seraph-body which is the "naked beauty of the soul" (66). Here is a crowning gem:

> Men scarcely know how beautiful fire is—
> Each flame of it is as a precious stone. . . .
>
> (27)

These, I think, reach the poem's core, a close realization of the magical and unearthly which is yet earth-twined and concretely imagined. The close interdependence of the vital and solid approaches Keats's larger, less com-pacted, symbolisms, while also resembling the sharp phrase-hardening of Yeats's later style. The linear rhythms also point to Yeats. The lines have a similar ring or rap, a terse, finished manner of statement, almost abrupt. My quotations have provided clear instances. Here is another:

> Beneath, the billows having vainly striven
> Indignant and impetuous, roared to feel
> The swift and steady motion of the keel.
>
> (46)

The imagery of fierce sea *controlled* resembles Yeats's "dolphin-torn" and "gong-tormented" sea. A consonantal technique and homely imagery may give tautness as in

> The steepest ladder of the crudded rack . . .
>
> (55)

and

> She ran upon the platforms of the wind.
>
> (55)

But, reserved though it be, no poetic idiom houses a more vital and un-earthly magic. The phrases are "atoms of inextinguishable thought," or vision. Each stanza makes a compact, terse, usually completed statement, and in no poem does Shelley so clearly obey Keats's advice to "load every rift with ore." Finally, the poetic rhythms often approach, but no more, a keen, almost Byronic humor; a pith and pregnancy of wit just left unde-veloped, thereby contributing to, without despoiling, the gossamer charm.

The Witch is a remarkable lady, whose title is quite unjustly derogatory. She is a dream-projection and, partly, an incarnation of poetry itself. Shelley's own poetic experience is clearly built into her, and we watch, even more clearly than in *Prometheus*, the myth-making faculty at work; that queer business of using one's imaginative experience to create something surprising to oneself. Self-objectifiction may prove uncanny and revelatory. Mental confession alone cannot study the human mind: the myth-making faculty can. Shelley here very subtly objectifies and personifies his own poetry to serve as an exploitation of magic.

From now on I shall not give references: my analysis moves in a sequence corresponding to the poem's own order.

You can see why the Witch is shown as knitting with light, since to her, and Shelley, light is substantial. Moreover, considering the sun as the ultimate behind all positive vision and the moon as nevertheless an *easier* romance-medium, we see why sun and moon references are in turn used to introduce her. Her mother is "one of the Atlantides"—almost, I think, Mother Earth; her father, the Sun, whose kiss dissolves her (the mother) to a golden joy from which she becomes in turn vapor, cloud, meteor, star. We may remember Panthea's precisely similar love-account. The "Mother of the Months," the Moon, has bent her bow "ten times" and as often commanded the seas since first in Atlas' cave the "dewy splendour" (cf. Cythna's birth-fantasy) took shape. The cave is, in fact, a womb, while the "cavern" and "secret fountain" at the start have as direct physiological meanings as the ten months' duration. Similar nature-human suggestion occurs in "Kubla Khan" and *The Triumph of Life*. The child is next an "embodied power" who warms the cave. Star-imagery has been inwoven into her mother's experience preceding, or during, the birth; and now the heroine's eyes are as openings into "unfathomable night" through a temple's, probably domed, roof. She *is* the dark prenatal magic of night, of sleep. While the fountain she lives by is now "sacred" and a normal enough birth-symbol, the cave-womb association becomes explicit: the "enwombed rocks" have brought her forth.

After this exceedingly complex and not quite clear attempt to explicate birth-mystery, the poem's lady becomes a personification of magic. She negates death-instincts, as does the conclusion to *Prometheus*, and animals are by her regenerated. The approach, in homage, of animals, nature-deities, rustics, and kings may suggest (1) the lower orders of creation integrated into a human birth, and (2) the adoration of a divine birth in the New Testament. When she clothes herself in mist, being too beautiful in nakedness, there is dual suggestion of the soul clothed in a body, a usual Shelleyan figure, and human dress: she resembles Asia. There follow gossamer stanzas concerning her magic properties, including power to make death a rich dream-joy. Often we had best equate her with the *poetic consciousness*, if only to assist our approach: Shelley is writing, you see, of a supernatural state, or person. Her cave has carvings of ancient lore, like that in *Prometheus*, concerning the proper path from man's fallen state back to a golden age matching in harmony the "sacred stars." The sense of natural sanctity here is comparable with that of Keats. Whether the cave still symbolizes the womb is doubtful: rather the Witch now personifies the birth-quality, in both its child-purity and magic unconsciousness. The cave's carvings are, however, things of ancient art and learning: the subconscious and superconscious meet. The Witch symbolizes a potentiality wherein all dangerous forces of the elements, time, and man's will are mastered: again, a reminder of *Prometheus*. Spirits do her bidding, penetrating, like Ariel, "the earth," "matted roots," and the "gnarl'd heart of stubborn oaks": her power interpenetrates the insentient. Yet she is herself independent of mortal nature. Her cave-roof is (to suggest a magic guided by sexual *instinct*) paradoxically *lighted* by her fountain: on it she reads her scrolls of ancient widsom. She also, being poetry itself, embroiders a "pictured poesy." The impressionism is Keatsian, the more so for the presence of "sandal wood, rare gums, and cinnamon."

She has a boat, which Apollo "bought"—strange term in such a poem—from Venus for whom it was first intended as a "chariot," though proving too weak. It was made from a love-plant, and perhaps also symbolizes poetry: Wordsworth uses the symbol similarly in introducing *Peter Bell*. True, the Witch is already such a symbol, but Shelley is nothing if not lavish, and we have yet a third following. The Witch creates out of "fire and snow" mingled with "love" a new being resembling Goethe's Homunculus, the mixture recalling the sunny-ice of Coleridge's dome, symbol of the purified, yet inclusive, poetic consciousness. This seraph-form is *sexless*, its bosom swelling "lightly" with "full youth," yet incorporates *the best of both sexes*, strength and gentleness, and is excessively beautiful with an artistic "purity." It is thus supersexual rather than asexual, as is the creative consciousness, and, perhaps, the evolutionary or transcendental goal of mankind. Coleridge's Apollo-form in "The Destiny of Nations" is a direct analogy; and the Witch herself is later called "sexless." Anyway, he sits in the boat's prow, a guiding force, like the Child-navigator in *The Revolt of Islam* who takes hero and heroine to Heaven, the seraph-consciousness there ruling and guiding the sexual partnership. Here he lies as an "image" with "folded wings and unawakened eyes," "busy dreams" playing on his countenance, with "rapid smiles" and "warm tears" aroused *"from that full heart and brain."* Though closely resembling the sleep-smiling Child in *Prometheus*, he is more mature: a child superman, as it were. He is close to Shakespeare's Ariel, spirit of poetry; yet perhaps more inclusive.

We now have various poetic expeditions. The boat of poetry voyages through Shelleyan scenery, sometimes reminiscent of "Kubla Khan" and *Alastor*. It flies on the wind or lingers by "pools" of "content." Next it descends cataracts that either "shiver" into "golden air" (i.e. paradisal vision) or "sepulchre" themselves in "unfathomable" "chasms" (i.e. more tragic vision), but remains always guarded and upborne by "circling sun-bows" (i.e. divine, dome-like assistance) that "light it far upon its lampless way." The symbolisms are normal. There are, also, labyrinths. To ascend from "the labyrinths of some many-winding vale" upward to "the inmost mountain," to attack that most difficult poetic job of moving *from river to dome* which elsewhere makes Shelley's streams flow uphill, the Hermaphro-dite's seraph-purity is especially needed. He is therefore now *awaked*, repre-senting poetry fully *conscious*, and, in glorious imagery mixing light and snow (Coleridge's sunny-ice again), is seen spreading his wings to speed "like a star up the torrent of the night," while the pinnace cleaves "the fierce streams towards their upper springs." Or they (witch, seraph, and boat) may voyage under a waning moon (another Coleridgian reminder), where the Lady cannot rest content with "visions," the relation of voyages to poetic experience being explicit. Now she makes herself a dome-paradise amid and above storm, a "windless haven" among stars, constructed of clouds' "windy turrets" *beneath* which stars twinkle, set among other clouds like inaccessible mountain crags. Here, where the "outer lake" under "the lash of the winds' scourge" "foamed like a wounded thing"—the imagery is tempestuously ferocious—and the cormorant momentarily lit by lightning seems a wind-wandering and wrecked "fragment of inky thunder-smoke," her haven remains a "gem," an "engraven" copy of Heaven: against sea and ethereal storm stands firm the minute precision of art's eternity. You can see how constantly our dome-structure remains basic in contrast or comparison with watery and ethereal turmoil.

She may play pranks before the late moon, "as a sick matron," starts her journey. An almost cynical turn of phrase deliberately tones down the glamor, as in Byron and the later Yeats. From their "hollow turrets" of white, gold, and vermilion clouds she calls her spirits, who arrive in "mighty legions," each troop, somewhat like Milton's Satanic host, "emblazoning its merits" on "meteor flags"; and these make "proud pavilions" out of the atmospheric textures upon the "calm mere," as many pleasure-domes over water. Such is their Queen's "imperial tent"

> as may be seen
> A dome of thin and open ivory inlaid
> With crimson silk—cressets from the serene
> Hung there, and on the water for her tread
> A tapestry of fleece-like mist was strewn,
> Dyed in the beams of the ascending moon.

The ethereal is often here given a textile expression, a newly concentrated extension of Shelley's continual use of "woven" in atmospheric description. So the Witch sits on a "throne" overlaid "with starlight," listening to tales from earth, growing moon-pale, weeping and laughing by turns. She rules waters and reptiles, riding a dolphin like Arion, "singing" through the "shoreless air," "following the serpent lightning's winding track"—a deliberate imagistic photography rendering almost still the inexpressibly swift —or running on the wind. How like Ariel she is! Yet these are all images of violent action, against which are set those of circular harmony, when she moves to soft upper regions "which whirl the earth in its diurnal round," and joins in the angelic chorus. On such days earth knows intimations of a mystic happiness.

The poem now changes to a more Keatsian tone. We have had moonlight, starlight, subdued fire, marvelous storms, and mystic dome-pavilions ethereally wrought. Next we explore a legendary Egypt and the wonders of sleep.

This movement is fittingly introduced by a voyage on the winding Nile as he "threads" Egypt and Aethiopia, leading to notice of "cities and proud temples" and many "a vapour-belted pyramid" on its banks: the heights as usual lifting above the winding river. There follows a striking image of blossom-strewn lakes and "naked boys bridling tame water-snakes" or "charioteering ghastly alligators" (cf. the dolphin-riding spirits in Yeats's "Byzantium"); and next boy and beast sleep together after the "pomp" of their "Osirian feast" within the "brazen doors of the great labyrinth." Again, see how boy-forms, seraph-forms, like the tyrant-comforting child in *The Revolt of Islam*, are safe with fierce antagonists. Remember the reptiles in "The Ancient Mariner." This impossible union, like Isaiah's of lion and lamb, child and asp (cf. child and basilisk in *The Revolt of Islam*, V, 49–50), preludes descriptions of sleep's labyrinthine mystery.

The Witch goes

> Through fane and palace-court, and labyrinth mined
>   With many a dark and subterranean street
> Under the Nile, through chambers high and deep
> She passed, observing mortals in their sleep.

These fanes, subterranean passages and chambers, the Nile itself, are more psychological than geographical. The Witch, like the Child in *Prometheus* and Shakespeare's Queen Mab, moves through the world of dream; seeing now two lovers linked pictorially in a beautifully plastic and Byronic image, their locks creeping "like ivy from one stem"; and now "old-age with snow-bright hair and folded palm"—the line limning the riches of age, sanctity, and marmoreal peace in one swift stroke. Unrestful dreams are passed over by this "holy song": she herself is, like Coleridge's dome, by them undisturbed, though mankind are as "weak mariners," only too troubled as they make an "unpiloted and starless" course over a "wild surface to an unknown goal" —to Coleridge's "caverns measureless to man." The Witch is now rather below, than above, that winding course, in "calm depths" among "bright bowers of immortal forms," beneath the "restless" tide of existence. Depth is always liable to replace height in these eternity-symbolisms. She sees *into* all sleepers, exploring the true "naked beauty" of an outwardly disfigured form. To those most beautiful she gives in "deep sleep" a magic drink; makes them men of genius, so that they live thenceforth "as if some control mightier than life were in them"; and to these death's eternity is a pleasure-house:

> as a green and over-arching bower
> Lit by the gems of many a starry flower.

This happy death is curiously described in lines powerfully illustrating the closely realistic and disciplined approach to a theme more usually given a fanciful expression. The Witch undoes the embalmers' work, shakes light from the funeral lamps. She took

> The coffin, its last cradle, from its niche,
> And threw it in contempt into a ditch.

We have a pulsing immortality in terms of sleep and magic vegetation:

> And there the body lay, age after age,
>   Mute, breathing, beating, warm, and undecaying,
> Like one asleep in a green hermitage,
>   With gentle smiles about its eyelids playing,
> And living in its dreams beyond the rage
>   Of death or life; while they were still arraying
> In liveries ever new, the rapid, blind
> And fleeting generations of mankind.

This suggests Shakespeare's Hermione-statue, the sleep-smiling child in *Prometheus* and Keats's pulsing architectures. But the Witch thwarts the purposes of those who are evil, making them comically reverse their behavior in dream, and two stanzas of pithy satire deal with Shelley's old antagonists, priests and kings. Yet how poetically fresh that aversion seems when accorded so precise and detailed, so truly creative and original an expression. Now soldiers in sleep beat their swords to ploughshares. Young lovers, not yet joined, dream of their union, but "ten months" shows the union, through the Witch's magic, to be real, as though this dream were very much more than a fancy-language after all. She also, through sleep, unites friends, like those in "Christabel," long-parted. Sleep in this poem is at once the source, nurse, and redeemer of waking life, which is felt as a shallow unreality in that comparison. The Egyptian tonings are kept up through these stanzas, since the mystic lore of ancient Egypt may be supposed to have possessed a more authoritative insight into sleep and dream than Western science can approach. The use precisely resembles Yeats's use of Byzantine civilization. In Shelley magic and moonlight, or dawn-awakening, are, of course, continually given Eastern associations. In *The Witch of Atlas* we tread the borders of a consciousness wherein sleep, not waking, is the truer life: which points toward Keats. And what then of death?

The Witch marks an attempt to create a composite figure of supernature from all Shelley's intuitions of sleep and dream, poetic creation and especially poetic symbolism, his own psychic conflicts and eternity insight, and, at the start, that even more final mystery than death, the darkly magic quality of birth. There is a steady progress from the mainly feminine "seraph"-child in *The Revolt of Islam*, through the pivotal and half-metaphysical Child in *Prometheus*, to the supersexual Hermaphrodite and alligator-boys in *The Witch of Atlas*. Shelley attempts to penetrate both the womb and purpose of creation through fine use of his mythopoeic art; to force that art to reveal the ultimate mystery.

"Hymns of Pan and Apollo"

by Milton Wilson

The most finished of Shelley's short lyrics is the "Hymn of Pan," written, along with its companion piece the "Hymn of Apollo," for the opening scene of Mary Shelley's verse play *Midas*. In this scene old Tmolus judges a singing contest between Apollo with his lyre and Pan with his pipe. Midas enters in the midst of preparations for the contest and, invited by Tmolus to remain and listen, tells the reader, in an aside, of his preference for "my guardian God, old horned Pan." [1] But, when Apollo and Pan have sung, Tmolus promptly awards the palm to Apollo, commending the wisdom, beauty, and divine power of his music. The infuriated Midas interrupts and expresses his own decided preference for Pan's song. He says, in the words given him by Mary Shelley,

> Immortal Pan, to my poor, mortal ears
> Your sprightly song in melody outweighs
> His drowsy tune; he put me fast asleep. . . .

Whereupon Apollo turns on Midas and gives him asses' ears as a symbol of his "blunted sense." [2]

Pan's hymn is addressed not merely to the judge, Tmolus, but also to Apollo, his rival. In fact, it is something of a reply to the other hymn.

> I am the eye with which the Universe
> Beholds itself, and knows itself divine,
> All harmony of instrument or verse,
> All prophecy, all medicine are mine,
> All light of Art or Nature,

sings Apollo. It is a sweeping claim, and old Tmolus is duly impressed. But Apollo does not shine in lonely, unapproachable eminence. He has to com-

"Hymns of Pan and Apollo" (Editor's title). From *Shelley's Later Poetry: A Study of his Prophetic Imagination* by Milton Wilson. (New York: Columbia University Press, 1959, pp. 30–37). Copyright © 1959 by Columbia University Press. Reprinted by permission of Columbia University Press.

[1] *Proserpine and Midas*, ed. by Koszul, p. 50.   [2] *Ibid.*, p. 56.

pete with Pan, and, although a hill-god like Tmolus may prefer him, a deluded mortal like Midas may prefer Pan. In reading the "Hymn of Pan," we must recognize in the background some such dialectic between the bright spiritual light of Apollo and the lush, sweet world of forests and fauns and dewy caves and moist river-lawns and shadowy mountains which surrounds the pipings of Pan. And the rapid, darting movement of the "Hymn of Pan" gains if we hear it against the equally light but nevertheless firm and solemn movement of the "Hymn of Apollo." We need to relate the pipe and the lyre.

No poem of Shelley's shows a subtler control of rhythmic variation than the "Hymn of Pan." Indeed, no poem I know surpasses it in the handling of that most difficult of all rhythms for an English poet, the anapestic. The loss of final "e" in late Middle English administered a sedative to English verse which, with occasional lapses, has been gradually taking effect ever since. By the time of Keats, rhythm can hardly be said to move at all; the saturation point of spondees has been reached. The modern reader reads Chaucer badly, not because he finds it hard to reverse the Great Vowel Shift, but because he finds it hard to imagine quick verse. Nineteenth-century poets, like Poe and Byron and Tom Moore, sometimes tried to lighten their rhythms by pouring their lines into ready-made anapestic patterns, and their failure spoiled the anapest for later poets. Even the sprung verse and free verse of Hopkins and Whitman did only a little to repair the damage which had been accumulating for centuries. Among the few nineteenth-century poets who successfully counteracted the spondaic tendency belong Coleridge, Byron (in *Don Juan*), Shelley, and Browning.

The metrical principle behind the "Hymn of Pan" is the alternation of anapestic and iambic feet. Or, to be more precise, iambic feet do not normally occur in succession, although anapests often do. Such a pattern noticeably lightens the usual rhythm of English verse, but does not confine it in a strait jacket, as persistent anapests generally seem to do. A line in the "Hymn of Pan" usually contains three feet, but some expansion is liable to occur near the end of a stanza. Run-on lines and decisive caesuras are infrequent.

In such a rhythmic world, a succession of iambic feet or even an initial trochee is a call to attention. One could drop a dozen spondees into a page of the *Idylls of the King* and hardly disturb the surface; a spondee or two in the "Hymn of Pan" or "When the Lamp is Shattered" could be a major event. We have already observed one unforgettable example from the end of the latter: "When leaves fall and cold winds come." The most significant examples from the "Hymn of Pan" also occur at the end. In the first stanza Shelley is mainly concerned to establish his norm, and he diverges from it with great restraint. He keeps his iambic feet well spaced and brings them together only for a simple effect in the short second line; if accents are juxtaposed, it is only in passing, perhaps to emphasize the attention of old Tmolus or of the noiseless waves.

> From the forests and highlands
>   We come, we come;
> From the river-girt islands
>   Where loud waves are dumb,
>   Listening my sweet pipings;
> The wind in the reeds and the rushes,
>   The bees on the bells of thyme,
> The birds on the myrtle bushes,
>   The cicale above in the lime,
> And the lizards below in the grass,
> Were as silent as ever old Tmolus was
>   Listening my sweet pipings.

The big effects are saved for the last few lines of the poem.

Before looking at the versification beyond the first stanza, we need to consider the plot of Pan's song, what sort of story or argument it presents. Roughly speaking, the poem is a dramatic monologue, an *apologia pro vita sua*, an account of his past success as a musician, aimed (unsuccessfully, as Pan realizes in the course of his performance) at arousing the sympathy of his present listeners. The places he has visited, the audiences he has charmed, the extent of his repertoire, all these are sketched in some profusion. Traditionally a forest and mountain god, he has extended his range to include a lowland world of "river-girt islands" and "moist river-lawns." The inhabitants of this region are as responsive to his songs as old Tmolus (a hill-god) has been in the past. In the second stanza Pan paints a vivid picture of his control over nature and its denizens. "Liquid Peneus" flows faster, and the shadows of night lengthen faster (the listening Apollo could hardly approve!), under the influence of his pipings. The demi-gods of the earth, water, and forest listen to him in "silent love":

> Liquid Peneus was flowing,
>   And all dark Tempe lay
> In Pelion's shadow, outgrowing
>   The light of the dying day
>   Speeded by my sweet pipings.
> The Sileni, and Sylvans, and Fauns
>   And the nymphs of the woods and the waves
> To the edge of the moist river-lawns,
>   And the brink of the dewy caves,
> And all that did then attend and follow

Were silent with love, as you now, Apollo!
With envy of my sweet pipings.

In stanza three Pan appeals to his unresponsive listeners by tracing the progress of his art to its climax in the lyric of disappointment and suffering, which, for Pan, are the fate of men and gods alike.

I sang of the dancing stars,
  I sang of the daedal earth—
And of heaven—and the giant wars—
  And Love, and death, and birth,
  And then I changed my pipings
Singing how down the vale of Menalus,
  I pursued a maiden and clasped a reed,
Gods and men, we are all deluded thus!
  It breaks in our bosom and then we bleed!
All wept, as I think both ye now would
If envy or age had not frozen your blood,
  At the sorrow of my sweet pipings.

But his present audience fails to respond. Both Apollo and Tmolus hear Pan's outcry with dry eyes. The silence of Apollo is the silence of envy not love (as Pan has already claimed at the end of stanza two), and the silence of old Tmolus is now revealed as the insensitivity of old age. So the poem ends with Pan singing his sweetest songs that tell of saddest thought to an audience which he regards as too prejudiced or insensitive to respond. The Apollo of the "Hymn of Apollo" would be, of course, incapable of envying the "Hymn of Pan," but he would be equally incapable of appreciating it. The lyre of Apollo is only the mutable instrument of an otherworldly wisdom; the pipe of Pan is the very substance of human disappointment and transformation.

The force of the climactic (and anticlimactic) third stanza is intensified by the skill of Shelley's versification. We recall that in stanza one a number of effective variations from the norm (such as successive iambic feet, the spondee, the emphatic caesura) were held back for later use. Stanza two is also comparatively restrained, although lines two to four show significant irregularities. Most significant is the versification of line eleven, where Pan addresses Apollo directly: "Were silent with love, as you now Apollo!" The direct address and the new emphasis on the present are pointed up by the caesura and the conjunction of accents in "you now."

The restraint of stanzas one and two is rewarded in stanza three, particularly after the structural shift in line five. In the early part of the stanza Pan outlines the range of his art. It includes poetry of nature (praising the vitality and intricacy of creation); poetry of supernature (about "heaven," whatever that may involve in this context—perhaps Shelley means hymns and dithyrambs); mythological narrative (about the wars of the Titans and the Olympians); and philosophical poetry (about the recurrent fundamentals of human existence, whose cyclical repetition is underlined by a striking change to a line of three successive iambic feet: "And Love, and Death, and Birth"). Normally the next line would bring the first part of the stanza to an end with a version of the refrain. But Pan's fifth and last genre is a new departure into the lyric of personal suffering. Shelley has the brilliant idea of making Pan's sudden change seem more radical by ending the first part in line four and turning the refrain line into the first line of the new part. And whereas stanzas one and two broke up clearly into two parts of one sentence each, this second part of stanza three is chopped up into a number of separate sentences. The continuity of the earlier stanzas is lost.

In the lines

> Gods and men, we are all deluded thus!
> It breaks in our bosom and then we bleed,

the "Hymn of Pan" reaches its moment of greatest impact. I can think of no lyric in which such a moment is achieved with more economy and coordination of means. A technical critic can only inadequately point to the initial strong accent (here created simply by omitting the weak accent which normally precedes it), the caesura after "men," the reduction of anapests to one in the line, and the expansion from trimeter to pentameter; the following line shows the same iambic concentration combined with a powerful alliteration.

Shelley still has some surprises to offer. Line ten begins with a spondee followed by a caesura, and the line as a whole is rigid with accents stronger than the reader anticipates.

> All wept, as I think both ye now would
> If envy or age had not frozen your blood,
> At the sorrow of my sweet pipings.

But in the last two lines the anapestic rhythm reasserts itself and takes control. The poem ends with a burst of speed and a return to normal, which submerge the "sorrow" beneath the "sweet pipings."

We need not look for such sorrow and liveliness, such a dramatic rise and fall of tension, in an Apollonian hymn. Nor would Apollo move from scene to scene, audience to audience, genre to genre. Apollo follows a prearranged cyclical pattern, like the sun-god he is, although he regrets the necessity of even that concession to time, preferring to remain at noon forever, rather than descend "into the clouds of the Atlantic even." Nor would Apollo ever fall upon the thorns of life and make sweet songs out of his own pain and delusion. He may describe his own activity, to be sure, but with a confident impersonality.

> Whatever lamps on Earth or Heaven may shine
> Are portions of one power, which is mine.
>
> I stand at noon upon the peak of heaven,
>   Then with unwilling steps I wander down
> Into the clouds of the Atlantic even—
>   For grief that I depart they weep & frown;
> What look is more delightful than the smile
> With which I soothe them from the western isle?
>
> I am the eye with which the Universe
>   Beholds itself and knows itself divine.
> All harmony of instrument or verse,
>   All prophecy, all medicine is mine;
> All light of art or nature;—to my song
> Victory and praise, in its own right, belong.

There could be no split between this singer and his audience, or, if there were, he would not be aware of it. He knows that his song deserves the victory "in its own right."

"The Two Spirits," *Adonais,* and *The Triumph of Life*

by Harold Bloom

"The Two Spirits: An Allegory"

Shelley wrote nothing so hopeful again.[1] The ruin and desolation that shadow the heart's affections in *Prometheus* haunt all of his later poetry.

The unwilling dross that cannot be tortured into spirit, the hardened element that will not wish its own redemption, becomes increasingly the feared antagonist in Shelley's poetry, until at last it wins over Imagination the triumph of life and closes Shelley's poetic career in the welter of a watery chaos. The episodes of that strife, with momentary escapes into visionary possibility, find their record in the series of marvelous poems that distinguish Shelley's last and most productive years, 1820–22. The great but imperfect structure of *Prometheus* is made out of hopes and desires that still seek their object, but the more perfectly structured later poems seek no resolution beyond their own form.

The most beautiful of Shelley's shorter poems, to me, is the neglected lyric of 1820, "The Two Spirits: An Allegory," published posthumously in 1824. Here Blake's theme of Spectre and Emanation, independently worked out by Shelley in his earlier poetry through *Prometheus*, finds its definitive statement as a dialectic of infinite desire and the finite limits that attempt to defeat desire. The First Spirit begins:

> O thou, who plumed with strong desire
> Wouldst float above the earth, beware!
> A Shadow tracks thy flight of fire—
> Night is coming!
> Bright are the regions of the air,

[1] Cf. the preceding discussion of the last lines of *Prometheus Unbound* in *The Visionary Company*. [ED.]

> And among the winds and beams
>   It were delight to wander there—
>   Night is coming!

The Shadow is the ruin haunting love, the Spectre that will displace the strongly desired Emanation after the desire is frustrated by the menace of coming night. But the Second and more Shelleyan Spirit is undaunted:

> The deathless stars are bright above;
>   If I would cross the shade of night,
> Within my heart is the lamp of love,
>   And that is day!
> And the moon will smile with gentle light
> On my golden plumes where'er they move;
>   The meteors will linger round my flight,
>   And make night day.

The shade of night is the shadow thrown into the heavens by our earth, and it ends at the sphere of Venus, the lamp of love which is the evening star and which the Second Spirit carries within him as an eternal and unfailing day. The First Spirit warns him again of the coming storm, but he utters a finer defiance:

> I see the light, and I hear the sound;
>   I'll sail on the flood of the tempest dark,
> With the calm within and the light around
>   Which makes night day:
> And thou, when the gloom is deep and stark,
> Look from thy dull earth, slumber-bound,
>   My moon-like flight thou then mayst mark
>   On high, far away.

This has the accent of Ariel scorning Caliban and marks the poem as containing the theme of Icarus' courage, the vision that makes night day. The dialogue between Spirits is over, and the poem resolves itself in two stanzas of myth-making:

> Some say there is a precipice
>   Where one vast pine is frozen to ruin
> O'er piles of snow and chasms of ice
>   Mid Alpine mountains;
> And that the languid storm pursuing
> That wingèd shape, for ever flies
>   Round those hoar branches, aye renewing
>   Its aëry fountains.

This would be the First Spirit's spectral interpretation of the Second Spirit's ruinous fate. In a Promethean setting of cyclic and frozen pursuit the winged shape expiates its daring by perpetual flight from the languid but ever renewed storm. But the poem's last stanza, the most exquisite in all of Shelley, tells a different story of the Second Spirit's destiny:

> Some say when nights are dry and clear,
>   And the death-dews sleep on the morass,
> Sweet whispers are heard by the traveller,
>   Which make night day:
> And a silver shape like his early love doth pass
> Upborne by her wild and glittering hair,
>   And when he awakes on the fragrant grass,
>   He finds night day.

The subtle mustic of De la Mare is anticipated in this perfect stanza. The traveler hears sweet whispers that make night day in a visionary sense, like the Second Spirit's earlier transfiguration of night into day. The shape of early desire, of lost youth and abandoned vision, comes to the traveler in the form of the inviolable Second Spirit, now revealed in its allegorical meaning of early love. When the traveler awakes from vision, it is literally to find night day, as Arthur awakes in *The Faerie Queene,* to find himself alone on the fragrant grass. Desire suffers both fates, the Spectre's prophecy of cyclic desolation, and the Emanation's fulfillment of a vision that cannot die, for it has the potency of renewable though wavering life. The mood of this enigmatic final stanza, the fantasy of realized wish, is extended at least once by Shelley in his most beautiful longer poem, *The Witch of Atlas,* composed in three days of inspired creativity in August 1820. The dream of love and beauty does not seek reality in *The Witch of Atlas,* but for once contents itself to move in a world entirely of Shelley's making.

Adonais

Shelley and Keats, brought together by Leigh Hunt, failed to become friends. Hunt puts it briefly: "Keats did not take to Shelley as kindly as Shelley did to him." Still, they saw enough of one another in the spring of 1817 for Keats to fear the other poet's personal and literary influence upon *Endymion,* and they continued to see one another until Shelley left England for a last time in March 1818.

In July 1820 Shelley, knowing of Keats's illness, asked him to come to Italy, to avoid the English winter. The invitation was for Keats to take up his residence with the Shelleys. Yet the same generous letter contains criticism of Keats's poetry which he was not likely to accept. After praising *Endymion* for "the treasures of poetry it contains," Shelley adds, "though treasures poured forth with indistinct profusion." This becomes a more general censure: "In poetry I have sought to avoid system and mannerism. I wish those who excel me in genius would pursue the same plan."

Keats's reply was equally apt. "You, I am sure, will forgive me for sincerely remarking that you might curb your magnanimity, and be more of an artist, and load every rift of your subject with ore." Each poet had hold of a limited critical truth about the other, but Keats, ill and irritated, understandably showed less graciousness in the exchange.

The poets did not meet again, for Keats came to Italy only to die, at Rome, on February 23, 1821. Shelley had, in the meantime, read the *Hyperion* fragment in Keats's volume of 1820 and thereby changed his estimate of Keats's poetry. "If the *Hyperion* be not grand poetry, none has been produced by our contemporaries." Shelley went to his own death with the rereading of Keats, evidently his last act. Trelawny, identifying his friend's body, catches this final and affecting detail:

> The tall slight figure, the jacket, the volume of Sophocles in one pocket, and Keats's poems in the other, doubled back, as if the reader, in the act of reading, had hastily thrust it away. . . .

Keats was only three months dead when Shelley composed his elegy. He said of the poem that it was "perhaps the least imperfect" of his compositions, and certainly it is a highly finished work. Responding to his friends' praise of it, he very truly observed: "The poet and the man are two different natures: though they exist together, they may be unconscious of each other, and incapable of deciding on each other's powers and efforts by any reflex act." We may apply this to the subject of *Adonais;* it is the formalized lament of Shelley the poet for Keats the poet. It has rather less to do with the very real but remote grief that Shelley felt for Keats as a man. As in Milton's *Lycidas*, the poet's concern is with the fate of poets in a world that resists their prophecies and a nature that seems indifferent to their destruction.

Shelley's form is the pastoral elegy, modeled on Bion's "Lament for Adonis" and Moschus' "Lament for Bion," Hellenic poems of the second century B.C. Shelley had translated fragments of both poems and turned to them as archetypes of the kind of elegy he wished to write. Bion laments the death of the vegetation god, Adonis, the doomed lover of Venus. Moschus adopts the form of his friend's poem as approriate for lamenting Bion's death and so initiates the tradition of one poet associating the death of another poet with the fabled death of Adonis. Spenser's lament for Sir Philip Sidney,

Astrophel, and Milton's for Edward King continue this tradition, which culminates in *Adonais.*

Shelley chooses to believe, for his poetic purposes, that Keats was slain by the attacks upon *Endymion,* particularly the one made in the *Quarterly Review.* What counts here is imaginative, rather than literal, correctness. Shelley means, as Northrop Frye observes, that the hatred of genius by mediocrity is a death principle in society.[2]

The epigraph to *Adonais* is a little poem attributed to Plato, which Shelley himself translated:

> Thou wert the morning star among the living,
> Ere thy fair light had fled;—
> Now, having died, thou art as Hesperus, giving
> New splendour to the dead.

Keats has passed from the sphere of Lucifer, star of the morning, to that of Hesperus or Venus, first light of evening. This is a prefiguration of his fate within the poem.

Adonais consists of fifty-five Spenserian stanzas, and falls into two principal movements, with the thirty-eighth stanza marking the point of transition. The last seventeen stanzas are much finer than what precede them. Shelley casts off his poem's machinery in its final third and chants an astonishing hymn that recapitulates his darkened quest and seeks at last the quest's realization in a transvaluation of death. The movement of the first two thirds of the poem is much clearer than that of the final third, but is considerably less inspired.

Adonais, or Keats, is dead as the poem opens, and the Hour of death mourns him, and is to call the other hours to similar mourning. The dead poet was the youngest and dearest son of the Muse Urania, patroness of his poems *Endymion* and *Hyperion,* who was slumbering in her paradise when the murder occurred. She is called upon to weep, and yet her lament will be in vain. The poet's creations lament with her. The poem's first crisis comes in the counterpoint between the rebirth of nature and the soul's failure to revive:

> Ah, woe is me! Winter is come and gone,
> But grief returns with the revolving year;
> The airs and streams renew their joyous tone;
> The ants, the bees, the swallows reappear;
> Fresh leaves and flowers deck the dead Seasons' bier;
> The amorous birds now pair in every brake,

[2] *Fearful Symmetry* (Princeton, 1947), p. 377.

And build their mossy homes in field and brere;
And the green lizard, and the golden snake,
Like unimprisoned flames, out of their trance awake.

Through wood and stream and field and hill and Ocean
A quickening life from the Earth's heart has burst
As it has ever done, with change and motion,
From the great morning of the world when first
God dawned on Chaos; in its stream immersed,
The lamps of Heaven flash with a softer light;
All baser things pant with life's sacred thirst;
Diffuse themselves; and spend in love's delight,
The beauty and the joy of their renewèd might.

The leprous corpse, touched by this spirit tender,
Exhales itself in flowers of gentle breath;
Like incarnations of the stars, when splendour
Is changed to fragrance, they illumine death
And mock the merry worm that wakes beneath;
Nought we know, dies. Shall that alone which knows
Be as a sword consumed before the sheath
By sightless lightning?—the intense atom glows
A moment, then is quenched in a most cold repose.

This is a first and relatively crude formulation of the poem's greatest
concern; the shaping spirit alone vanishes, while everything grosser turns
over and reappears in cycle. This grief becomes that of Urania when she
seeks her son's death chamber. She desires to join him in death, but she is
"chained to Time, and cannot thence depart." After her lament, she is joined
by the Mountain Shepherds, the surviving poets, including Byron, Thomas
Moore, and Leigh Hunt, only the last of whom, in fact, cared for Keats.
Once again, Shelley deliberately ignores the poets as men, and emphasizes
only their symbolic aspect. Amid the others, comes Shelley himself:

A pardlike Spirit beautiful and swift—
A Love in desolation masked;—a Power
Girt round with weakness;—it can scarce uplift
The weight of the superincumbent hour;
It is a dying lamp, a falling shower,
A breaking billow;—even whilst we speak
Is it not broken? On the withering flower
The killing sun smiles brightly: on a cheek
The life can burn in blood, even while the heart may break.

In his other stanzas of self-description here, Shelley compares himself to

Actaeon, Cain, and Christ. Like Actaeon, he has "gazed on Nature's naked loveliness," and Nature strikes back by turning his own thoughts upon him, as Actaeon was pursued by his own hounds. Like Cain, he has perhaps failed to be his brother's keeper, though he had tried to preserve and shelter Keats. Again, like Cain, he is in fact an outcast from his family's and nation's society, for he is more reviled in orthodox English circles than Keats or Byron or any other contemporary writer. The Christ comparison is frankly impious; Shelley means to parallel his sufferings for mankind with those of Christ, for he desires to make his own sufferings vicarious, though not an atonement. In the stanza just quoted he compares his own power to the mutable strength of natural process, caught at the moment of its downward passage, "a falling shower, a breaking billow." Like the confronted reality of Asia or Emilia, his power can scarcely be apprehended before it wavers and vanishes. He has caught for us, imperishably, the basis of his style, its deliberate evanescence, and has given us its thematic justification: to be true to what *he* observes as most vital in nature.

Renewed lament for Adonais is followed by the poorest stanza in the poem (XXXVII) in which the Quarterly Reviewer is castigated as a "noteless blot on a remembered name." From this bathos the next stanza recoils, and the poem soars into greatness:

> Nor let us weep that our delight is fled
> Far from these carrion kites that scream below;
> He wakes or sleeps with the enduring dead;
> Thou canst not soar where he is sitting now.—
> Dust to the dust! but the pure spirit shall flow
> Back to the burning fountain whence it came,
> A portion of the Eternal, which must glow
> Through time and change, unquenchably the same,
> Whilst thy cold embers choke the sordid hearth of shame.

Shelley remains agnostic as to literal immortality; Keats "wakes *or* sleeps with the enduring dead," and survives only as they survive. But though he agrees with Ecclesiastes on "dust to the dust," he affirms the return of creative spirit back to a source neither temporal nor mutable, "the burning fountain" where life-giving water is aflame with the energy of imagination. In the light of that fountain, the dead poet is neither dead nor asleep, but "awakened from the dream of life" by having "outsoared the shadow of our night." Urania is represented in the heavens by Venus, the star of evening, to whose sphere Keats has soared. As the shadow of earth stops at the sphere of Venus, the poet is now free "from the contagion of the world's slow stain," and becomes a presence of transcendent Nature:

> He is made one with Nature: there is heard
> His voice in all her music, from the moan
> Of thunder, to the song of night's sweet bird;
> He is a presence to be felt and known
> In darkness and in light, from herb and stone,
> Spreading itself where'er that Power may move
> Which has withdrawn his being to its own;
> Which wields the world with never-wearied love,
> Sustains it from beneath, and kindles it above.

There is a touch of Keats's "Ode to a Nightingale" here. More vital, Shelley moves in this stanza to his most overt affirmation of the benevolence of the unknown Power he has pursued since *Alastor*. The Power is withdrawn, and has taken Keats into that remote tranquility, but it still dominates and directs the world with love, by both giving reality a firm existence at a phenomenal level and kindling the spirit rising out of phenomena:

> He is a portion of the loveliness
> Which once he made more lovely; he doth bear
> His part, while the one Spirit's plastic stress
> Sweeps through the dull dense world, compelling there,
> All new successions to the forms they wear;
> Torturing th' unwilling dross that checks its flight
> To its own likeness, as each mass may bear;
> And bursting in its beauty and its might
> From trees and beasts and men into the Heaven's light.

This majestic stanza completes one aspect of Shelley's imaginative apprehension of reality. The Spirit itself now directs the successions of mutable appearances, as part of its ultimate desire to mold the world into its own likeness. The unwilling dross of things resists, but finally in vain, as the Spirit bursts triumphantly through the forms of nature and man up into the light of Heaven. Until the Spirit kindles itself for a last time in the final four stanzas, this is all that Shelley is willing to put in terms of a faith.

Keats, like Chatterton or Sidney, is one of "the splendours of the firmament of time," and he goes now to join them, the Vesper of their throng. But Shelley's thought returns to groundling earth, where he himself still abides. As he ponders the problem of earthly consolation, his mind turns to Rome, scene of Keats's death and burial, and to the Protestant cemetery where lie the remains of Keats, and where he himself was to lie not so long after. Though the Spirit's breath moves, the world's wind remains bitter:

> From the world's bitter wind
> Seek shelter in the shadow of the tomb.
> What Adonais is, why fear we to become?

This is the poem's great moment of transition, its dialectical resolution as Shelley chooses the fate of Keats for himself. In a stanza justly celebrated two opposing realities are brought together, with neither negating the other:

> The One remains, the many change and pass;
> Heaven's light forever shines, Earth's shadows fly;
> Life, like a dome of many-coloured glass,
> Stains the white radiance of Eternity,
> Until Death tramples it to fragments.—Die,
> If thou wouldst be with that which thou dost seek!
> Follow where all is fled!—Rome's azure sky,
> Flowers, ruins, statues, music, words, are weak
> The glory they transfuse with fitting truth to speak.

Though life *stains* the white radiance of Eternity, the staining is not all loss, for the dome produces the colors that Eternity merely subsumes. Death smashes the dome and tramples it into fragments, but the fragments are at least brightly colored, for they are identical with the azure sky, with flowers, ruins, statues, music, and the words of Shelley's own poem. Yet he turns from them and seeks the deathly glory they transfuse:

> Why linger, why turn back, why shrink, my Heart?
> Thy hopes are gone before: from all things here
> They have departed; thou shouldst now depart!
> A light is passed from the revolving year,
> And man, and woman; and what still is dear
> Attracts to crush, repels to make thee wither.
> The soft sky smiles,—the low wind whispers near:
> 'Tis Adonais calls! oh, hasten thither,
> No more let Life divide what Death can join together.

The low wind that rises here is like the west wind of Shelley's "Ode," the creative and destructive agent, which begins by destroying. The year revolves again, yet a light has passed away from it forever, and everything left behind is caught in the strife of contraries, "attracts to crush." For a last time Shelley states his now pragmatically hopeless faith:

> That Light whose smile kindles the Universe,
> That Beauty in which all things work and move,
> That Benediction which the eclipsing Curse
> Of birth can quench not, that sustaining Love
> Which through the web of being blindly wove
> By man and beast and earth and air and sea,
> Burns bright or dim, as each are mirrors of
> The fire for which all thirst; now beams on me,
> Consuming the last clouds of cold mortality.

In this straining upward, the natural world that is given to us becomes only a darkness, into which we are born by an eclipsing Curse, and within which we weave our sustaining web of Love quite blindly. This is the under-song of the Spirit's immense declaration, for the overt emphasis here is on the salvation that brings us finally back to the burning fountain. The poem now refers us back to the "Ode to the West Wind," as the force invoked there now descends on its prophet:

> The breath whose might I have invoked in song
> Descends on me; my spirit's bark is driven
> Far from the shore, far from the trembling throng
> Whose sails were never to the tempest given;
> The massy earth and spherèd skies are riven!
> I am borne darkly, fearfully, afar;
> Whilst, burning through the inmost veil of Heaven,
> The soul of Adonais, like a star,
> Beacons from the abode where the Eternal are.

We mistake this triumph of rhetoric if we read it as other than a triumph of human despair. The imagination holding life open to death is not the burden of this great but suicidal stanza. Shelley is surrendering to Heaven, though it is the Heaven not of any orthodoxy but of his own agnostic will. A known is yielding to an unknown, and a vision collapses into mystery. *Adonais* is an imperishable poem, but it is also the sepulcher of a humanist and heroic quest.

The Triumph of Life

William Hazlitt reviewed Shelley's *Posthumous Poems* in 1824, and complained of the paradoxical title of Shelley's last poem:

> The poem entitled the *Triumph of Life*, is in fact a new and terrific *Dance of Death;* but it is thus Mr. Shelley transposes the appellations of the commonest things, and subsists only in the violence of contrast.

The *Triumph* is in *terza rima* and shows the influence of Dante throughout, particularly of the *Purgatorio*. Keats was dead when Shelley composed the *Triumph*, and Keats's *Fall of Hyperion* was not published until 1856, so there is no question of mutual influencing or example in the extraordinary fact that both poets left as their last considerable fragments work dominated by the *Purgatorio*. Both were attempting visions of judgment, and Dante seemed the inevitable model.

The *Triumph*'s vision is of a public way:

> Thick strewn with summer dust, and a great stream
> Of people there was hurrying to and fro,
> Numerous as gnats upon the evening gleam,
>
> All hastening onward, yet none seemed to know
> Whither he went, or whence he came, or why
> He made one of the multitude, and so
>
> Was borne amid the crowd, as through the sky
> One of the million leaves of summer's bier. . . .

This recalls the opening stanza of the "Ode to the West Wind." The people are as dust, as gnats, as dead leaves, crowding along to their own destruction. They lack individuality and will, and all the objectives of their trek are equally unreasonable. As Hazlitt said, this is a dance of death, compulsive and busy, replete with meaningless activity and serious folly:

> Old age and youth, manhood and infancy,
>
> Mixed in one mighty torrent did appear,
> Some flying from the thing they feared, and some
> Seeking the object of another's fear. . . .

Down the sterile, flowerless path they run the way of competition. As the poet gazes in wonder, the passing crowd's dance becomes wilder:

> And as I gazed, methought that in the way
> The throng grew wilder, as the woods of June
> When the south wind shakes the extinguished day,
>
> And a cold glare, intenser than the noon,
> But icy cold, obscured with blinding light
> The sun, as he the stars. Like the young moon . . .

The glare comes from an advancing chariot, which rolls over the fierce dancers in its path, and whose blinding cold glare, light without heat, obscures the warm light of the sun, even as the sun's light obscures the light of the stars. We have touched the optical theme before in Shelley, but in the *Triumph* it assumes a new importance. The chariot's glare is the light of life; the sun's, of nature; the stars', the visionary light of imagination and poetry. Nature's light obliterates that of the poet, only to be destroyed in turn by the light of life, the moonlike cold car of Life. The chariot of Life is introduced by the sinister image of the new moon with the old moon in its arms, prophetic of an oncoming storm:

> So came a chariot on the silent storm
> Of its own rushing splendour, and a Shape
> So sate within, as one whom years deform,
>
> Beneath a dusky hood and double cape,
> Crouching within the shadow of a tomb. . . .

Like Ezekiel's visionary chariot, Shelley's comes in a storm. Ezekiel's cherubim each have four faces and four wings; we see no beasts drawing the chariot because so divine a vehicle can be moved by no force external to itself. Shelley's charioteer has four faces, and we are not allowed to see the shapes drawing it, for they are lost "in thick lightenings." The vision in Shelley is a deliberate "diabolic" parody of the chariot of Ezekiel, as well as its derivatives in the *Purgatorio* and *Paradise Lost*. Shelley's Shape, within the chariot, is called simply "Life," is deformed, dusky, and also shrouded and indefinite:

> And o'er what seemed the head a cloud-like crape
> Was bent, a dun and faint aethereal gloom
> Tempering the light.

The Enthroned Man in Ezekiel's chariot, or the Christ in *Revelation*'s chariot modeled after Ezekiel, nakedly blazed with light, and had the hard, definite form of agate. The Shape of Life is hooded, and rather less human, being merely natural, to be identified with all the life lived by the natural man. With the Shape we see her charioteer:

> All the four faces of that Charioteer
> Had their eyes banded; little profit brings
>
> Speed in the van and blindness in the rear,
> Nor then avail the beams that quench the sun,—
> Or that with banded eyes could pierce the sphere
>
> Of all that is, has been or will be done;
> So ill was the car guided—but it passed
> With solemn speed majestically on.

The four-faced Charioteer is derived from the Ezekiel-*Revelation*-Dante-Milton tradition of a divine chariot made up of four-faced cherubim. Every text in that tradition emphasizes the innumerable eyes of the cherubim. Blake, in his illustration of the *Purgatorio*'s Triumphal Chariot of the Church, carries this emphasis to an extreme, for his painting is dominated by a plethora of eyes over everything else in the scene. The eyes are open; like Keats's "intelligences," which were "atoms of perceptions," these eyes also "know and they see and they are pure, in short they are God." But every one of the four faces of Shelley's Charioteer "had their eyes banded." The Charioteer cannot guide, and so the light given off by the chariot is of no help to him in his blindness. This chariot's progress is therefore meaningless, for all its majestic appearance and solemn speed.

The chariot passes on, and the poet sees a horde following it, captives in its triumphal procession:

> —all those who had grown old in power
> Or misery,—all who had their age subdued
> By action or by suffering, and whose hour
> Was drained to its last sand in weal or woe,
> So that the trunk survived both fruit and flower;—
>
> All those whose fame or infamy must grow
> Till the great winter lay the form and name
> Of this green earth with them for ever low;—

Counting up all these *alls*, one counts up to everybody as having been conquered by Life, except for "the sacred few" who are considered next in the poem. "The sacred few" escaped this defeat only by choosing to die to this life, like the poet at the end of *Adonais:*

> All but the sacred few who could not tame
> Their spirits to the conqueror's—but as soon
> As they had touched the world with living flame,
>
> Fled back like eagles to their native noon.
> For those who put aside the diadem
> Of earthly thrones or gems till the last . . .
>
> Whether of Athens or Jerusalem,
> Were neither mid the mighty captives seen,
> Nor mid the ribald crowd that followed them
>
> Nor those who went before fierce and obscene.

These sacred few certainly include Socrates and Jesus, though many of their followers are later seen among the captives, whom Shelley divides into three groups. These are: the mighty ones chained to the chariot (Rousseau will describe them later, after he makes his striking entrance into the poem); the ribald old following the chariot; the young dancing to destruction before it. The young at least are destroyed by the failure of love, like the poet in *Alastor,* but the old sink to corruption "with impotence of will." The given condition of natural man is depicted in its dual modes of hopelessness, after which the poem mounts to its first climax:

> Struck to the heart by this sad pageantry,
> Half to myself I said—"And what is this?
> Whose shape is that within the car? And why—"
>
> I would have added—"Is all here amiss?—"
> But a voice answered—"Life!"—I turned, and knew
> (O Heaven, have mercy on such wretchedness!)
>
> That what I thought was an old root which grew
> To strange distortion out of the hill side,
> Was indeed one of those deluded crew,
>
> And that the grass, which methought hung so wide
> And white, was but his thin discoloured hair,
> And that the holes he vainly sought to hide,
>
> Were or had been eyes. . . .

This is what remains of Rousseau, who has attained completely to the state of nature, Blake's Vegetative universe of Generation. Rousseau enters the poem as the chastened prophet of the state of nature, the disillusioned poet of natural religion and natural passion. As Virgil guided Dante, so the relic of Rousseau is to guide Shelley, to purify his vision. Rousseau himself can no longer see; Life's chariot has blinded him. He hears Shelley's words and replies to them. Out of his grim knowledge he gives the younger poet a warning not to join the dance, "which I had well forborne." He passes judgment upon himself in the poem's finest lines:

> Before thy memory,
>
> I feared, loved, hated, suffered, did and died,
> And if the spark with which Heaven lit my spirit
> Had been with purer nutriment supplied,
>
> Corruption would not now thus much inherit
> Of what was once Rousseau,—nor this disguise
> Stain that which ought to have disdained to wear it. . . .

Rousseau began with flame in his spirit, a spark that had both heat and light. He needed only to supply proper nutriment for this spark, but he failed, and he recognizes his own responsibility for the failure. Corruption veils the aged victims of the chariot (line 174) but not Rousseau, merely "what was once Rousseau," is thus disguised by the contagion of the world's slow stain. The disguise stains "that which ought to have disdained to wear it," imagination. Rousseau is now as corrupt as any of Life's victims, but the way of his corruption was nobler than that of other "sages":

> —The wise,
>
> The great, the unforgotten,—they who wore
> Mitres and helms and crowns, or wreaths of light,
> Signs of thought's empire over thought—their lore
>
> Taught them not this, to know themselves; their might
> Could not repress the mystery within
> And for the morn of truth they feigned, deep night
>
> Caught them ere evening. . . .

These leaders include bishops, warriors, rulers, and canonized saints and mystics; their headgear indicates "thought's empire over thought," tyrannies of the spirit. No system of belief has brought them knowledge of the selfhood or mystery within, and so their truth is only "feigned" and they too are conquered by Life.

Among them is Napoleon, the fallen Titan, whose appearance now inspires the central statement of Shelley's poetry:

> —I felt my cheek
> Alter, to see the shadow pass away,
> Whose grasp had left the giant world so weak
>
> That every pigmy kicked it as it lay;
> And much I grieved to think how power and will
> In opposition rule our mortal day,
>
> And why God made irreconcilable
> Good and the means of good. . . .

The last and subtlest Fury had reminded Prometheus that goodness and power, wisdom and love, were antithetical, "and all best things are thus confused to ill." The contraries are now sharper; power and will are in opposition, and thus good and the means of good are irreconcilable by the very nature of things. Life, our life, can be met only by quietism or by willful self-destruction.

What remains in this poem of total despair is the story closest to Shelley's individual fate, the overcoming by Life of the poet's unextinguished imaginative spark. While Shelley broods on the irreconcilable contraries, Rousseau completes his naming of the mighty captives by listing the "spoilers spoiled," Voltaire and his disciples, the "benevolent despots":

> For in the battle Life and they did wage,
> She remained conqueror. I was overcome
> By my own heart alone, which neither age,
>
> Nor tears, nor infamy, nor now the tomb
> Could temper to its object. . . .

None of Life's weapons succeeded in limiting Rousseau's desire by reducing his heart's infinite capacity to desire. If his heart had been so tempered to its object, then it would have been content with Life's gratifications, and so would have been conquered by Life. He has been overcome nevertheless, but by his own heart alone, not by Life. He is self-defeated, and his account of how this came to be forms the closing movement of the poem as we have it.

Rousseau's story resembles that of Wordsworth in the "Intimations" ode, for both describe a process of rebirth, of the transition from Innocence to Experience, from boyhood to manhood, from absolute dependence upon nature for imaginative vision to the realization that nature's vision fails its seer.

In the April prime of the year the young Rousseau falls asleep in a cavern with an opening to the west, actually a deep ravine that cuts through a mountain, probably to be related to Dante's mountain of Purgatory. The mountain is north-south, the ravine through it east-west. On the east of the mountain Rousseau passed his infancy and early childhood. He progresses through the mountain as he grows older, until as a young man he reaches a center point within the cavern where a fountain or well takes its rise. The fountain issues in a west-flowing gentle rivulet, the sound of which lulls Rousseau to sleep. The rivulet broadens into a stream and then a river as it flows westward out of the mountain.

As Rousseau sleeps under the rivulet's influence his childhood vanishes into oblivion. When he awakens, he faces the Wordsworthian situation of the fading of an earlier phenomenal glory:

> I arose, and for a space
> The scene of woods and waters seemed to keep,
>
> Though it was now broad day, a gentle trace
> Of light diviner than the common sun
> Sheds on the common earth, and all the place
>
> Was filled with magic sounds woven into one
> Oblivious melody, confusing sense
> Amid the sliding waves and shadows dun. . . .

For a while he can still see the diviner light, and still experience the fused or organic sense that haunted Coleridge and Wordsworth. But then the light of nature has its way with him. The vision of a Shape, representing Wordsworthian Nature, now appears to him:

> there stood
>
> Amid the sun, as he amid the blaze
> Of his own glory, on the vibrating
> Floor of the fountain, paved with flashing rays,
>
> A Shape all light, which with one hand did fling
> Dew on the earth, as if she were the dawn,
> And the invisible rain did ever sing
>
> A silver music on the mossy lawn;
> And still before me on the dusky grass,
> Iris her many-coloured scarf had drawn. . . .

The rays of the sun flow in from the eastern side of the cavern. The "sun's image" burns on the fountain, and a rainbow appears within that image. The rainbow is the emblem of salvation, of a continuity in nature, in Wordsworth's "Ode," but here it is employed ironically, against Wordsworth's vision. The Shape moves upon the surface of the water, a movement that parodies Dante's *Purgatorio* XXVIII–XXIX, where the poet meets Matilda in her earthly paradise, on top of the mount of Purgatory. Dante sees Matilda across the water of the river of Lethe, a draught of which will wash away all memory of sin. Rousseau sees the Shape all light upon the waters of a Lethe-like river, but she carries a crystal glass the contents of which will wash away all memory whatsoever, including the divine youth of Rousseau, the spark with which his earlier spirit was illuminated. As the Shape approaches Rousseau, her pragmatic malevolence becomes unmistakable:

> And still her feet, no less than the sweet tune
> To which they moved, seemed as they moved to blot
> The thoughts of him who gazed on them; and soon
>
> All that was, seemed as if it had been not;
> And all the gazer's mind was strewn beneath
> Her feet like embers; and she, thought by thought,
>
> Trampled its sparks into the dust of death;
> As day upon the threshold of the east
> Treads out the lamps of night, until the breath

> Of darkness re-illumine even the least
> Of heaven's living eyes. . . .

The Shape tramples the sparks of Rousseau's mind, thought by thought, "into the dust of death." Day treads out the stars, "the lamps of night," which are equivalent to the poets who are the lamps of earth and who are extinguished by the light of common day.

The Shape is like Keats's Belle Dame, and from her tempting him to a strange drink, Rousseau will awaken to Shelley's version of Keats's cold hill's side. She offers her nepenthe, Rousseau drinks of it, and suddenly his brain becomes as sand where tracks are more than half erased. And the cold vision of Life bursts upon him:

> —so on my sight
> Burst a new vision, never seen before,
>
> And the fair Shape waned in the coming light,
> As veil by veil the silent splendour drops
> From Lucifer, amid the chrysolite
>
> Of sunrise, ere it tinge the mountain-tops. . . .

Even as the sun dims Lucifer, the morning star, now the glare of Life's chariot dims the rainbow, emblem of the sun. Rousseau has surrendered to Nature, but Nature either cannot or will not keep faith with him. The mature Wordsworth would have said the first, Blake the second, for Shelley's Shape is very like Blake's Vala in her effect. Either way, the rainbow fades, and the memory of it replaces the now extinct memory of an earlier and more divine light. Rousseau is swept into the chariot's procession until at last he falls by the wayside. The poem breaks off in the despairing cry of Shelley or Rousseau:

> "Then, what is life?" I cried.

The poem has already provided the answer. Life is what triumphs over nature, even as nature triumphs over imagination. Life is death-in-life, Ulro, a cold, common hell in which we wake to weep. The quest of Shelley comes full circle from *Alastor* to *The Triumph of Life*, and the total structure of his poetic canon is seen to resemble the ironic cycle of Blake's "Mental Traveller." Shelley was too honest an agnostic and too good a poet merely to repeat the cycle again. He went forth to suffer a sea change, abandoning behind him the rich strangeness of his poetry.

Chronology of Important Dates

1792	*August 4.* Percy Bysshe Shelley born at Field Place, Horsham, Sussex, the son of Timothy Shelley (later Sir Timothy), a prosperous landowner and Whig Member of Parliament.
1802–04	At Sion Academy.
1804–10	At Eton.
1810	*March.* Publishes *Zastrozzi*, a gothic novel.
	September. Publication of *Original Poetry by Victor and Cazire* (Shelley and his sister Elizabeth).
	November. Publication of *Posthumous Fragments of Margaret Nicholson* (by Shelley).
	Michaelmas Term (October 10–December 17). Goes into residence at University College, Oxford.
1811	*March 25.* Expelled from Oxford for writing pamphlet, *The Necessity of Atheism* (with his friend T. J. Hogg, who was expelled with him).
	August. Elopes with Harriet Westbrook, whom he marries in Edinburgh.
1812	*February–April.* In Ireland, active in political agitation on the radical side.
	October. Meets William Godwin, whose *Political Justice* he had read at Oxford, and with whom he had corresponded.
1813	*May. Queen Mab* published.
	June. Birth of daughter Ianthe.
1814	*July 28.* Elopes to continent with Mary Godwin. Returns in September.
1815	*January.* Death of Sir Bysshe Shelley (grandfather) gives Shelley a regular income.
1816	*January.* Birth of William (to Mary).
	February. Alastor published.
	Summer. Shelley, Mary, and Claire Clairmont (Mary's half-sister) join Byron in Geneva. (Claire had had relations with Byron in London.) Leave for England, August 29.
	December. Body of Harriet Shelley found in a pond in Hyde Park. Shelley marries Mary.
1817	*September.* Birth of Clara.
	December. Laon and Cythna printed.
1818	*January. Revolt of Islam* published (version of *Laon and Cythna*).
	March. To Italy, henceforth to be his home.
	September. Death of Clara.
	Autumn. Begins *Prometheus Unbound*.

1819   *June.* Death of William.
                 October. Writes "Ode to the West Wind."
                 November. Begins *A Philosophical View of Reform* (published 1920).
                 Birth of Percy Florence (later Sir Percy).
1820   *Spring. The Cenci* published.
                 June. Writes "To a Skylark."
                 Summer. Publication of *Prometheus Unbound.*
                 August 14–16. Writes *Witch of Atlas* (published in *Posthumous Poems,*
                 ed. Mrs. Shelley, 1824).
1821   *February–March. A Defence of Poetry* written (published 1840).
                 Summer. Adonais and *Epipsychidion* published.
1822   *May–June.* Writing *Triumph of Life.*
                 July 8. Drowned at sea.

Notes on the Editor and Contributors

GEORGE M. RIDENOUR, the editor of this volume, writes on nineteenth century English poets, especially Byron and Browning. He is Professor of English at the University of New Mexico.

RICHARD HARTER FOGLE is the author of *The Imagery of Keats and Shelley*, and of other works on the Romantic period. He is Professor and Chairman of the Department of English at Tulane University.

LEONE VIVANTE is an Italian philosopher now living near Siena. T. S. Eliot wrote of the essay drawn on in this volume that it "has brought me to a new and more sympathetic appreciation" of Shelley.

The late HUMPHRY HOUSE was Fellow of Wadham College and Senior University Lecturer in English at Oxford. In addition to an important volume on Coleridge, he has also published on Dickens and Hopkins.

CARLOS BAKER, the author of *Shelley's Major Poetry*, is Professor of English at Princeton University.

EARL R. WASSERMAN, the author of important studies on Shelley and Keats, is Professor of English at Johns Hopkins University.

MELVIN M. RADER, who wrote *Presiding Ideas in Wordsworth's Poetry*, is a member of the Philosophy Department at the University of Washington.

G. M. MATTHEWS is best-known for his publications on Shelley. He teaches at the University of Leeds.

FREDERICK A. POTTLE, Sterling Professor of English at Yale University, best known for his work on the life and writings of James Boswell, has long taught courses in the English Romantic poets.

G. WILSON KNIGHT taught at the universities of Toronto and Leeds. He has written at length on the Romantic poets, especially Byron.

MILTON WILSON, the author of *Shelley's Later Poetry*, teaches at the University of Toronto.

HAROLD BLOOM has written on all of the Romantic poets, notably in *Shelley's Mythmaking* and *The Visionary Company*. He is Associate Professor of English at Yale.

Selected Bibliography

See credit notes on the first page of each essay in this volume for studies not listed here.

WORKS

The Complete Works of Percy Bysshe Shelley, eds. Roger Ingpen and Walter E. Peck. The "Julian edition." 10 vols. New York, 1926–30.

The Complete Poetical Works . . . , ed. Thomas Hutchinson. Oxford, 1905.

The Poems . . . , ed. C. D. Locock. 2 vols. London, 1911.

Shelley's Prose, ed. David Lee Clark. Albuquerque, New Mexico, 1954.

The Letters . . . , ed. Frederick L. Jones. 2 vols. Oxford, 1964.

LIFE

Newman Ivey White, *Shelley*. 2 vols. New York, 1940.

Edmund Blunden, *Shelley: A Life Story*. London, 1946.

CRITICISM

Gaston Bachelard, *L'Air et les songes*. Paris, 1943, pp. 49–65.

Harold Bloom, *Shelley's Mythmaking*. New Haven, 1959.

A. C. Bradley, "Shelley's View of Poetry," in *Oxford Lectures on Poetry*. London, 1909.

Douglas Bush, in *Mythology and the Romantic Tradition in English Poetry*. Cambridge, Mass., 1937.

Kenneth Neil Cameron, "The Political Symbolism of *Prometheus Unbound*," in *PMLA*, LVIII (1943), 728–53.

John Holloway, Introduction to *Selected Poems of . . . Shelley*. London, 1960.

Christian Kreutz, in *Das Prometheussymbol in der Dichtung der englischen Romantik*, *Palaestra*, vol. 236. Göttingen, 1963.

F. R. Leavis, in *Revaluation*. London, 1949; also in M. H. Abrams, ed., *English Romantic Poets: Modern Essays in Criticism*. New York, 1960.

C. S. Lewis, "Shelley, Dryden, and Mr. Eliot," in *Rehabilitations*. Oxford, 1939; also in Abrams (see above).

G. M. Matthews, Introduction to *Shelley: Selected Poems and Prose*. Oxford, 1964.

Sister M. Eunice Mousel, "Falsetto in Shelley," in *Studies in Philology*, XXXIII (1936), 587–609.

David Perkins, in *The Quest for Permanence*. Cambridge, Mass., 1961.

Frederick A. Pottle, "The Case of Shelley," in *PMLA*, LXVII (1952), 589–608; also in Abrams (see above), with revisions.

C. E. Pulos, *The Deep Truth: A Study of Shelley's Scepticism*. Lincoln, Nebraska, 1954.

Donald H. Reiman, "Structure, Symbol, and Theme in 'Lines Written Among the Euganean Hills,'" in *PMLA*, LXXVII (1962), 404–13.

I. A. Richards, "The Mystical Element in Shelley's Poetry," in *The Aryan Path*, XXX (June, 1959), 250–56; (July, 1959), 290–95.

Earl R. Wasserman, "*Adonais*: Progressive Revelation as a Poetic Mode," in *Journal of English Literary History*, XXI (1954), 274–326; reprinted in *The Subtler Language*. Baltimore, 1959.

William Butler Yeats, "The Philosophy of Shelley's Poetry," in *Ideas of Good and Evil;* reprinted in *Essays and Introductions*. New York, 1961.

TWENTIETH CENTURY VIEWS

Forthcoming Titles